# THE BRADFORD REGION

## STUDIES
## IN ITS
## HUMAN GEOGRAPHY

### C. RICHARDSON

*To Ruth, Ian and Ed*

Page Layout by Highlight Type Bureau Ltd., Bradford
Printed by Hart & Clough Ltd., Bradford
Published by Bradford Libraries Archives and Information Service
Central Library, Prince's Way, Bradford, West Yorkshire BD1 1NN
ISBN 0-907734-62-6
© C. Richardson
November 2002

# TABLE OF CONTENTS

# LIST OF FIGURES

# LIST OF TABLES

# ACKNOWLEDGEMENTS

I wish to thank the reference librarians at Bradford, especially Bob Duckett; and the staffs of Bradford Central Library, Keighley Library, and the University of Bradford Library for their considerable help during the researching of the book.

I would also like to thank Dr Nigel Copperthwaite, Chairman of the Department of Environmental Science of the University of Bradford. Throughout the writing of this book Dr Copperthwaite's valuable help and interest in the progress of the book has been stimulating, invaluable and always encouraging. He has been most generous in reading some of the sections of the book, offering helpful comment and making useful suggestions on points of detail. My task was eased by his allowing me to use the duplicating facilities of the Department. To this I would also add my thanks to the staff of the Environmental Science Department for their help.

In the year 2000, Dr Stephen (Ludi) Simpson of Bradford Council's Strategic Management Unit, suggested that I should update my "Geography of Bradford" (published in 1976), and this prompted me to write this book extending its coverage both in space and time, to the region focusing on Bradford. Dr Simpson involved himself most generously in giving his time in reading some of the draft chapters, and making available to me contemporary or recent statistical material on which I have been able to draw. His expertise on the demography of the Metropolitan District has enabled me to complete the last chapters by giving me access to material that would otherwise have been difficult to obtain, but more than that, I appreciate his advice in clarifying some of the detail of the chapters on the demography and the economy of the Region.

I am indebted to Dr Stuart Wrathmell of the West Yorkshire Archaeological Service, for allowing me to produce the map (figure 5) of the archaeology of Rombalds Moor. Dr Wrathmell was also helpful in referring me to resources on Roman Britain and to the place- names, which I was able to use.

However, in thanking Drs Copperthwaite, Simpson and Wrathmell I must take responsibility for any omission or shortcomings in the book.

Figures 3 and 4, based on the works of the Geological Survey, are reproduced with thanks, with the permission of British Geological Survey and are copyright to the National Environmental Research Council.

Dr Jason Ball of Yorkshire Water, kindly supplied me with up to date data on rainfall in the Bradford Region.

As the citations show, I have referred to the works of a number of local scholars, amongst which I include with gratitude, the following: Dr B Barnes, who wrote the book "Man and the Changing Landscape"; Dr Margaret Gelling author of "Place- names in the Landscape"; Dr E.M. Sigsworth for his definitive work on Black Dyke Mills; Dr Hilary Long who researched the industrial archaeology of Bowling and Low Moor ironworks; Ian Dewhirst for his classic work on the history of Keighley; Dr R.A. Schofield who researched the Irish localities in Keighley; Dr G Sheeran who wrote "Brass Castles" - studies of buildings and their owners in the Region- excited me; and to Dr Sarah Hinds for her study on commuting focused on Bradford.

Finally, my task was made easier by the efforts of my daughter Ruth Richardson, who proof-read the text and prepared the index, and not least important, she 'rescued' me when I got into difficulties with the word-processor.

Clem Richardson
Department of Environmental Science
University of Bradford
2002

# INTRODUCTION

# THE BRADFORD REGION
## Place          Time          People

This is the story of Bradford and its neighbours in Airedale and Wharfedale. It is about a place and its people. For three millennia people have entered the area, established their homes, built their settlements and lived out their lives. Although it is written by a geographer it cannot be separated from its history, nor can it ignore the human interaction, not only with place, but also with neighbours. It is therefore also very much a social study of human behaviour related to place. As a social and economic study, it is concerned with the way people in the past have interpreted and used this Pennine environment, as well as how they interacted with each other. In the development of the themes of the book we see how the geographically separate places in this area of the Pennines have come together to be treated as a unit forming the Bradford Region, and as can be seen, the Region that is so defined, conveniently corresponds closely to the area of the Bradford Metropolitan District.

In its Report, the Royal Commission on Local Government in England 1963-69 identified the economic and public service connections of the towns and villages in the middle reaches of Airedale and Wharfedale with the City of Bradford County Borough. The Commission concluded that these places should be incorporated to form a single all-purpose city regional authority. Its findings were largely accepted by the central government and the Bradford Metropolitan District came into existence.[1] In a separate study, the author in his *A Geography of Bradford* also produced evidence to show the various ways in which the urban districts were related to the central city of Bradford. He called this Pennine tract 'Greater Bradford'.[2] (See Figure 1) Since then there have been studies detailing travel-to-work connections, and commuter links between the inner Bradford centre and the outer area settlements of Airedale and Wharfedale.[3] The latter are reviewed in chapter 11 of this book. These separate studies confirm the close correspondence between the Metropolitan District and the Bradford Region.

Some years ago the Bradford Metropolitan Council published a series of posters entitled **'Bradford is a Surprising Place'.** Large parts of the less attractive areas of the older populated centres of the Region were the product of late 18th and 19th century industrialisation, and outsiders might be forgiven for thinking that their poor environment typified other parts of the Region. But the posters reminded us that even in the most congested parts of the largest urban area, Bradford, there are many attractive rural areas, and in outer Bradford, the deeply entrenched valleys of the rivers Aire and Wharfe constitute a rural expanse of high scenic value, while the intervening moorlands of Keighley, Thornton, Rombalds and Ilkley are justifiably classed as areas of outstanding natural beauty. The physical background forming this Pennine expanse of moorland and dale is discussed in **chapter 1,** where the Carboniferous block structure, its sculpturing, its relief, climate, soils and plant life are reviewed. For fifty centuries, ever since man began to appear on the Pennines, the region's natural resources have had different values to the many cultures which have occupied its surface. Over the years successive cultural groups have entered the area, beginning with the hunters and gatherers of the Old Stone Age.

Later at about the time when Stonehenge was being built, incomers of the New Stone Age began their occupation. They were followed by Bronze Age and Iron Age people. These early

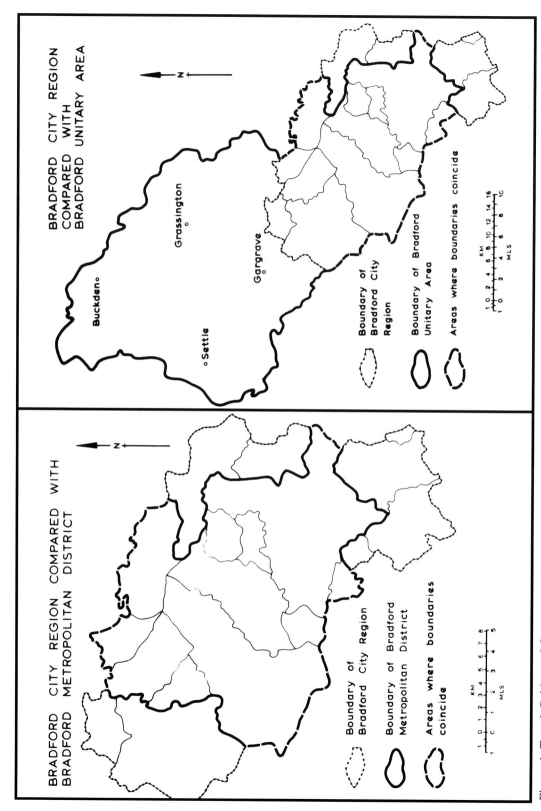

Figure 1. Two definitions of Greater Bradford.

inhabitants began to farm the moorland fringes and the valley benches. They left their mark in the many carved stones and other structures which dot the upland surface. As **chapter 2** shows, the geographer has to draw on the interpretation of the archaeologist to appreciate the nature of the human relationship with the land in those remote times. As the chapter notes, the fort at Olicana (Ilkley) was built to police the Brigantian tribal lands against incursions by the Pictish Scots and it is a reminder of more turbulent times during the Roman occupation.

From the evidence of place names and the Domesday survey, **chapter 3** shows that the present-day regional pattern of urban places such as Bradford, Keighley, Bingley, Baildon, Shipley, Ilkley, Burley and other towns and villages in the Region had its origin in the manors carved out of the forest and the waste by the Anglo Saxon occupants well before the Norman Conquest of 1066. The decision to make Bradford the centre of the feudal manorial administration, and the grant by its lord of a market charter may be seen as a beginning of the extension of Bradford's influence and an early example of sub-regional integration. In addition we see that even in those early times future industrialisation is foreshadowed, although production was small scale and only capable of satisfying the needs of the feudal farming communities.

**Chapter 4** looks at land use and the land tenurial processes which contributed to the creation of the modern fieldscape; the emerging settlement forms; and the greater use of the Region's mineral wealth prior to the industrial 'take off' of the late 18th century.

Undoubtedly the isolation of the Bradford region limited large scale industrialisation and as **chapter 5** shows, that isolation was not broken until the construction of the turnpikes and later, the canals. With the construction of the Leeds and Liverpool Canal and the Bradford Canal the Aire valley towns and villages were joined to the national communication system that linked them to the ports of Liverpool and Hull. This development completely transformed the industrial potential of the Region's natural wealth of water power, coal and iron. The railway network speeded transport and contributed further to regional development. These improvements in transport coincided with major technological developments in the manufacture of textiles, metal goods, engines, machinery and the organisation of industrial production in factories.

As **chapters 6 and 7** show, Bradford acquired the title of 'Worstedopolis' because of its pre-eminence in the production of worsted cloth, a function it shared with the former water-powered mills sites in the valleys of the River Aire and its tributaries. Here we see the growth of specialisation which gave a further impetus to the areal definition of the Region. To the physical connections made by the growing communication network were added the economic links of the cloth market and the specialisation in worsted cloth manufacture. Furthermore, the wool trade based on the Bradford cloth hall (the Piece Hall) also assisted in establishing Bradford's centralising influence vis-a-vis its neighbours.

Even in prehistoric times it is noted that people were migrating to the Region, a process that continued during the early middle ages. As **chapter 8** shows there was a period of slow growth in the population of the Region. Also there was relative demographic stability as a consequence of high birth rates being matched by equally high death rates. There were periodic outbreaks of plague and the prevalence of killing diseases which kept numbers down. The great change came with the increased accessibility of the Region and the rapid development of its coal and steam-based textile economy, to which large numbers of migrants were attracted from all parts of the British Isles. This influx contributed to the rapid increase in population of all the textile towns and villages in the Bradford Region, particularly during the 19th century. Amongst the arrivals, most notably, were the famine-stricken Irish victims of eviction, disease and starvation, who concentrated in limited areas in the inner parts of Bradford and Keighley. As we see, this poverty-stricken population contrasted with the tiny group of prosperous and economically influential German merchant settlers.

The early evolution of the human Region is discussed in the first eight chapters. The Region contained an apparently fragmented collection of free-standing settlements separated from each other and the rest of the country by a poor communication system and there was only limited differentiation between one place and another, but as we note, a beginning had been made in region formation with the construction of the transport and communication networks to provide the inter-connecting linkage. It served the common economic activity of wool and worsted cloth manufacture throughout the region and helped create a functional unity oriented towards Bradford centring on its Piece Hall. Here, as elsewhere, we are reminded of the role of the entrepreneural decision-maker in the creation of urban space and the construction of the human geography of the Region.

In **chapter 9** the spatial organisation of the urban centres - the built environment, is discussed with the emphasis on the buildings, especially housing, and the human problems arising from the creation of places that grew too quickly as a result of poor central management of the urban environment. **Chapter 10** is a critical examination of the connection between the sanitary condition and resultant unhealthiness of the Region's human environment. It discusses the health of towns and the weakness of local town governments in dealing with the environment where the property owning decision-maker was the real power. The chapter also looks at the social and economic reasons for the lack of progress in improving the health of the 19th century town. Chapter 10 also deals with the growing pressures to ensure more effective overall management of the urban areas and the progress of town government.

The regional concept has often exercised the thinking of geographers. In it they searched for the unifying characteristics of an area. It had value in application to the physical region. In dealing with the urban region, however, a different approach is required. The town extends its influence beyond the built-up area giving rise to the notion of 'rural-urban' space. It recognised that the town was not just a collection of buildings and streets merely confined to the built-up area, but extended its influence into the surrounding country area, so that thinking was directed towards human behaviour and locational choice. This aspect involved choice and decision-making, notably on the location of residences in relation to workplace. In this, the differences in income distribution within and between human groups are critical because they refer to the means and the opportunity to fulfil peoples' choice, leading to the creation of homogeneous single class social areas. Poor people however, are less able to choose where to live than the more affluent. In our area we see in chapter 11 that the interaction between the geographical separation of residence, workplace, shopping and service areas, manifests itself in movement, and in **chapter 11** the role of transport and communication in facilitating movement is also examined. Attention is drawn, therefore, to what might be called 'functional space', which as chapter 11 shows, depends on the movement of goods, and of people in particular. It is this movement that defines the city region, in which the transport and communication network provide the means, and the commuter flows help to quantify the relationship. It is the geographical pattern of this human interaction that helps define the Bradford city region.

The Bradford Region's industrial structure at the end of the 20th century is described in **chapter 12.** It notes the decline of the Region's basic manufacturing industries, especially of textiles, and offers an explanation for the change. It discusses the consequential unemployment of redundant workpeople, noting that it affects the largely male Asian textile workers more than the women employees because women are more readily absorbed in the growing service sector. Nevertheless manufacturing employment in the Region remains above the national average. The redundant former cloth mills are not easily adapted to the needs of modern industry, although there are a few examples of innovative use, including their use for cultural purposes such as museums, an art gallery and a business centre. Against the over-specialised economy which characterised the first sixty years of the 20th century there are examples of industrial diversification. Although there are some large firms, the small to medium firm is more typical of the Region's industrial structure. The examples of  the value of production, turnover, and profits in the review of the final year of the century present a healthy picture, not only in the economic buoyancy revealed in the financial statistics but many of the new businesses are in the 'growth sectors'.  The Region's contribution to the national economy is shown in its substantial export earnings. Thanks to the involvement of the local Council as industrial partner, new industrial distributions are being created through the development of business, retail and science parks, where the Bradford Council is an important  facilitator. There is no doubt that the creation of the University has been beneficial, not just as an employer but it is significant that the Lister Hills Science Park is sited next to the campus.  The service industries are important as employers and have their own geography. City centre shopping malls in Bradford and Keighley have helped in supporting the economy of the central business areas and they represent a relatively new feature in the Region, though older Bradfordians often express regret at the loss of the Swan Arcade.  In reviewing the business economy, the role of the ethnic shop in providing a service for the wider community and Asian restaurants, are strong features in the leisure economy of the Region.

**Chapter 13** studies the demographic geography of the Region.  Bradford's population at the beginning of the 20th century was 410,000.  In 2001 it was 481,000.  However by the end of the century its composition had changed considerably, largely due to changes in family size and the arrival in the Region of new ethnic groups from Europe, Africa, Asia and the Caribbean area. In the immediate post-war years people came from eastern Europe, many of whom were ex-service personnel, some were displaced by the transfer of territory in the re-drawing of the political map of Europe. Unlike the concentrations of the Asians from Pakistan and Bangladesh in the inner areas of Bradford and Keighley, they are dispersed throughout the Region and have been absorbed into the community, so there are few inner city  concentrations of these groups, but their social clubs and their churches are still in the inner urban areas. As regards Asian settlement a few began to settle in Bradford during the second World War, but the main influx has been since then.  They now form a sizeable minority.  In dealing with ethnicity however, it is important to note its diversity. In Chapter 13 the differences in the distribution of the social and ethnic groups are mapped and discussed, and we note the social contrasts between the inner urban and the outer urban commuter areas of Bradford and Keighley. The study focuses on the origins and the  phasing of the migration and the pattern of class and ethnicity. The socio-economic differences of the inner urban areas, especially in Bradford and Keighley, are contrasted with the outer commuter areas. Economic indicators which relate to income, such as car ownership, education, and property tenure help explain the differential social pattern.  The affluent are able to choose where to reside and can afford to commute to the city for work and to use the city centre facilities. The less well-off have less choice where to live, many live in the estates or the  terraced streets, and in the ethnic neighbourhoods of the inner city.  The reasons for the Asian migration are seen as the operation of 'push' factors and 'pull' factors. Between places in the Indian sub-continent and places like Bradford, where the attraction of work and of family ties have generated migration to the Region. In the case of Asian settlement the relationship between numbers and cultural self-sufficiency is noted, and  illustrated in maps. Using the data of the census, the ethnic maps locate the ethnic neighbourhoods and give a 'broad-brush' view of social distributions within the Region based on the electoral ward divisions.

Undoubtedly **Bradford is a surprising place** with a diversity of landscapes, and an interesting  history. It has a lively cultural life, which has been enriched by the people it has attracted from other parts of the world who are the new Bradfordians. It has had its bleak periods but it has shown resilience and a capacity to absorb newcomers and accommodate change.

## REFERENCES
1. H.M. Stationery Office: *Royal Commission on Local Government in England 1966-69*,  vol I. Report. 1969 p.194
2. Richardson, C. *A Geography of Bradford*.  University of Bradford 1976 Chapter 12
3. Hinds, Sarah  'Commuting and Transport Trends' Appendix 3, National Census 1971-1991 - 10% Sample 1996
   West Yorkshire Metropolitan  County Council: *West Yorkshire: an Archaeological Survey  to A.D. 1500*, 1981.

CHAPTER ONE

# THE PHYSICAL SETTING

## RELIEF AND DRAINAGE

The Carboniferous rocks of the Millstone Grit and the Lower Coal Measures series underlying the Bradford Region have had a profound influence on its relief, drainage, climate, soils, vegetational cover and human activity. The Millstone Grits are the oldest rocks, and as figure 2 shows, produce the high relief of the Pennine Moors to the west; and the more rewarding Coal Measures which continue the plateau surface to form the basin-like Bradford-dale which occupies the eastern tract. The Coal Measures have contributed greatly to the economic development of the lower-lying areas especially in Inner Bradford. From the high points of Addingham High Moor at 384 metres above ordnance datum (O.D.) and 443 metres O.D. on Keighley Moor, the Grits of the Pennine plateau dip towards the southeast, and this gently sloping surface continues across the Lower Coal Measures to a height of about 160 metres O.D. on the boundary between Bradford and Leeds. Into this dipping surface have been excavated the main valleys of Airedale and Wharfedale, the lowest points of which, lie at about 70 metres above ordnance datum. Although the moorland Grits constitute a major scenic asset, a local 'lung', and a valuable recreational area for the local urban population; their poor soils and harsher climate have inhibited human activity, so that settlement, has been confined to the lower land and to the valley benches. The generally northwest to southeast trending valleys show a marked steepening of the north facing slopes compared with the gentler south facing slopes, to produce an asymmetrical cross-sectional valley profile in Airedale and Wharfedale. The impressive scarps which fringe Rombalds Moor contribute to the grandeur of its landscape, especially at Rivock Edge on the western edge; in the rocky scarp south of Addingham, and in the majestic vertical faces of the Cow and Calf rocks which overlook Ilkley. In the Keighley Moor region the steep sides of the Worth valley, the appropriately named Thwaites Brow, and the north-facing slopes south of the River Aire, are supported by the same resistant Grits. On Rombalds Moor this worn-down surface appears as an eastward sloping, largely unrelieved, horizon, partly interrupted by the newer Lower Coal Measures' outlier of Baildon Moor. South of the Aire the Pennine plateau has a similar inclination. On the northern edge of Rombalds Moor there is little development of tributary streams draining from the Moor into the Wharfe. In contrast, south of the River Aire a number of streams flow into the Aire to drain the moorland surface. The deep valley of the River Worth gathers water from the Grits of the Keighley and the Haworth moors, to be fed by waters collected on the Oxenhope Moor. Further east Harden Beck takes its rise near Denholme Gate.

In addition to forming locations for settlement and industrial development, including waterpower for the corn, fulling and worsted mills strung along their sides, these valleys provided sites for the construction of reservoirs intended to satisfy the increasing industrial and domestic water needs of Bradford during the 19th century, starting with the reservoirs at Manywells and Chellow Dean (on Lower Coal Measures), 1855; Stubden, Doe Park, 1860; extending to the Thornton and Oxenhope Moors in 1885. However it was the Bradford Beck valley which became the most important of these Airedale tributary valleys. At the same time it should be said its catchment and value as an industrial water power source proved to be too limited and Bradford Corporation had to go further north to Nidderdale to satisfy the City's needs.

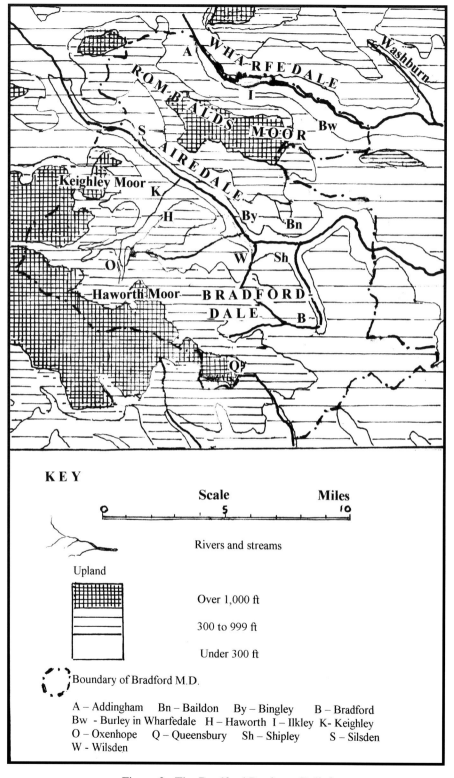

**KEY**

Scale       Miles

0       5       10

Rivers and streams

Upland

Over 1,000 ft

300 to 999 ft

Under 300 ft

Boundary of Bradford M.D.

A – Addingham    Bn – Baildon    By – Bingley    B – Bradford
Bw - Burley in Wharfedale   H – Haworth   I – Ilkley   K- Keighley
O – Oxenhope    Q – Queensbury    Sh – Shipley    S – Silsden
W - Wilsden

Figure 2. The Bradford Region – Relief

# GEOLOGY

## SOLID GEOLOGY

The solid geology of our area consists typically of sequences of sediments in both the Millstone Grits and the Lower Coal Measures. Faulting has occurred throughout, determining the northwest-southeast orientation of the main valleys, and bringing near the surface, or concentrating in some localities, assemblages of coals and other valuable raw materials. (See figure 3). Though of enormous importance to the 19th and 20th century industrial and domestic economy of Bradford, production had almost ceased by the mid-1920s.

**MILLSTONE GRIT**  Millstone Grit, the total succession of which is more than 305 metres thick, varies in thickness in different localities.  As well as being a dominant feature of the moorland landscape, so significant in the leisure economy, we should not forget its economic importance in other income-earning ways.  For example, the stone has been quarried at a number of places.  Its hard, resistant grit, as the name implies, was used in the manufacture of grindstones in milling.  Nor should we forget the value of the gritstone as a building material, particularly in the older built-up areas where it can be seen in the older buildings to  give the local  urban landscapes a distinctive 'regional character'.   The grit strata vary in texture, sometimes they contain very coarse sandstone and pebbles.  The succession also includes coarse sandstone interbanded with shale, clay and mudstone, and at Silsden iron bearing shales occur. Occasionally thin seams of coal are found; e.g. at  Bingley Brick Pit where a 3 inch (7.6cm) seam is recorded; and coal 'smuts' are mentioned in the geological memoir on the area at High and Low Bradley, Riddlesden, Stanbury and Thwaites. The coal, rarely thicker than 5cm, was of poor quality, so exploitation where it occurred, was consequently small scale. The Grits are given different names depending on locality, as for example, in  the Silsden Moor Grit where it is 61 metres thick.  Similarly a local name was given to the Grit deposits south of Addingham where it is distinguished by the fossil content and designated, Addingham Edge Grit. This member of the grits series extends eastwards to the Ilkley and Burley moorland.

## LOWER COAL MEASURES

Lower Coal Measures cover the remaining part of the Bradford district. They are shown in the generalised section in figure 3 and form the northwestern section of the Yorkshire Coalfield. The base of the series lies at the top of the Rough Rock Group of the Millstone Grit succession and has a maximum thickness of 335 metres. In reviewing the geology of this succession it is important to remember that the presence of a number of different coals offering different industrial uses often occurs at the same site in a number of favoured locations, leading to the establishment of  large mining, metalworking and engineering works in Bradford-dale in the late 18th and the 19th centuries. The lowest  member of this series is the **Pot Clay Coal.**  It was found at Thornton Moor reservoir where the coal was 5cm thick;  and deposits were found at Cottingley Moor Bridge where it was known as Cottingley Crow Coal. Here its thickness was12.7cm. However, the **Soft Bed Coal**  is the lowest occurring coal of economic importance in our area. It has a  geographical spread extending from Denholme, located on a site near the church, at the Road Side Pit in Thornton, at Heaton Royd Colliery and on Baildon Common

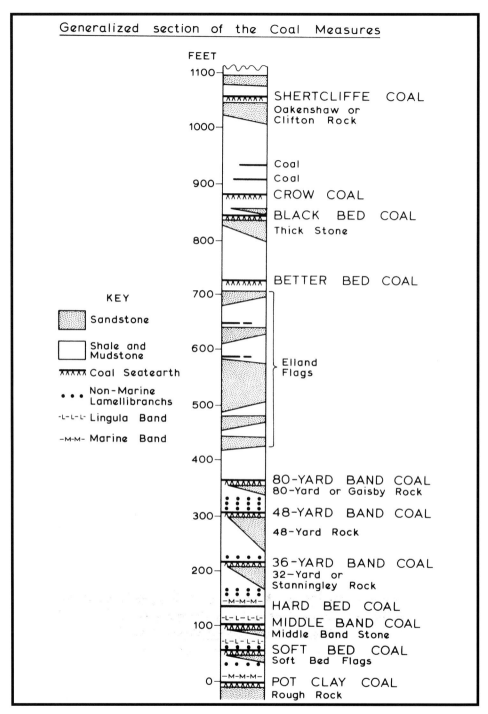

Figure 3. Generalised Section through the Lower Coal Measures in the Bradford Area.
The breaks in the section consist of sandstones, shales and mudstones, with no
commercially productive seams of coal.
Based on the Geological Memoir, Geology of the Country between Skipton and Bradford
H.M.S.O. 1953 – Copyright British Geological Survey c NERC All rights reserved

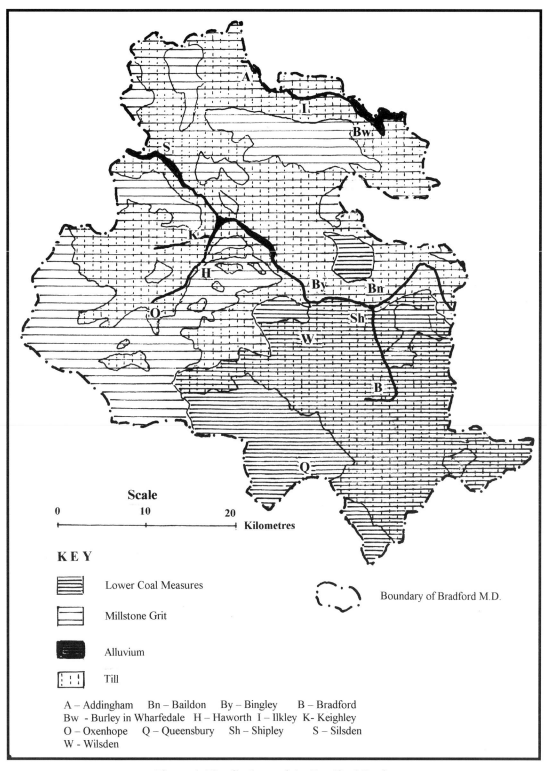

Figure 4. The Geology of the Bradford Region.
Based on the Geological Memoir, Geology of the Country between Skipton and Bradford
H.M.S.O. 1953 – Copyright British Geological Survey c NERC All rights reserved

11

where its thickness was 46cm. The seat earth of this coal has been worked for fireclay. The **Hard Bed Coal** described as of poor quality, is found over most of the Bradford basin, achieving a thickness of between 61 and 69cm in the west of Bradford-dale. It thins out to between 43cm and 51cm in the east. Above the **36-Yard Coal** lie thin coal seams separated by shaley mudstones and sandstones. Of the latter, Gaisby Rock is quarried at Bolton Woods on the eastern edge of the North Brook. By far the most widespread sandstone type is the Elland Flags sequence which reaches a thickness of 92 metres. The flags split into thin slabs and are frequently separated by shales. The hard wearing flag element is important in its scenic effect because of its near-horizontal alignment as a capping feature on the plateau which surrounds the rim of Bradford-dale, and in the dale's stepped slopes. Its versatile use as a building material can be seen in the stone walls, the roofs of the older houses and factories; and its hard-wearing properties make it ideal as a paving material in the footpaths of the dale. Above the Elland Flags stratum, in measures totalling 83 metres, are found the coal seams which were of greatest significance in Bradford's development, namely the **Better Bed Coal** and the **Black Bed Coal.** The Better Bed Coal had low ash content. It reaches a thickness of about a metre in the west of the Dale decreasing towards the east. It was important in the town's iron-smelting industry because of the absence of such impurities as sulphur and phosphorous. The seat earth of this seam was also worked for fireclay, and the ganister has been used in making firebricks. Thirty three metres above the Better Bed Coal lies the Black Bed Coal, where the seam ranges between 20cm and 27cm in thickness. Associated with the Better Bed Coal and forming the roof deposits is the **Black Bed Ironstone** group of carbonaceous shale 3 metres deep containing thin layers of clay ironstone, which yielded an ore of 30% metalic ore. The iron industry of Low Moor, Bowling, Bierley and Farnley was based on this assembly of coals, iron ore and the useful seat earth. In the southeast of Bradford-dale **Shertcliffe Coal** comes to the surface, of which the **Crow Coal** was of importance as a gas and a domestic fuel.

## STRUCTURE

The block structure of the Pennines has been subjected to earth movements since its original uplift. During and after these upheavals there were long periods of erosion which removed the overlying rocks, eventually to produce today's eastward dipping plateau. The block was subject to some folding west of our area in the form of the Skipton anticline and the Bradley syncline; but faulting is the dominant structural element affecting the plateau surface. A number of major faults, which have a mainly southeasterly trend, cross the region. They have influenced the direction of the valleys of the Aire and the Wharfe. Further south the Hewenden and the Denholme Clough faults follow the same alignment. Between these principal faults the land has been subject to numerous minor faults, described in the district geological memoir as a 'shatter belt'. Vertical displacement of the strata resulting from this faulting, has had the effect of making accessible, at or near the surface, minerals of economic value, notably coal, iron and other industrial materials, thus favouring the industrial development of particular locations.

# DRIFT GEOLOGY

## GLACIATION

The plateau was covered with ice during the Pleistocene geological period (the Ice Age) now evidenced by the presence of boulders and pebbles on its surface. Some of these glacial deposits included limestone derived from areas to the west. The latter occurred in sufficient quantity to support lime working at some places on the plateau; for example, at Lanshaw Delves on Ilkley Moor, at Keighley Moor, at Bingley, and at Beckfoot. In the later stages of the glacial epoch glaciers occupied the Wharfe and Aire valleys ponding melt waters in the side valleys to form lakes. These lake levels, which can be inferred by their outfall 'nicks', reached a height of over 360 metres on Keighley Moor and over 335 metres on the moor west of Addingham to give us some idea of the thickness of glaciers flowing down the Aire and Wharfe valleys. The greatest development of the late-glacial lakes was on the south side of the Aire valley. Wharfedale, with fewer side valleys was, less affected by the glacial lake phenomenon. As noted, notches corresponding to the outfall level of these lakes occur in succession down valley, Lake Bradford being the largest. At its head a delta developed forming flat surfaces near Leaventhhorpe Hall and further west at Bell Dean. In Wharfedale the ice receded at a slower pace than that of Airedale, resulting in the formation of drumlins as the Wharfedale ice turned south through the Guiseley Gap into Airedale. Some of the dry valleys occupying the outfall notches have been used as reservoirs, such as the storage reservoir at Chellow Dean. Moraine left behind by the ice, covers large parts of the lower-lying terrain, filling in the lowest parts of the main valleys and the Bradford Beck valley, to form flatter surfaces, while morainic bench-like features can be seen along the valley sides of the Aire. Overlying the moraine, more recent *alluvium* flanks the rivers and smaller streams. Parts of the valley bottoms on the low flat areas of the Aire and Wharfe are liable to flood. Landslips occurred at the Cow and Calf and below the scarp at Addingham High Moor in Wharfedale, and at the Chevin further east outside our area. A layer of *peat* covers the high moors of Keighley and Stanbury. At Clough Hey Allotment it reaches a thickness of 2 metres; and there are patches on Ilkley Moor about a metre deep, sufficient to have been worked, for example, at Crawshaw Moss, and peat deposits are found on some valley terraces in Airedale. There are several references to rights of *turbary* in the court rolls of earlier times.

# CLIMATE

## TEMPERATURE (see table 1)
With a difference of over 360 metres between the highest and the lowest parts of our area, relief plays a major part in influencing precipitation, temperature and such aspects as cloudiness and therefore the hours of bright sunshine. Temperature falls 0.65 degrees Celsius for every 102 metres of altitude so that Keighley Moor (443 metres) is almost two degrees cooler on average than Lister Park at 133 metres O.D, suggesting a mean difference between the two places of l.3 degrees Celsius during the months of January and February. In addition the growing season (i.e. for grass, the months averaging 4 degrees Celsius or more) is about one month shorter on the high ground on Keighley Moor and Rombalds Moor compared with the Lister Park Weather Station (see table 1). But in evaluating the limiting impact of the lower temperatures on agriculture, especially for sensitive plants, we should remember that the averages conceal the occasional killing frost. For example during the period 1924 to l950, there were only two years, 1924 and 1937, when ground frost did not occur in May, and in thirteen of the years there was at least one occurrence of frost in the month of September.

## Table 1. Temperature Bradford Lister Park (135m) 1950

| Temp C° | Jan | Feb | Mar | Apr | May | June | July | Aug | Sept | Oct | Nov | Dec | Year |
|---|---|---|---|---|---|---|---|---|---|---|---|---|---|
| | 3.3 | 3.4 | 5.1 | 7.4 | 10.4 | 13.9 | 15.5 | 15.01 | 12.9 | 9.4 | 5.8 | 4.1 | 8.7 |

Source - Meteorological Office - Average Temperature Gt. Britain and Northern Ireland

# Table 2 Bright Sunshine, Bradford Lister Park (135) 1931-1960

| Average Daily and Monthly Hours for the years 1931-1960 | | | | | | | | | | | | |
| --- | --- | --- | --- | --- | --- | --- | --- | --- | --- | --- | --- | --- |
| | Jan | Feb | Mar | Apr | May | June | July | Aug | Sept | Oct | Nov | Dec | Year |
| Daily | 1.54 | 1.92 | 2.79 | 4.52 | 5.58 | 6.36 | 5.44 | 4.87 | 3.73 | 2.43 | 1.3 | 0.76 | 3.4 |
| Monthly | 32 | 54 | 86 | 136 | 173 | 191 | 169 | 151 | 112 | 75 | 39 | 24 | 1.242 |

Source: Meterological Office - Gt Britain and Northern Ireland

## RAINFALL (see table 3).

## Table 3 Annual Average Rainfall - The Bradford Region 1961-1990 (millimetres)

| Weather Station | Marley Sewage Works | Otley | Bradford Lister Park | Lower Laithe Res. | Silsden | Chelker | Wilsden |
| --- | --- | --- | --- | --- | --- | --- | --- |
| Annual Rainfall mm. | 866 | 743 | 873 | 1233 | 925 | 976 | 1061 |
| Approx. height above O.D. metres | Under 100 | 60 | 135 | 160 | 160 | 230 | 240 |
| Grid Ref. SE | 087412 | 209460 | 149352 | 015367 | 044475 | 052517 | 088349 |

Source: Yorkshire Water

Rainfall differences are also evident on higher ground compared with lower-lying areas. Thus at Heaton Reservoir (162 metres O.D.) the annual average totalled 867mm, and at Stubden Reservoir (326 metres) the annual mean was 1277 millimetres. Table 3 gives further information. Compare the low-lying Otley (60m O.D.) average of 743 mm. per year with that of Wilsden at 240 m. O.D. where annual rainfall is1061mm. The 'rain shadow' effect can be seen when compared with the heavy rainfall of the high Pennine moors and the lowland section of the Wharfe valley lying in the lee of the the Pennine upland at Otley. April to July appear to be the driest months, and October to January is the wettest time of the year. Overall however, the Bradford Region's average rainfall is high compared with that of the Vale of York where the annual precipitation is 627mm, indicating its drier and sunnier climate, thus making it more suited to arable cultivation than the Bradford region which favours pastoral farming. Similarly, table 2 shows less sunny conditions in Bradford, which has an annual total of 1242 hours of bright sunshine compared with the 1304 hours at Askham Bryan in the Vale of York.

## SUNSHINE
The seasonal distribution of bright sunshine in Bradford-dale is shown in table 2. During the period l93l to l960 the sunniest months on average were May and June. But the most cloudy months may be inferred from the fact that 40% of rainfall of Bradford-dale occurs during the period October to January. High land is subject to greater cloudiness. Fog frequency was measured by S.R. Eyre in his study of 'Fog in Yorkshire' which showed that the higher parts of Bradford-dale in the Wibsey and Bradford Moor areas were subject to above average fogginess.

## WIND DIRECTION

The prevailing wind in Bradford is from the northwest-southwest quadrant. This was revealed in the analysis of the Lister Park records of wind direction in the author's '*A Geography of Bradford*'. It also showed that during the period for which data were available (1918-1939), winds from the south blew for only 5.6 percent of the year, and there was a marked increase in wind from the east and from the north in March and April.

## THE EFFECT OF CLIMATIC CHANGE

In evaluating the climate data discussed above, it is important to remember that the global temperature is rising, and this is likely to have an effect on rainfall and other aspects of climate covered by the above data. However, the tables are useful in showing climate differences between high and low land and in the distribution of the climatic variation through the year.

## 'NATURAL VEGETATION'

As the following chapter shows 'Natural Vegetation' has continually changed since the time of the disappearance of the Pennine glaciers. In late *Devensian* times (11,000 to 9,000 B.C.) tundra occupied the surface in our region. Since then climate changes and successions of plant colonisation have changed the natural environment. But also intervention by hunters and gatherers, and graziers and farmers, has resulted in changes in the vegetational cover. Today, therefore, we see a mixture of heather, acid tolerant grasses, and mosses; also in the cloughs a scatter of moorland shrubs may occur, together with lichen-covered patches of the bare rock of the Millstone Grit.

## SOILS

A large part of the Bradford Region can be classed as farmland, though Outer Bradford contains large moorland areas. It is in the lower parts of Bradford-dale, Airedale and Wharfedale that we find better environments for agriculture. Until the industral developments of the 19th and 20th centuries soil was the main local economic resource and it can still be treated as significant in the local economy today. On the higher western moors of Outer Bradford, raw peat soils are found. They vary in thickness from a few centimetres to over 9 cm, tending to be shallower on steeper slopes. On Rombalds Moor, where leaching is greater, *gley* soils are evident. Gley soils develop where soils are subject to the movement of the water table through the soil profile according to the season, so as to saturate it at one time and partially to dry it out at other times. Their texture is clayey. Being semi waterlogged, they are the result of leaching and chemical change and consequently are poorer in plant foods. In freer drained sandy, or gravelly areas *podzols* may develop. In contrast, on the lower land of the valleys more fertile *Brown Earths* occupy their flatter parts. Thus in most of Inner Bradford below 160 metres and on the lower terraces and benches of the Aire and Wharfe valleys where less harsh climatic conditions prevail, soils benefit from the richer vegetation which adds to the organic content of the soils. But in general the soils of Bradford-dale are poor and were incapable of supporting large populations that were mainly dependent on agriculture. The author in his *Geography of Bradford* refers to a number of farmland soil samples he had taken from different parts of Bradford-dale, which revealed soil pH values of 5, indicating acid conditions. While considerable variations are evident in local soils due to slope, orientation and intensity, and microclimate, it is possible to make certain generalisations. Firstly all the local soils tend to be moisture retentive and are naturally acidic, partly due to the higher rainfall (above 160 metres the average annual precipitation is over 867mm). This leaches out neutralising minerals such as lime. Soil acidity is also partly due to the mineral content of the drift material which makes up the skeletal content of the soil. However, on steep slopes soils are thinner as the important humic layer is removed by water wear. The following chapters examine the part played by natural factors as well as showing the importance of human action in the development of the Bradford Region.

## SITES OF SPECIAL SCIENTIFIC INTEREST (S.S S.I.)

Within the Bradford Region there are sixteen designated Sites of Special Scientific Interest (S.S.S.I) where some of the generalisations on the geology discussed above may be studied in the field. Their location is shown in Appendix I.

## APPENDIX I - REGIONALLY IMPORTANT DESIGNATED SITES OF SPECIAL SCIENTIFIC INTEREST IN THE BRADFORD REGION

1. Horton Bank Reservoir
2. Ponden Clough
3. Royds Hall Beck
4. Goitstock Waterfall
5. Baildon Bank Quarries
6. Addingham Edge Millstone Quarry
7. Wrose Hill
8. Noon Nick glacial overflow channel
9. Lanshaw Delves Moraine
10. Cow and Calf Rocks
11. Dimples End Quarry
12. Shipley Glen
13. Baildon Moor
14. Throstle Nest
15. Double Stones
16. Eldwick Crag

Source: West Yorkshire Regionally Important Geological Sites Group

## REFERENCES

1. *The Geology section is based partly on Green A.H. et al. The Geology of the Yorkshire Coalfield and Geological Survey of Great Britain: The Geology of the Country between Skipton and Bradford, and the local sheets of the Geological Survey Drift Sheets 69 and 77. 1955 and exracts from map Sheets SD93-94,SEO2, SE O3, SE O4, SE 12, SE 13, SE 22 and SE23.* COPYRIGHT NERC by permission of British Geological Survey, IPR /26-44C.
2. *Proceedings of the Yorkshire Geological Society.* Vol 24; p. 129, contributions by Sissons J.B. and Hudson R.G.S. and Dunning A.V. 1941.
3. Air Ministry - Meteorological Office. *Tables of average Temperature Great Britain and Northern Ireland 1921-1950.*
4. Air Ministry - Meteorological Office. *Tables of Bright Sunshine Great Britain and Northern Ireland 1931 - 1960.*
5. Yorkshire Water. Data provided by the Company covering the period 1961-1990.
6. Wind direction frequency derived from the weather records of the Lister Park Meteorological Station, Bradford.
7. Sir John Russell. *The World of Soil* 1957.
8. Pearsall, W.H. *Mountains and Moorlands* 1970.
9. Richardson, C. A. *Geography of Bradford* 1976.

# CHAPTER TWO

# THE HUMAN LANDSCAPE BEFORE 500 A.D.

It is possible there was some migration of paleolithic people from the mainland of Europe into Britain in early post glacial times, while the country was still joined to the continent; and before the rise in sea level severed the land connection to form the English Channel. Figure 5 shows in simplified form, the importance of Rombalds Moor in prehistoric times. Table 6[4] shows the climatic and vegetational changes which can be related to the cultural phases in the Region before 500 A.D. In interpreting the table it should be noted that in the Pennine region the human events would more likely have taken place many years later than in lowland Britain because of the harsher environment of this upland region. Archaeological evidence apparent from figure 5, also suggests a continuum of human activity rather than the sharp divisions between one culture and another. For example, Mesolithic triangular arrowheads may be found on the same site alongside Neolithic leaf-shaped types, and Neolithic, with Bronze Age artifacts.

With the rise in global temperature at the end of the Ice Age the northern European ice-cap retreated and the Aire and Wharfe valley glaciers shrank. Tundra vegetation began to colonise the denuded land following the disappearance of the ice. From about 8000 B.C. birch and pine began to occupy the British Isles, to be replaced by mixed oak with hazel, and pine woodland in the following two millennia. By the end of the post glacial era wetter conditions led to the increase in alder woodland and peat formed on the higher land. The Paleolithic Age in Britain dates from between 10,000 and 5000 B.C., and it is from about this time that evidence of Old Stone Age man is found. However, it is likely that the arrival of this cultural group in our area would be later. As a generalisation, in spite of a few examples of archaeological finds, it does seem that the heavier soils of Inner Bradford and the lower valley land were avoided by early man until the early Mediaeval period.

## PALEOLITHIC AND MESOLITHIC (MIDDLE STONE AGE - 8000 TO 5000 B.C.)

The change in vegetation at the end of the Atlantic climatic period was no doubt partly due to the intervention of man as well as to climate. Barnes[2] refers to the possibility of 'slash and burn' activity reducing the denser tree canopy to a more open type of woodland on the upland fringes. The occurrence of arrowheads and geometric microliths beneath eroded peat deposits on the high moors indicate a hunting and gathering culture, though there have been a few discoveries of tranchet axes associated with the later Mesolithic. The evidential geographical range of Mesolithic artifacts, extends from the region south of the Aire including: Haworth Brow Moor, Harden Moor, Stanbury Moor, Keighley Moor, Oxenhope Moor and Thornton Moor, and across the valley on to the upland moors between the Aire and the Wharfe. But significantly the *West Yorkshire Archaeological Survey (WYAS)* notes the 'dearth of Mesolithic finds from the Bradford basin' and it notes that favoured settlement sites were located on the better drained terraces above flood levels. North of the Aire large numbers of broad blade microliths were found, on Hope Hill and Pennythorne Hill on Baildon Moor, and at Charlestown, where archaeologists associate the finds with the early period of the Mesolithic. The West Yorkshire Survey notes that there were settlement sites in the lower Washburn Valley, and at Chevin and that these were base sites, as was evidenced by the presence of micro cores, blades and flakes.

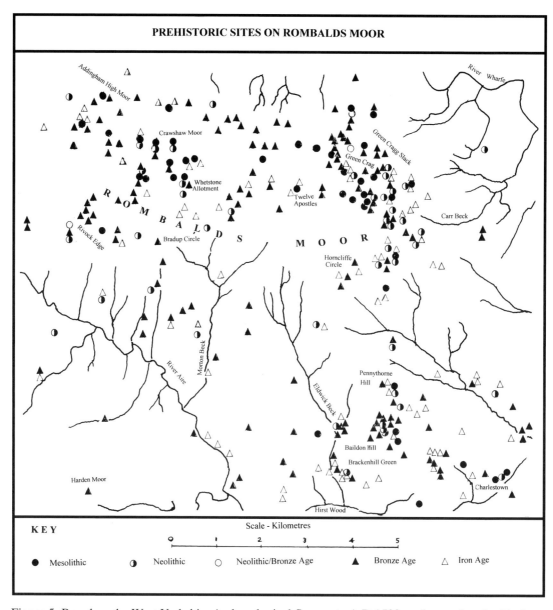

Figure 5. Based on the West Yorkshire Archaeological Survey to A.D.1500, and reproduced with the permission of the West Yorkshire Archaeological Service

The Archaeological studies of Green Crag and Green Crag Slack, on the eastern side of Rombalds Moor all lying at or above 244 metres, revealed a predominance of broad blade microliths and a marked absence of microliths such as scrapers[3], supporting the view that these sites possibly were not permanent sites but used by the hunters and gatherers on a seasonal or temporary basis. But at the same time the general point can be made that the whole upland area was exploited on a seasonal basis as a hunting ground, a function which continued in later cultural periods.

**Table 4. Climate and Vegetational Changes[4]**

| STAGES | CLIMATIC PERIOD | VEGETATION | DATES B.C |
|---|---|---|---|
|  | Sub Atlantic | Upland Peat Forest Clearance in stages | 0 |
|  | Sub Boreal | Increase Ash Birch | 500 1,000 1,750 |
|  |  |  | 2,000 2,500 2,500 3,000 4,000 |
| Post Glacial | Atlantic | Increase Alder and Peat on higher land | 5,000 |
|  | Boreal | Mixed Oak with Hazel and Pine | 6,000 7,000 |
|  | Pre-Boreal | Birch and Pine | 8,000 |
| Late Glacial | Upper Dryas | Tundra | 9,000 10,000 |
|  | Lower Dryas |  | 11,000 |

## NEOLITHIC PERIOD (5000 to 1500 B.C.)

Radio carbon studies show that the British Isles experienced marked climatic changes during the Neolithic Age. Climatic warming would favour development of farming in favoured lowland areas. Pollen analysis shows a reduction in some tree species, e.g. elm, during Neolithic times. According to archaeologists an altitudinal division exists covering the area below 305 metres O. D. and the higher land, from which it is inferred the upland was used as hunting and gathering territory and the terraces and valley benches lying between 122 and 183 metres O.D. as settled land. Quantities of flint on the alluvium of the River Aire were found north west of Idle and similar evidence suggests occupation during the Neolithic period at Baildon, Bingley and Shipley, Green Crag Slack on Baildon Moor and on Hawksworth Moor, from which it is suggested that these places were being more permanently settled. Notable finds of axes, e.g. as at Silsden and Keighley, infer some clearance of forest, possibly for pastoral or farming activity. The Neolithic enclosure on Rombalds Moor would no doubt substantiate this view.[5]

## BRONZE AGE (1500 to 500 B.C.)

The Bronze Age of 12th and 11th centuries B.C. was a period of major climatic change which influenced changes in such important aspects of human occupation as land use and settlement. There is considerable evidence of Bronze Age occupation in the moorland region of the Bradford Region, especially on the Rombalds, Ilkley, and Baildon Moors. (See figure 5) Here are found barrows, ceremonial monuments, stone circles, and what are considered to be ancient field systems. Some of the evidence comes from the finds of bronze artifacts and ceramics. Radio-carbon dating and the archaeological analysis of peat formation associated with the presence of socketed axes and pegged spearheads also point to a change in human activity coinciding with the wetter phase of the sub-boreal. Most of the pollen analyses show tree cover on the uplands and the valley slopes giving way to the spread of peat, heather, cotton grass and the development of podsols. The discovery of Bronze Age axes such as palstave broad butt types at a number of widely spread places including Keighley, Cullingworth, Silsden and Riddlesden, suggest a greater emphasis on tree removal by the Bronze Age inhabitants, demonstrating their role in changing the vegetational cover as well as changing the moorland area's land use to pastoral and possibly, shifting cultivating farm practice. It is worth noting that the parallel banks on Baildon Moor have been interpreted as a Bronze Age field system. There was also an enclosure at Brackenhall Green (Shipley Glen), at ditched enclosures at Hirst Wood north of the Aire, and at Catstone Ring on Harden Moor. Archaeologists have described the Baildon and Rombalds Moor sites as an area of major occupation by Bronze Age people. Certainly, sites yielding a variety of flint and other artifacts such as those at Green Crag Slack and Baildon Moor point to a long and more or less permanent occupation of those localities. As does the widespread presence of burial sites like that at Harden Moor south of the Aire, where there was a circle surrounding four or five urns; or the ring barrows of Birch Close, Dobrudden and Pennythorne Hill on Baildon Moor; and Thornecliffe and Great Skirtfull of Stones on Rombalds Moor. In addition, Thornton and Chellow Dean yielded funerary finds providing further evidence of the extent of Bronze Age involvement in our area. Over one hundred cup and ring and other monuments have been discovered on Rombalds Moor, Addingham Moor, Bingley and at Riddlesden also dating from the Bronze Age, emphasising the cultural importance of this part of the Pennine moorland to the inhabitants of that period.

## IRON AGE (500 - 0 B.C.)

Pollen evidence indicates that the Iron Age was a period of less favourable climatic conditions characterised by the heavier precipitation of the sub-Atlantic. Barnes notes that dense woodland persisted into the Roman period. There would be increased cloudiness and lower temperatures, both being less favourable to arable farming.

During the sub-Atlantic climatic period, peat bog increased on the higher ground and there was a general deterioration of soils. Population was thin even in favoured areas like the Vale of York. By the later part of the Iron Age our region had become Brigantian tribal territory. Although generally thinly settled, there is an accumulation of evidence of settlement in the Aire valley, notably in the Baildon, Bingley and Keighley areas. Also the discovery of an iron loom weight at Harden, and the finding of sherds on Burley Moor hint at a wider distribution. Iron artifacts are less likely to survive, especially in the acid soils of the Grit regions, and there are only a few pottery fragments referred to in the literature. Thus identification of occupation comes largely from the interpretation of earthwork structures correlated with radio carbon dating. These settlement phases may be divided into those related to defence such as Almondbury to the south and outside of our area, and those identified as serving an agricultural purpose. Prehistoric walls on Cullingworth Moor, similar structures at Harden Moor, and at Wilsden, as well as the earthworks at Crossley Wood Bingley and Hirst Wood are all considered to relate to a pastoral economy, probably of a transhumant nature.

## THE ROMAN PERIOD (0 to 410 A.D.)

At the time of the Roman annexation of Britain in A.D. 43 the area identified here as the Bradford Region, was part of the tribal territory of the Brigantes. Although they were the biggest tribe in Britain, their tribal organisation consisted of war bands, and the many valleys penetrating the Pennines favoured this kind of social fragmentation. Sheppard Frere in 'Britannia'[6] refers to their organisation as 'federal'. In a footnote she states that they could hardly have numbered fewer than 10,000 'to judge by the (Roman) garrison that was required to control them'. They were brought under central control by an energetic queen Cartimandua and her consort Venutius. Their capital was *Isurium* (Aldborough). Brigantia occupied an area covering North and West Yorkshire, Lancashire, Westmorland, Cumberland and County Durham. By A.D.51 it had become a client state of the Romans under Queen Cartimandua, who had helped the Roman rulers by assisting in the extradition of the rebellious Caractacus. However, she had quarrelled with Venutius who in A.D. 69-70 led an invasion of Brigantian territory, causing Cartimandua to seek Roman help. So effectively, the Roman occupation of our area began in A.D. 71, and Brigantia became a 'buffer state' in the Roman defences against raids by the Scots. To secure their control of the conquered province, the Roman occupation of Britain depended on a system of strongholds to defend and police this part of their empire. The fort to control Wharfedale at *Olicana* (Ilkley) formed part of this system. A levelled, rectangular expanse of green with a wall fragment, by the Manor House Museum overlooking the River Wharfe marks part of the site of the fort. Olicana was founded during the time of Agricola (A.D. 37-93) as governor of Britain, evacuated during the reign of Hadrian ( A.D. 76-138) and was re-occupied from about A.D.160 until the end of the Roman occupation (A.D. 410). The West Yorkshire Archaeological Survey shows a Roman route (road?) linking Olicana with Adel and Tadcaster. A reminder of the nature of the land use in Roman times is provided by the agricultural sites in Airedale at Crossley Wood and Hirst Wood, Bingley. These are attributed to the Roman period from the evidence of datable finds at the Crossley Wood excavation. Here there was a length of walling which is believed to have been a cattle pound. The flanged dish of third century provenance, which was found built into the wall, and a sherd of Samian ware, also helped date the site. Nearby were enclosures also considered to be of this period, as were similar structures at Hirst Wood east of the Crossley site. The West Yorkshire Archaeological study lists a number of isolated finds in the study area, e.g. brooches at Harden Moor, Idle and Keighley; pottery at Gilstead Lane, Bingley, and at Silsden; also a coffin at Leeds Road, Bradford; and inhumations at Idle.

## AFTER THE ROMANS

The Roman Empire came to an end as a result of attacks by Barbarians from the east. Rome itself was sacked by Alaric the Hun in A.D. 410, by which time Roman troops previously stationed in Britain had been withdrawn. With this, the British tribal areas lost the protection of Rome. The Pictish invaders from Scotland crossed the Roman Wall and threatened Brigantia, which was weakly organised because it was split into small kingdoms. In the north was Deira, corresponding approximately to the modern County Durham, south of that was Bernicia and Elmet. It is believed that to the northwest of Elmet lay the Celtic-speaking kingdom of *Cravenscire*. Proof of the extent of the area of the British kingdom of Elmet is found today in the number of place names bearing the name Elmet in the district east of Leeds. Our study area includes a part of the *Cravenscire* region. Even during the Roman era Teutonic pirates had begun to raid the eastern coastal areas of England eventually establishing control and colonising eastern Yorkshire, from where they penetrated westward. The British resisted these attacks but resistance was broken and the combined British forces were beaten by the Anglo Saxon invaders at the battle of Catterick c.A.D. 600. Using place name evidence there are only a few examples of Scandinavian intrusion in our area, compared with the areas to the east.

In this review of the Bradford Region in prehistoric times, thousands of years of change in the local landscape due to natural environmental factors can be recognised, but at least from Mesolithic times, human action has played a significant part in changing the natural plant cover and the soils, to produce, for example, the moorscapes of today. During most of the period pastoralism largely influenced by climate, seemed to have been the main kind of farming, even into Roman times. The widespread use of the heavier soils of the boulder clay areas was avoided until Mediaeval times and the more rewarding better-drained soil environments of the valley terraces continued to be preferred. Of special interest is the continuous occupation of these more elevated settlement sites through a number of early cultural periods.

## REFERENCES

1. West Yorkshire Metropolitan County Council. "West Yorkshire an Archaeological Survey to A.D. 1500" Vol 4 Map no.7 - (WYAS)1981.
2. Barnes, B. *Man and the Changing Landscape* 1982 p.36.
3. WYAS op.cit.p.75.
4.. Barnes, B. ibid. p.19.
5. Barnes, B. ibid p.42.
6. Sheppard Frere. *Britannia - A History of Roman Britain* 1987, p.67.

Note - The author acknowledges with thanks his debt to the WYAS Survey and to Dr B Barnes' work in the writing of this chapter.

# CHAPTER THREE

# THE MEDIAEVAL GEOGRAPHY
# OF THE BRADFORD REGION 500 – 1500 A.D.

For tangible signs in the form of buildings and other structures there is very little to see in the Bradford Region as a 'developed' area between the departure of the Romans and well into the Medieval period. The oldest structures in Bradford-dale are the tower of Bolling Hall and the Cathedral, both of late 15th century origin. There was however, a church in the vill* two centuries before the date of the present building, and as the following discussion shows, monastic lands in the form of granges are distributed throughout the area of the Bradford Region. Clearance of woodland is perhaps the most striking change in the landscape, and perhaps we take for granted the connection between the well-established settlement pattern that existed in the tenth century and earlier, and its connection with the modern distribution of towns, villages and fields. The Domesday Book provides written proof of the existence of a scatter of agricultural settlements in late Anglo Saxon times. The survey was carried out between 1080 and 1086 and it gives information about the manors of our region at the time of Edward the Confessor 1042-1066. Later we are able to draw on the Manorial Court rolls, which cover the medieval period; and by relating them to tithe and other maps of later date; and to place name and field name studies, it is possible to re-construct the geography of this period, as can be seen in figure 8 on page 34.

In historical geography we can liken the regional landscape of today to a *palimpsest,* an early parchment, a surface which has been used more than once; where the erasures of one period are only partly removed, and where those earlier inscriptions have been over-written by later scribes. This is evident in the settlement sites; in their street patterns, in the linking roads, and in the field systems of former years.

At the time of the Norman Conquest the regional tract we have designated the Bradford Region was shared between overlordships known as *Honours* (i.e. owing service directly to the king). Most of our area was included in the Honour of Pontefract, which was an area much larger than today's Bradford region. These honours were grants of land made up of a number of Saxon manors, in the first instance distributed as rewards, to William the Conqueror's supporters who had assisted him in his conquest. Another division of this nature was the Honour of Skipton comprising parts of Keighley; and the Wharfedale manors of Addingham, and Kildwick. In Wharfedale, the former Anglo Saxon lands of the Archbishop of York formed another tenurial division, though still subject to the system of feudal obligations. In Yorkshire the parish from which the church was supported has always been an ecclesiatical territorial unit, i.e. the area served by an individual church from which the tithes supported that church, and parishes comprised groups of vills*. Bradford parish provides a good example of this grouping. The other division was the *wapentake,* which was an administrative area covering a number of manors. However, of greater importance from our point of view, was the territorial economic unit of the feudal manor, as it formed the basis of land use management as well as being a populated place. It was this same distribution of mediaeval manorial centres which corresponds substantially to the present day settlement pattern of city, town and village, and we might add,

*vill = a collection of houses which had an active church.

to a large part of the connecting road system. As is shown later on a local scale, even the typical strip field division of the ancient open fields of the manor can be recognised in the more modern street patterns. In the same way, in some places, medieval enclosures (the assarts) have left their mark in the present fieldscape. The Saxon lands of Britain were invaded and occupied by Scandinavian groups in the ninth century and the Viking Kingdom of York was established, with its centre at York. Although we can identify a few places with Scandinavian connections derived from their place names, with some places acquiring names from the Danish intrusions including Micklethwaite, Eldwick, Silsden and Kildwick, but the majority of place names in our area are of Old English, i.e Saxon, origin.

Using place names[1], it is possible to identify the sequence of settlement by these early peoples. According to Cameron,[2] Old English forms date from between the fifth and the eleventh century, and within that period Scandinavian settlement took place during the ninth century, with some places acquiring names from the Danish intrusion. Middle English, of which there are some place names in our locality,  belong to the period 1150-1500, examples being Bentley and Boldshay in Bradford-dale.   Reaney[3] states that, 'names regarded as 'early' in general terms are those ending in -ham and -ton'.  The suffixes -ley and  -den, meaning clearing and valley respectively, are the names of topographical features, indicating a later date of origin. The suffix 'ley' derived from the Old English *leah* is the commonest form of place-name in England. Margaret Gelling notes that it is believed to relate to the O.E. *leoht,* modern 'light' and the sense of glade or clearing, and in reference to chronology she notes, quoting Cox, the great increase in the frequency of this place-name form after 730 A.D.[4] It is suggested that the place names incorporating *ing* or *inga,*  such as Addingham and Cullingworth, belong to an early Saxon  period. Thus to sum up, we may generalise that the places ending in  -ton, although not all are mentioned in the Domesday record for the Bradford region, existed at an earlier date, probably as  far back as the seventh century, and those ending in -ley  indicating a clearing in the forest or waste, represent a  secondary stage of settlement. As noted, in this connection, the frequency of places in our area, incorporating the -ley suffix is important. Most of them occupy sites below the 230 metre contour in the valleys, for example: Burley, and Ilkley, in Whardedale; and Harden, Keighley, Utley, Riddlesden, Cottingley, and Shipley in Airedale.

Place names once had a literal meaning, though this has been lost in the passage of time as a result of the errors of scribes, who, listening to oral statements, sometimes mis-heard what was said, or they copied wrongly.  Most of the names have prefixes, such as Bol-*ton,* (a bowl) and Brad-*ford,* which describe the setting of the place, and the prefixes, such as *Aller-ton* (indicating an association with alder trees), are often adjectival. Examples of the kind of place names associated with local topography are: Baildon *(Bageltune)* meaning a  bend by the hill, Bradford *(broad ford)* and Bolton already noted, Burley *(Burghelai)* forest glade near fort, Halton *(Havelton),* Harden *(Haredon)* -rock valley, Micklethwaite *(Mucelfuuit)* great clearing, Oxenhope *(Uxhusflat)* ox house flat, and Shipley *(Scipelai)* meaning sheep clearing. For many places in our area their names originated from the name of the folk occupying the area. These include Addingham *(Ad(d)a's)* place, Bingley *(Binghelai)* Bynna's folk clearing, Cottingley *(Cottingelai)* Cota's folk forest glade, Cullingworth *(Colingauuorde)* Cula's folk clearing, Keighley *(Chichelai)* Cynna's clearing, Silsden *(Siglesden(e)s)* (Old Norse) Sig(g)el's  valley, and Eldwick *(Helguic )* Helgi's farm.

The interpretation of these names can help us build up a picture of the landscape features which impressed the early settlers in the Bradford Region and enables us to obtain approximate locations of the phenomena they describe. In particular, field names give a more detailed picture.

As we have noted above it is possible to identify clearances from the waste or the forest and even details of plant cover. The prefixes referring to trees are significant, especially when supplemented by the Domesday and manorial records. Thus in Bradford-dale we have Allerton i.e (elder), Burley (Ellersham- alder), Ilkley (Wicken- rowan Tree Crag), Oakworth (oak clearing), Halton (heather place), Keighley (bracken bank) and (alder wood), Bent Ing (bent grass); and there are several fields described as Whin (gorse).

## DOMESDAY GEOGRAPHY[5]

The region was thinly populated in 1066 A.D. (the time of Edward the Confessor) even before the punitive 'Harrying of the North' of 1070 following the conquest. The Domesday Book 1086 was a thorough survey of the assets of King William's newly conquered kingdom. What it recorded was a region laid waste. Each manor was assessed not only at the time of the survey, but the Domesday Book also stated who were the tenants, how the land was used, and what other taxable assets existed in 1066. It is therefore a valuable source book on the economic geography of the eleventh century. Between the two dates all the manors in our area showed a marked drop in their taxable value due to the depopulation following the 'harrying'.

## DOMESDAY WHARFEDALE

Burley, Hawksworth, Ilkley, and Menston were berewicks (outlying estates of a manor) which along with fifteen others, formed part of the Otley *(Othelai)* estate of the Archbishop of York. King Athelstan (927-939) had given the Manor of Otley (along with others) to the Archbishop of York. The entry reads:

*Land the Archbishop of York*
*Manor Othelai with these berewicks Stubbing Farm, Middletune, Dentune, Cliftun,*
*Bichetun, Fernelai, Timbe, Ectone, Pouele, Gisele, Henochesuuerde (Hawksworth)*
*Beldon (Baildon in Airedale), Merasintone (Menston), Burghelai (Burley),*
*Ilechelieue (Ilkley)*

Together these territories contained sixty carucates or an estimated 2,525 hectares, averaging 168 hectares each (NB a carucate was as much land as could be ploughed in a season, the accepted area of this ploughland measured 104 acres or about 43 hectares). Also recorded were: 35 ploughs, in the time of Edward the Confessor in 1066 when the estate was held by the Saxon, Eldred. The Norman, Thomas who was a former canon of Bayeux, had helped William by lending him money for his conquest and was rewarded by receiving the Archepiscopal lands.[6] In 1086 the Archbishop had in demesne 2 ploughs, 6 villains and 9 bordars with 5 ploughs. There was a church with a priest and one villain, and one plough (the church was one of the very few named in the 1086 survey in our area). Meadow comprised 4 acres (1.6 ha.); and wood pasture measured two miles and three furlongs long and the same broad. Coppice wood accounted for an area nine miles long by nine miles broad, and the extent of arable was two miles long by 2 miles broad; while moor belonging to this manor of the Archbishop, was two miles long and one mile broad. In 1046 the manor was valued at £10, but had fallen to £3 in 1086. The Domesday Book records that *'the greatest part of the manor is waste'*. The Archbishop held extensive lands in the East Riding and the North Riding, and he had land in the

West Riding in Airedale (see below).[7]

Addingham, till the tenth century, had formed part of the Otley Estate. It was held by the Saxon Gamelar in the time of the Confessor, had one carucate, half a plough, wood pasture one mile by half a mile broad; and was valued at ten shillings. The Survey recorded 'it is the same now'.

## DOMESDAY AIREDALE

In 1046 the Saxon Gospatric had 4 carucates and 2 ploughs in Bingley. The manor by the time of the Domesday Survey was held by Ernegis de Burun.
The entry reads:

> *Land of Ernis de Burun* (An ancestor of Lord Byron the poet)
> *Manor Bingheleai (Bingley) Gospatric had 4 carucates for geld. There is land for 2 ploughs Ernegis de Burun has (it) and it is waste. T.R.E. £4 wood pasturable 2 leugae long and one in breadth. The whole manor is 4 leugae in length and two in breadth. Within this boundary is contained this soke Beldune (Baildon) 2 carucates, Cottingelei (Cottingley) 2 carucates, Helguic (Eldwick) 1 carucate, Muceleuoi (Micklethwaite) 1 carucate, Mardelai (Marley) 1 carucate, Hateltun (Harden) 1 carucate together for geld 8 carucates. the land has 4 ploughs they are all waste.*

There was wood pasture two miles long by two miles broad. Included in the Manor was the soke (land subsidiary to a manor) of Baildon with 2 carucates. In 1086 Ernegis also held the berewicks of Marley, one carucate, (car.); and the following places measuring six carucates all being taxed together: Halton (?) two car., Cottingley two car., Cullingworth two car., and Haworth half a carucate. All were recorded as waste by the Domesday surveyors.[7] King's Land in Crave (Craven) included the manor of Morton. It was held by the Saxon Ardulf, where there were four carucates and two ploughs valued at thirty shillings; and Archil had three carucates, with two ploughs valued at ten shillings. Riddlesden was recorded as King's land. It was a separate manor with one carucate to tax. The berewick of Halton, which was a soke of Bingley, comprised six carucates. The six carucates of Keighley manor were shared between four tenants Ulchel, Toli, Ravensuard and Wilhelm. Gamelbar had three carucates at the manor of Wilsden, and shared one carucate at Oakworth with Wilhelm. Archil held two carucates at Kildwick, Wilhelm also had in Utley manor one carucate and the same at the berewick of Newsome. Ravensuard had two carucates at Laycock.[7] The manor of Shipley was held by Ravenschil who had three carucates and two ploughs taxed at ten shillings in 1046, with wood pasture measured at one mile long by half a mile broad. Thus the lands in Airedale amounted to fifty seven carucates, or 2,400 hectares, averaging 57 hectares each.[8]

## DOMESDAY BRADFORD-DALE

Bradford was divided into a number of manors recorded in the Domesday Book. The area which might be defined as Inner Bradford included the manors of Bradford, Bowling, Bolton, Heaton, Tong and Bierley. The entry for Bradford reads: *"M.in Bradford cu' vi berewicis vi Gamel - xv ca'rt're ad g'ld ubi poss. e' viii carcuce Ilbert h't & wast. e T.R.E. val' iiii l'b. Silva past. 1 m long and 1m lat."*. Which freely translates as: 'Bradford Manor had six berewicks, which in the time of King Edward (1042-66) had been held by the Saxon, Gamel, of which there were fifteen carucates to tax, where there may be eight ploughs, and wood pasture 1 mile long by 1 mile broad, its value is £4. Ilbert has it, and it is waste'. The six berewicks probably included Manningham and the Hortons. Bradford-dale included the manor of Bierley (including present day Wibsey and Odsal); part of Calverley (Idle), Bolton, Heaton, and Shipley (included with Airedale above). Bolton manor held by Archil with 4 carucates and 2 ploughs also included Allerton, Chellow, Clayton and Thornton, which together shared 10 carucates and 6 ploughs. Bierley, held by Stainulf, had 4 carucates and 2 ploughs. Other holdings of Stainulf in Bradford-dale were Tong and Wyke each with 4 carucates and 2 ploughs and wood pasture. The tenant of Bowling manor was the Saxon Sindi with 4 carucates. Heaton manor held by Dunstan and Stainulf had 6 carucates and 3 ploughs. All were returned as waste, and their value was reduced considerably between 1070 and 1086. Eccleshill was a berewick of Wakefield. The average size of the manors in Bradford-dale was 137 hectares. The author[9] estimated Bradford-dale's population in the eleventh century as between 300 and 400, a figure slightly less than that of James[10] who produced the figure of 500. Using the same value of 6 ha per person at the lower level for more fertile land, or 8.1 p.p. ha for less fertile land, in Domesday times the total population of the three dales would be between 900 and 1500 (if all of the Archbishop of York's lands in Wharfedale are included).

The area of Queensbury was included in Northowram which was in the graveship of Hipperholme, which in turn was part of the Wakefield manor. (The graveship was a division for the collection of rents, which were usually collected by a tenant of the lord).

The pre-conquest land system was based on the manor, the land of which was farmed in open fields on a two or three year rotation that included a fallow year (i.e. a resting period). On poorer land the two-year rotation was more likely to operate and we may reasonably postulate that a two year rotation probably operated on the poorer land of our area of study.

In summary, from the Domesday Book it can be concluded that during the mid-years of the eleventh century the area of the Bradford region was thinly settled, its agrarian population was contained in the vills of the manors of the three dales. The siting of these vills or settlements, corresponds substantially to the present pattern of towns, villages and hamlets of the Bradford Region. The record also shows that the Saxon lords had been replaced by Normans. Everywhere the land was laid waste, and the value of all the manors had fallen drastically between 1066 and 1086. This was no doubt due to the reduction in the population, in particular because of the loss of the able-bodied males in the 'harrying of the North' who had been required to work the manor. Men would either have been killed or enslaved in the punitive action of the conquerors, leaving only the aged, the women, and the children. Again from the record, we can visualise that a land use map of the time would have shown the manorial territories as islands of arable and meadow-land in the surrounding woodland. In addition, the wooded land, either as forest or as coppice land with pasture, was sufficiently valuable in the manorial economy to be included in the survey. It constituted a valuable resource for the manor, as a provider of fodder for the animals of the manor, of timber for buildings and tool-making, and for fuel and game.

## THE EVIDENCE OF THE MANORIAL COURT ROLLS[11]

From the 13th century onwards detail about the spatial economy of the Bradford Region begins to build up. By 1251 Bradford had assumed local importance as a commercial and administrative centre, as a result of the administrative act of Edmund de Lacy, the tenant in chief, who in that year acquired a market charter for the township. The charter stated that Edmund de Lacy and his heirs should have *one market every week, on Thursday, at his manor in Bradford in the County of York, unless the market should be to the injury of the neighbouring markets'*. Similar weekly markets were granted at Bingley (1212), Ilkley (1293), Keighley (1305). Associated with these commercial developments embryonic towns were emerging, a point noted by Hopper in his *History of Communications in Bradford,* where he refers to the ancient streets of Ivegate, Kirkgate and Westgate in the town[11a]. The Court Rolls in1295 record the yield £17. 6s. 8d. from market tolls, and in 1311, there were 30 burgages in Bradford. (Burgage = a tenure held by a burgess, who enjoyed certain specified privileges and freedoms from feudal obligations in return for payment of rent). By 1272, the lordships and townships of Thornton, Allerton, Clayton, Heaton, Bowling and Wyke had been appropriated to the Liberty and Leet of Bradford. But its court's jurisdiction extended into the valley of the Aire and its tributaries. It can be seen therefore, that by the 13th century the small market town of Bradford had acquired an ascendancy in the economy and administration of the sub-region. However, it remained a poor area, testified by the references to the low value of the Pennine manors in contemporary records.

The court rolls of the constituent manors are particularly valuable in helping in the understanding of the human geography of the Bradford Region in the Middle Ages. As can be seen from the discussion of the monastic lands below, similar patterns of land use and land management to those of Bradford-dale were repeated elsewhere in the region. For example it is recorded in the survey of 1342 in Bradford, that there were 16 acres of unenclosed woodland with its herbage valued at two shillings and underwood at 6/8 (33.3p) every fourth year for pannage. (Pannage = the right to pasture swine in woodland in return for a rent). Also in the same year, John Renge is recorded as a villein rendering one shilling yearly for the right to feed swine in the wood, and at Manningham, John and Alice Renge were fined sixpence because they gathered acorns in the lord's wood against the order of the baillifs. Two things are of interest here: firstly the mention of acorns in quantity is evidence of the presence of oak woodland, and secondly, that there was some evidence of woodland management to conserve the tree cover (and the game). In 1356 the pannage of the wood of Bradford was sold for 20 shillings (£1), and in 1357 seventeen people were fined because their pigs had trespassed on the Lord's wood. The manorial records make frequent reference to corn, and on occasions state what kind. Thus in 1346 William was fined because his beasts had trodden down and consumed the corn of William Attekirke with his cattle to damages which are taxed at 2d. Entries about depasturing occur in 1343, when Richard Forester had eaten corn of John Reins; and when William Attekirke was again in trouble because his animals had depastured the corn of Robert Idle. In Great Horton Thomas Walker's cattle depastured William Coke's oats; also in 1362, the pigs of Alice Gibwife depastured William Drynker's wheat.

In the above discussion it was noted that cattle and swine were common grazing animals, but stray horses, sheep, geese and a stag and bees are mentioned in the court rolls. The Beck was a fishery as can be seen from the entry of 1359, when William Coke complained that Thomas Walker had dug up turf in his meadow to dam up the water of Bradford Beck 'to his damage 12d'. William de Wilsden was accused of taking four swarms of bees which ought to have been the Duke's (of Lancaster).

In the subsistence economy of the mediaeval manor it was necessary for the inhabitants to process their own produce near to where it was grown, so mills were a common feature of all manors, and a source of revenue for the lord of the manor who charged the tenants in goods, later in money, for their use. The Pennine rivers and the streams provided the power which was used to grind corn, but also there were fulling mills to beat the cloth, replacing the simpler system of treading the cloth by walking, (hence the surname Walker of our day). There were water mills belonging to Manningham and Bradford. The Bradford mill can be located approximately by the street named Millergate, and by the Goit, the medieval mill race, which can still be seen in the line of large flags covering this water channel which once carried water to power the mill.  In the1311 inquisition it was valued at £10. The manor court records show the presence of mills in both Wharfedale and Airedale, there is an early reference in Keighley for example, when Adam FitzPeter endowed the Priory of Haversholme in Lincolnshire with a 'mill and two carucates of land' (1154) in that township.  The mill was later transferred to Kirkstall.[12] Later there is a reference to a fulling mill there. At Oxenhope the mill complex also included a  kiln to dry corn. At Ilkley in Wharfedale, Euphemia, wife of  Walter de Heslerton was granted a third of the mill in dower (1367).

The manors had to be self-sufficient as communications were very poor. True, there were connections between markets and the manors, but these were often more of the nature of  rights of passage, than roads as we know them today. For example the local markets at Bradford, and in those mentioned earlier in the other dales, required connections with the vills which they served. Again the increasing presence of monastic holdings within the manorial territories required linking routes with the monastic centres.  Sometimes there are clues in the court rolls or the monastic chartularies to indicate some degree of specialisation and land use diversification, e.g. from craft names mentioned in the manorial records, such as smith, or collier (charcoal burner); or references to forges and iron working; or bercaries (sheep grazing areas or enclosures) and vaccaries (cattle enclosures) many of which were established by the monasteries.  The monastic holdings became increasingly important from the 12th century onwards. Mills to grind the corn, fulling mills to process the cloth, and forges were important elements in the manorial economy and constituted a source of revenue for the lords of the manor who had the monopoly and charged for their use. Along the Aire and Wharfe valleys, the records refer to fishponds, as for example those at Bingley, at Riddlesden and at Ilkley.  The mill at Baildon recorded in the roll of 1469 was located at Baildon Bridge. Bingley was an iron-working site belonging to Rievaulx Abbey at Halton and at Faweather, and there was another site at Harden which according to the West Yorkshire Archaeological Survey was sited where the Beck joins the Aire.  As an indication of Baildon's involvement in trade there was the case of  Henry de Bayldon who in 1387 was sued for debt by a merchant of Florence.


## MONASTIC LANDS AND THE GRANGES

Monasteries occupied a privileged position in the economic geography of the Middle Ages. They became more important from the beginning of the 12th century onwards as their wealth grew, and were a significantly innovative element in the regional economy until their dissolution in the Reformation of the 16th century. They had acquired land by gifts over a number of centuries. It is noted by H.L. Judson[13] that abbeys acquired land *in liberam perpetuam elemosinan or in franc almoign* (i.e. free of temporal charges saving the just and reasonable service of the king). Thus, unlike the secular tenants whose lands might revert to the tenants in chief on the death of the tenant without heirs, the monasteries, being excused these feudal obligations, were 'immortal', and thus were able to retain their holdings and add to them.  The term grange implies a monastic farm or a farm building. It was important as an outlying possession serving the monastery's economic needs. A number of granges were located in  the Bradford region most of which belonged to the Cistercian Order, whose  main base was at Citeaux in France. The list in table 5  was taken from a compilation by Dr Donkin which showed a wide distribution in West Yorkshire. Their location in the Bradford Region is given in the following table.[14]

**Table 5 Cistercian Monastic Lands in the Bradford Region**

| Religious House | Township | Site | Location |
|---|---|---|---|
| Drax Priory | Bingley | Micklethwaite Grange | SE104414 |
| Rievaulx Abbey | | Faweather Grange | SE142418 |
| | | Halton Grange (now St Ives) | SE093389 |
| Kirkstall Abbey | Bowling | Newhall | SE170302 |
| Selby Abbey | Heaton | Chellow Grange | SE122352 |
| Bolton Priory | Silsden | Gill Grange | SE067459 |

Source West Yorkshire Archaeological Survey Vol.3 page 798 1997-1998

The grange sometimes defines a farm or a single structure, or a group of buildings, as for example in the grant to Rievaulx Abbey of the whole of the vill of Harden in the late 12th century. Harden's original place name was that of Halton which was changed to Harden in 1538, and to St Ives in the 19th century.[15]   A bovate of land was granted to Drax Priory at Faweather Grange in 1130, to be confirmed by Adam de Birkin in 1150-60. A later agreement between Drax and Rievaulx concerned 'one piece of land with crofts around it', indicating some enclosure of land.[16]. Although the *Grangia* at Silsden is mentioned in the Bolton Priory accounts of 1297, there is some doubt about the site, but the West Yorkshire Archaeological Survey refers to the evidence of earthworks and enclosures north of the present Grange.  In Bowling, John, son of Reginald, the clerk of Bradford granted three bovates of common pasture from his fee at Newhall to Kirkstall Abbey, later confirmed 1242-43.  Also John De Lacy confirmed the gift of land by Robert de Everingham at Chellow to Selby Abbey, and the land seems to have been granted to Rievaulx Abbey before 1143. Later Adam de Birkin granted the removal of dead wood and minerals and the whole of the vill to Selby Abbey.[17]

Many of the monastic lands within the manors were in the nature of demesne land i.e. farmed or developed, as was the case with mineral working, for the benefit of the geographically separate monastic centre.  Their distribution was widespread in the area of the Bradford Region, covering Bingley (Drax and Rievaulx - recorded in 1230), Harden, Cullingworth (Esholt Priory - from a grant in 1234), Bowling (Kirkstall 1248), Esholt (Bolton Priory  for land in Yeadon), Oxenhope (Nostell Priory), Ilkley (Sawley Abbey 1253), Keighley (Bolton Priory and Rievaulx early 13th century) (Kirkstall Abbey 1250), Morton and Riddlesden (Kirkstall and Drax Abbeys early 13th century), Shipley ( Rievaulx-1166) and Silsden (Bolton Priory). The monastic houses became wealthy innovators. Through their membership of an organisation with widespread national and European connections they were well placed to trade, especially in wool.  Some of the grants were specifically to provide grazing land for sheep, as for example in the grants to Kirkstall Priory to graze 200 sheep. A similar grant of grazing land in Kildwick for 200 sheep was made to Bolton Priory.

**THE MANORIAL FIELD SYSTEM**
Figure 6 based on the first six inches to one mile Ordnance Survey map of 1852 shows the fields of Baildon, Ilkley Keighley and Heaton. The small, narrow fields near the historic core of these settlements can be readily identified. They contrast with the larger fields of later enclosure away

## Figure 6.   EXAMPLES OF FIELD SYSTEMS IN  AIREDALE AND WHARFEDALE
### (In Baildon, Ilkley, Keighley and Heaton)

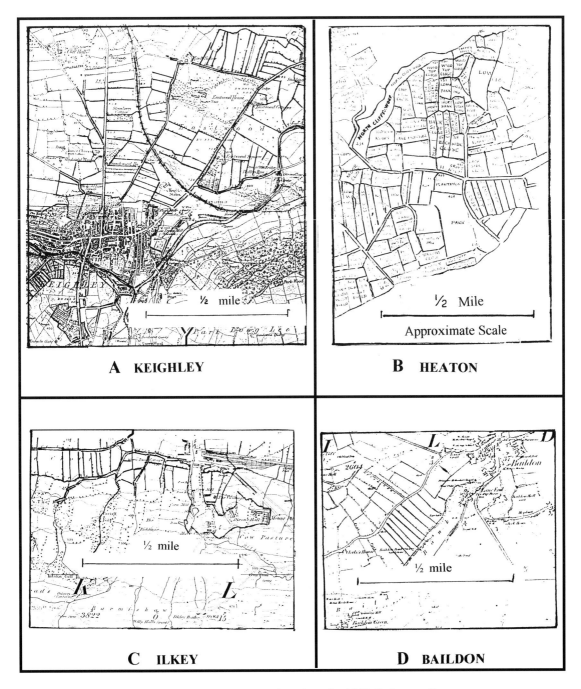

**A   KEIGHLEY**

**B   HEATON**

½ Mile

Approximate Scale

**C   ILKEY**

**D   BAILDON**

Note – Maps A, B and D are based on the 1852 Ordnance Survey
Map C on the 1839 Enclosure map.

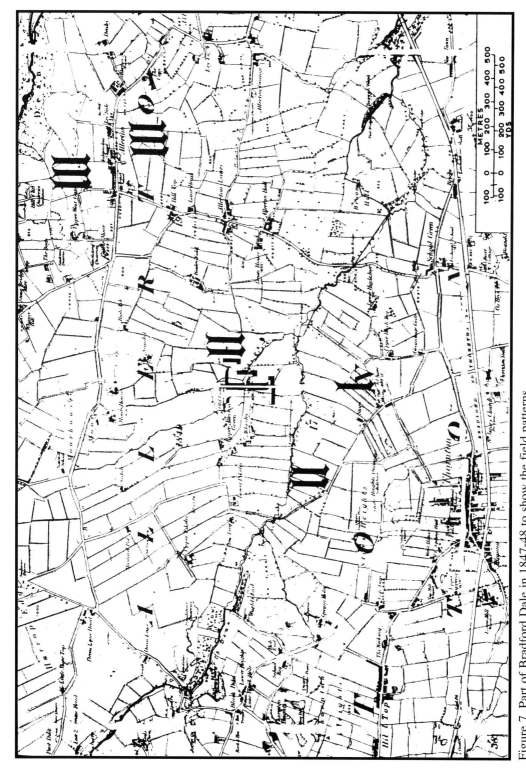

Figure 7. Part of Bradford Dale in 1847-48 to show the field patterns.
I - Early mediaeval strip fields; II - later enclosures; III - 18th and 19th century - types of enclosure

from the centres. In the Bradford map (figure 7) an attempt is made to classify the field types. As will be seen in figure 9 it is possible to relate the early field pattern to the modern system of roads and streets.

The analysis of the map of Robert Saxton of the fields of the Manor of Manningham was made by the author in his *Geography of Bradford*.[18] From the examination of the first Ordnance Survey maps and tithe maps the pattern was repeated throughout our area. The Saxton map is very accurate and can be fitted exactly to the first 6 inch to one mile O.S. map published in 1852. Saxton's survey showed the great fields, their divisions into strips, the nucleated settlement of Manningham, the scatter of tenancies, and the ancient local road pattern (see figure 9). The author[19] noted how the early field pattern was recognisable in the layout of urban streets. Although the Saxton survey was carried out in connection with the enclosure of the Manningham lands it shows that the pre-existing field system survived intact, and because it included the names of the tenants it was possible to see how the land was allocated between the occupants of the manor. There were 290 field divisions, mostly in narrow strips. In 84% of the fields the occupier's name does not appear in the immediately adjacent fields, and there was only one instance where the occupier had succeeded in having four of his fields grouped (see table 6). The tenant's holding was scattered throughout the manor thus involving much unnecessary movement between fields and making the management of the holding more difficult. Enclosure facilitated the enlargement of fields in some cases, allowing for differential cropping and eventually the re-siting of farmsteads as we see below in chapter four where the Harden enclosures are discussed.

**Table 6 Manningham Fields 1613 - showing the extent to which field amalgamation had occurred**[20]

| Degree of contiguity - of the occupier's name appearing in adjacent plots | Frequency | |
|---|---|---|
| | No. | Percent |
| No contiguity | 130 | 84 |
| 2 adjacent fields | 19 | 12 |
| 3 adjacentfields | 5 | 3 |
| 4 adjacent fields | 1 | 1 |
| Total | 155 | 100 |

Source Richardson C A Geography of Bradford

## ASSARTS

Examples of early enclosure appear in the records of other manors, and are often referred to as *assarts*. Their location can be associated with the place-name element *royd* which indicates a clearing in the waste, and the court rolls show that these areas were fenced alongside a ditch. Thus, William de Bayldon complained that at Oxenhope a group of people from Haworth had broken his hedge and ditch and allowed cattle to stray into his corn and meadow. Again, in Bradford Manor in 1483 'Adam Nutbroun (of Bradford) had allowed his hedge to be enclosed which prevented Thomas Harper from having access to his herbs and peas growing there'. Other examples of assarting are referred to in Stanbury and in the Shibden valley.

Figure 8 attempts a reconstruction of the geography of Bradford-dale in the Middle Ages[21], as it might have appeared in the late 14th century. It is based on place and field name study,

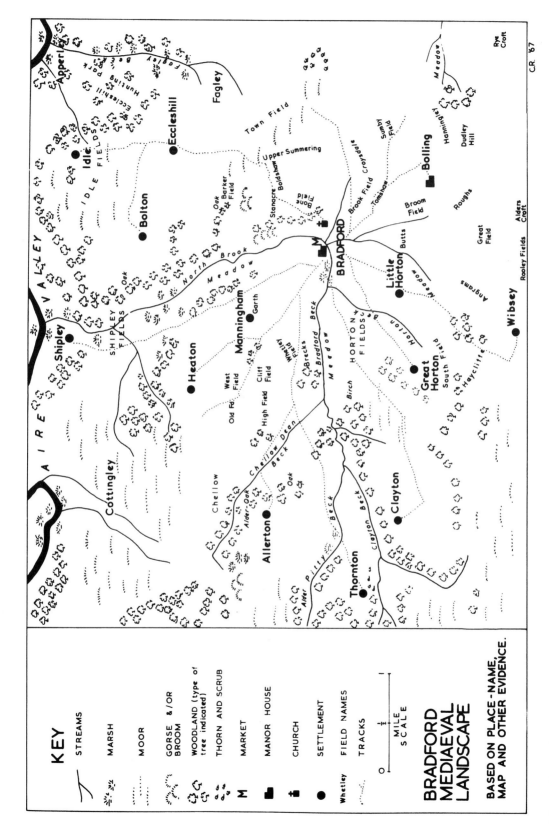

Figure 8. Mediaeval geography of Bradford-Dale – A reconstruction

34

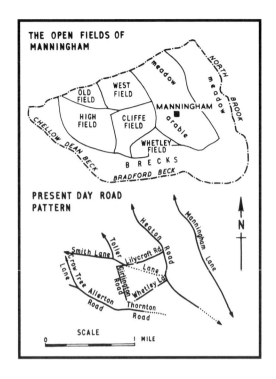

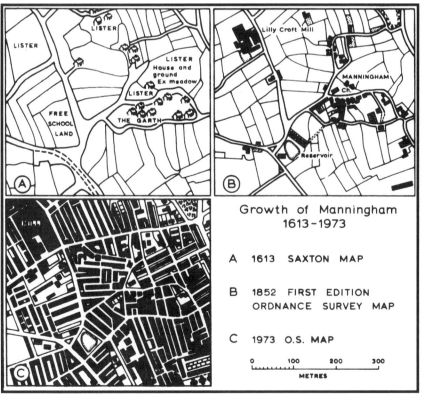

Growth of Manningham
1613-1973

A  1613  SAXTON  MAP

B  1852  FIRST  EDITION
   ORDNANCE  SURVEY  MAP

C  1973  O.S.  MAP

Figure 9. The Field Systems of Manningham in 1613 and 1847-48 related to the modern street pattern
Maps B and C are based on the ordnance survey and are reproduced with the sanction of the Controller of
H.M. Stationery Office. Crown Copyright reserved.

early maps such as that of Saxton, and tithe maps. The marking of the trees and other vegetational cover on the map is derived from the work of A.H. Smith's place name interpretation, and from the location of the field names shown on the tithe and early maps. The names of fields such as Hanningley, Barkers Field and Alders Croft point to early tree associations and in some instances early enclosure, e.g. at Fagley and Whetley. The word *carr* derives from two linguistic sources. In the old Norse it is *kyarr,* i.e. bog, marsh, and it appears as *ker* in its Middle English form, indicating brushwood. Smith's interpretation in the examples shown on the map, is that they belong to the old Norse form. The wooded valley, partially cleared, and surrounded by high moors, is strongly expressed on the map. The avoidance of the valley floor by the early settlers is also a striking feature of the manorial pattern of constituent vills and hamlets. Bradford appears to be the only exception, but as has been stated above, it developed above the wet flat land occupied by the ancient ford, which crossed the Beck. The Hall Ing was on the floor of the valley on the east side of the Beck, and it may provide a hint of the early manor house site, though it is shown on the west side in figure 8, corresponding to a later siting. In fact the Bradford Manor House shown on 19th century maps was built in 1705. Just north of the Beck, near the present Co-operative store stood the water mill, with an open leat (the Goit) leading from a weir near the present Water Lane. This was paved during the l9th century. The mill was used both as a corn mill and for the fulling of cloth. The church, now the cathedral, stood on a prominent bench overlooking the township.

In medieval times the tiny nucleated hamlets were surrounded by large open fields, which were divided into narrow strips. Some had been enclosed, evidenced by early references to *crofts, closes* and *tofts.* Some of the woodland would have been pollarded to supply timber for charcoal for the forge, and fuel for the manor. The position of the field known as the butts should be noted.

Shallow pits for the quarrying of coal had begun to appear by the 14th century, testified by the court references to cases involving cattle falling into them (cf. the Manorial Roll entry of 1346) when 'Robert Smith of Stanbury commanded to answer why he had opened the soil of the carriage of iron ore'.

Some of the fields near the village were used to bleach and stretch cloth, e.g. Thomas Walker in 1349, *'took of the Lord one plot of the Lord's waste for a home to be situated there and for the enlargement of his tenter the Lord to dig coal'.* In the previous year William Senleder was fined 2d. *'for treading the Lord's soil by the carrying of coal'.* The waters of the Beck were stained from time to time by effluent from the dyers' vats. The name Barkerend may indicate the presence of tanneries.

As can be seen from figure 7, the medieval field (marked I on the map), and the local road patterns (described in chapter 4, figure 9) have fundamentally influenced the present day townscape of the City of Bradford, a pattern which can be repeated in other parts of the Bradford region.

## REFERENCES

1   Smith, A.H.English Place Name Society. Volume XXXII *The Place Names of the West Riding of Yorkshire* 1937.

2   Cameron, K.  *English Place Names* 1961. p.128 and Chs. 4,5 and 6.

3   Reaney,  P.H. *The Origins of English Place Names*, Ch 6 1964.

4   Gelling, Margaret  *Place-names in the Landscape*,  p.198.  This is a fully researched  text, adding to Skaife's local detail listed below.

5   Skaife, R.H  *Domesday Book of Yorkshire* Transcript, 1895.

6   Speight, H "Hawksworth Hall and its associations" in *Bradford Antiquary*, Vol 4  1905 p.247.

7   Bawden, Revd. Wm.  *Dom Boc, A translation of the record called Domesday Book*, p.52 and 53; and Skaife, R.H. op.cit. p.496.

8   Bawden, Revd Wm  op.cit. p.145.

9   Richardson, C. *A Geography of Bradford*,   1976 p.24.

10  James, J  *The History and Topography of Bradford*,  1841 p.376.

11  Skaife, R.H.  Transcript  p.137.

11a Hopper op. cit. Typescript in Bradford Central Library.

12  Skaife, R.H.  ibid. p.139.

13  West Yorkshire County Council (WYCC) *West Yorkshire - An Archaeological Survey* Vol. 3, 1981 p.797-798.

14  WYCC   op. cit. p.325-6.

15  WYCC  ibid. p.795.

16  WYCC ibid. footnote p.800.

17  WYCC  re Selby Abbey p.397.

18  Saxton, Robert  Map of the Township of Manningham 1613 Facsimile in Bradford  Antiquary, Vol VI, 1921 p.11.

19  Richardson, C ibid. p.29.

20  Richardson, C ibid. p.28.

21  Richardson, C p.32.

# CHAPTER FOUR

# PRELUDE TO GROWTH 1550 - 1750

## ENCLOSURES

The process of change in the agricultural landscape reviewed in chapter three continued during the 250 years from 1500 to 1750. These changes, by enclosure of land, transformed the common land of open fields and their surrounding waste into a landscape of gated and fenced fields and by 1760, the date of the Enclosure Acts, the process of enclosure had been made simpler. Cudworth refers to the process of voluntary enclosure of glebe lands in Bradford; *'We, therefore considering that the said Sir Richard Tempest and the said freeholders have mutually considered and agreed among ourselves for the meeting and bounding of the aforesaid lands and laying them together and the enclosing of the same to the end etc.'* [1]

The tenurial system which had seen some changes in late medieval times, also changed as service tenures gave way to money rents and outright ownership. All parts of the Bradford Region were affected. Large areas of land had been enclosed in most of the manors in the region as can be seen from the court records. Assarts from the common land of the waste are often referred to, and there are frequent references to *closes,* during the mediaeval period. Most of these enclosures involved small plots usually described as *crofts,* but some were quite large areas. This was specially the case after the Dissolution of the Monasteries (1536-1540), and the Dissolution of the Chantries Act 1547, when areas of land previously belonging to church authorities often described as closes, frequently contained large acreages. Much concern was expressed by governments of the 15th and 16th centuries, and by contemporary writers concerning the enclosure of the common lands, mainly because of the social disturbance it caused as a result of unemployment, increased vagrancy and depopulation. For this reason there were attempts to limit the conversion of common lands from arable to sheep pasture which required fewer people to work the land. But the attempts to legislate to limit enclosure met with little success. However, the Dissolution of the Monasteries released large areas of land, which the 'new men' of the 16th century were ready to buy and/or to lease. The crown benefitted in the revenue from these land sales, and the new owners or lessees, were given greater freedom to fence the land and to vary its use. E.Dodd[2] writing about the enclosure of Riddlesden and Morton in 1790, Cullingworth (1800), Harden Moor (1853), Romels (sic) Moor (1861) and Hainworth and Lees Moor (1862) noted that these enclosures were 'a mopping up operation' as the remaining farm land was already enclosed. In 1591, 500 acres (202 ha) of moorland 'divided or to be divided into thirteen equal parts' covered an area stretching from High Eldwick to the edge of Baildon Moor[3]. An early map of Wilsden, showed all the land immediately surrounding the village area had been enclosed by 1670, and in Keighley in 1612 160 acres (64 ha) of land was sold containing 62 acres (25.1 ha) of meadow, 12 acres (4.85 ha) of pasture, 10 acres (4.05 ha) of woodland and common turbary and common 'for all manner of cattle', indicating the importance of land sales of common land in freeing choice in cropping and other land uses for the landholder following the Dissolution of the Monasteries and the Chantries.[4] Further evidence that the term *closes* no longer meant small plots of a few acres, is shown in the deed of sale of a close of 21 acres (8.50 ha) in Burley in 1650, and in the same year two closes of 12 acres (4.86 ha); and another sale of two closes totalling 36 acres (14.7 ha).[5] Enclosure became much simpler after the passage of the Enclosure Acts in 1760.

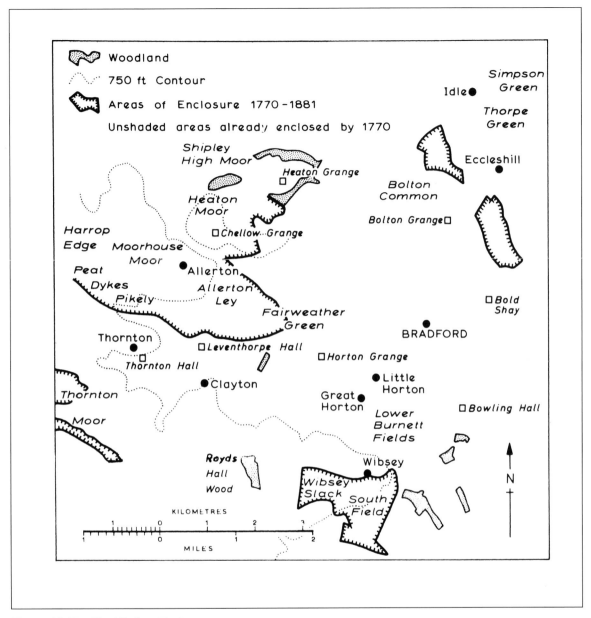

Figure 10. Bradford Dale – Enclosure

For example, according to Clifford Whone, there were large areas west of the village of Harden which were divided into holdings with farm houses away from the village. These included: Whitecote established in 1571, Lum Hirst (1593), Currer Laithe (1571), Birks (1571), Ellercroft (1572), Beckfoot Mill (1593), Ravensroyd (1593), Marley Banks (1593), Marley Old Manor (1600), Harden Brow (1613), Cockcroft Fold (1613), Marley Hall (1623), Jackfields(1625), Harden Grange (1636), Hill End (1650), and Woodbank (1654). Just how far this process of 'voluntary' enclosure had gone on in Bradford-dale may be inferred from the relatively small area of land that remained to be enclosed in the dale as may be seen in figure 10 and table 7.

The Bradford Manor lands were enclosed by 1611 and the tenants were enfranchised as copyholders of its divided waste and common in 1638. The lands of the manors of Clayton, the Hortons and Bowling were enclosed by 1770, which was the date of the first Parliamentary enclosure award in Bradford-dale. Even in the areas where tracts remained unenclosed, as for example in Wibsey, there is evidence of the partial enclosure of strip fields at an early date. Deeds dated 1609 and 1624, refer to *closes,* and the Wibsey Manor court rolls record instructions to certain farmers to repair their fences. Small areas in other manors of the dale remained in open fields or common until the period of the Enclosure Act awards, 1770-1881.

From the detailed study of the first edition of the six inches to one mile map of Bradford-dale, published in 1852, a section of which is reproduced in figure 7 on page 32, it is possible to distinguish three types of field corresponding to the three phases of field formation. The first of these is the medieval strips indicated in area **I** on figure 7. This kind of narrow field is found immediately adjacent to the house plots of the old manorial centres. They are small and markedly linear. The second type of enclosure, area **II**, belongs to the period of the late middle ages, extending into the eighteenth century. The fields are still linear, sometimes square, but frequently small. They may be surrounded by curved fences, suggesting probable origins as assarts. The Thornton Enclosure Award map shows a number of elliptical fenced areas subdivided into smaller fields, which are described on that map as 'already inclosed'. These were early intakes from the waste. The third category of enclosed fields is that of the Enclosure awards of the period 1770-1881 in Bradford, exemplified by area **III** in figure 7. These fields are larger and not elongated like those of the preceding types.[7]

Figure 10 shows that the area below the 230 m. contour had been largely enclosed by 1770. The exceptions were, the manor of Allerton, the western part of Thornton, the moors of Heaton amounting to 575 acres (323 ha.); two large areas of Wibsey manor, and parts of Idle. Bolton, Eccleshill and Wyke were also enclosed at this time. The dates of these enclosures are set out in table 7. As figure 10 shows, a swathe of unenclosed land extended into Bradford-dale as far as Fairweather Green. This was part of Allerton Manor. The map also shows Heaton Moor and the small areas on the eastern side of the dale; and two large open areas of Wibsey. But even allowing for these, the most striking conclusion to be drawn from the map is that by 1770 the lower land of Bradford-dale was contained in fences, and much of it was still in strips.

# Table 7 Land Enclosure Bradford 1770-1888[9]

| Area enclosed | Date of enclosure | Land affected |
|---|---|---|
| Allerton | 1840-1850 | Common lands and waste |
| | | Fairweather Green, Allerton Ley, |
| | | Moorhouse Moor, Guide Moor, |
| | | Harrop Edge, Peat Dyke |
| | | Pikeley Upper Green |
| | | |
| Bolton | 1819-1824 | Bolton Common |
| | | |
| Eccleshill | 1814-1848 | The township of Eccleshill |
| | | The common lands and moors of Eccleshill |
| | | |
| Heaton | 1780-1781 | The commons, moors and wastes of Heaton |
| | | |
| Idle | 1809-1814 | Part of Idle Moor, Tithe Laithe Green |
| | | Thorpe Green, Simpsons Green buildings |
| | | Thackley Common, Wrose Brow Common, |
| | | Gawcliffe Cragg  Buildings |
| | | |
| Shipley | 1815-1825 | The common and wastes of: High Bank, |
| | | Low Moor |
| | | |
| Thornton | 1770-1772 | Part of Thornton Common |
| | 1881-1888 | Wibsey Slack, Low Moor |
| | | |
| Wyke | 1813-1821 | The open common and other waste of the |
| | | Manor of Wyke |

Source  Richardson  p 38  Table  8

## SETTLEMENT FORMS

It has been said that Bradford was a large 'village', in fact it was made up a number of villages which have expanded and begun to coalesce with neighbouring settlements. This is what happened in Bradford-dale, where the many village centres in the dale have been joined to form a relatively high density continuously built-up area. From the historic nucleated centres roads stretch out, initially flanked by low one-storey, stone-roofed buildings bordering the roads leading out of the centres. Many of these early stone cottages remain.  In the above discussion of the Bradford Region in the Middle Ages, mention was made of the pattern of medieval manorial centres corresponding to the present distribution of towns and villages. The dominant settlement form is that of agglomeration, and in those areas where earlier buildings survive, the arrangement of buildings and 'snickets' is frequently random, exemplified by Lower Green in Great Horton, Little Horton Green and the old part of Wibsey.  In outer Bradford the clustering of Church and old buildings by the bridge at Bingley is a fine example of a surviving form of an  ancient nucleated settlement.  Local topography  in Wilsden has  resulted in an elongated form which was imposed by the restriction of the deeply incised valley causing the concentration of the old village structures by the Beck.  Also valley benches of the Aire and Wharfe influence the alignment of the older parts of these settlements to produce a linear form. As was shown in the previous section, enclosure of the village lands enabled some dispersal of dwellings to outlying farmsteads. The weavers' cottages of the Pennines constitute a distinct type of vernacular building in which the long low stone-mullioned-window is a dominant feature. A number of more substantial structures, sometimes located on the sites of the monastic granges, and no doubt built by the farmer beneficiaries of the Dissolution, are found. Of these the Paper Hall (1648), Leaventhorpe Hall (17th century), and Chellow Grange in Bradford, and Ilkley Manor (16th century) and Riddlesden Hall(17th century), Esholt Hall (1706-09), High House Addingham (1697) are good examples. They also demonstrate the opening up of settlement that had been made possible by the enclosure of the common lands, and significantly, date mostly from the late 17th century. Bolling Hall is a museum piece in itself, as it brings together in one structure, architectural styles of periods ranging from late 15th to the early 18th century.[10]

## INDUSTRY

Leland in 1540, could write of Bradford that it was *'praty quik town and standeth much by clothyng'*. Lord Clarendon in 1640 said that *'Leeds, Halifax and Bradford were three very populous rich towns depending wholly on clothiers'*. As far as Bradford is concerned, these statements give a misleading impression of this thinly settled part of England.

Heaton provides a map showing the broad distribution of the cloth making industry at the beginning of the 18th century.[11] West of a line drawn through Shipley, Wibsey and Wyke and extending into the Pennines for a distance of fifteen miles, worsted was the principal type of manufacture. Heaton called this the 'worsted field'. In the rest of Bradford, east of the line, white cloth was the main product, except that Idle produced both white and coloured cloth. Thus wool cloth-making was more important in the townships of Bradford, Bowling, Eccleshill, Idle, Wibsey and Wyke.

At this time cloth-making was a cottage industry, which meant that its distribution corresponded closely to the distribution of population in this area. Cloth making was carried on in the home of the cloth worker and it involved the whole family. The activity was combined with small-scale farming to support the clothworker's family. Important in the organisation of the domestic system of production was the wool merchant who supplied the raw wool to the weaver and his family who carried out all the cloth making processes from cleaning, combing spinning, and weaving in his home workshop. The clothier collected the cloth, later to be traded in the cloth halls in Halifax, Bradford or Leeds. We get an insight into this system and the status of the 'middle man' *vis-a-vis* the cloth-maker, from Sigsworth's work in which he refers to the inventory of William Greenwood on his death in 1779. He noted that the warehouse adjacent to William's house contained worsted goods valued at £1500; and referring to Robert Heaton of Ponden Mill, Oxenhope, who was a fuller who dealt in wool and soap, as well as farming, he took wool to forty spinners living in that part of the Pennines. The tenants paid rent to Heaton through combing and spinning and weaving the wool; but also by walling, helping build the dam, cutting peat from the moor, providing coal, and haymaking.[17] The industry had its landscape effects in a number of ways, for example in the form of specially equipped fields and in the design of the home workshop. The cloth-worker's holding included a tenter ground where frames were erected on which to stretch and hang the cloth. The special nature of these plots was evident at an early date, for the Bradford Court rolls record in 1326 that Thomas Walker took one plot of the Lord's waste to enlarge his tenter ground. The stone-built weavers' houses with their long mullioned windows, are a common landscape feature of the Pennines. As we see, the clothier controlled all the processes connected with cloth making, other than the finishing process. He had a warehouse where the wool was cleaned, sorted and classified, later to be delivered. Heaton[11] notes the sides of the hills around Halifax were spread with enclosures from two to six or seven acres each, seldom more, and all parts of the West Riding exhibited the same feature.

The wool stapler was an important element in the trade. He collected the wool from a wide area and distributed it to the home-based cloth workers. From the accumulated wealth of this activity, these thrifty merchants supplied the capital to construct the roads, canals and other facilities which were to trigger the growth of the urban centres flanking the Pennines. John Hustler typified this group. When he gave evidence to the House of Lords he said that he was accustomed to buying wool from nineteen counties, and his partner and other agents bought wool from another fourteen to the cottage worker.[11]

By 1773, the trade in Bradford had grown sufficiently for a piece hall to be erected. This was built on a site which can still be recognised as the Piece Hall Yard in the centre of the city. Before closing this section it is necessary to stress that the town occupied a very modest position in the Yorkshire cloth industry until the 18th century, and even then it lagged behind Halifax. Bradford produced inferior quality narrow cloths, which measured 14 to 17 yards long (12.8m to 15.5m) and one yard wide (91cm). By the middle of the 17th century however, it was making cloths of 30 yards length (28.3m). Heaton provides evidence of the insignificance of Bradford as a producer of cloth in this early period, quoting the aulnage returns of 1473-75 (aulnage = the statutory grading of cloth dating back to Richard I, to restrain the export of wool and the import of cloth). York had 2,346, Halifax 1,493 and Ripon 1,386 cloths (74% of the total) and Bradford came eighth in rank, with a mere 178$^1$/$_2$ pieces. By 1750 however, it was poised for the phenomenal growth which characterised the first three quarters of the 19th century. Jenkins shows that factory production was becoming more important from 1778, with the building or conversion of existing mills, for example at Baildon Gill Mill (1778), Esholt (1786), Addingham (1787), Ilkley (Hawksworth and Curtis 1788) and became cotton by 1790), Shipley Dumb Mill Worsted (1789), and Haworth Leeming Mill (1790).[12]

## COAL AND IRON WORKING

As was shown in chapter one, coal and iron are found in Airedale and in Bradford-dale. There are references in the manorial and monastic records to coal being mined, one of the earliest of which was in 1230. In 1342 Thomas del Halghes complained of 'the trespass of John, the villain of Mickle Horton in that *the said John made divers wells in his land and dug on the same Carbones Marinos*' (sea coal).[13] The monasteries were quick to exploit the mineral resources of their granges. In the late 12th century Rievaulx was granted rights to extract iron ore by Adam son of Peter de Birkin in Halton (Bingley township), Chellow, Heaton, and Shipley. In the Bradford Court rolls there are entries referring to the mining of *urston* (ironstone) and the presence of forges. Initially charcoal was the main smelting material but from the beginning of the 18th century coal became important and bell pits, appearing as dimples in a few areas in the present day landscape, can also be seen on the earliest O.S. sheets of the region (see figure 18). To give some idea of the scale of the monastic production, Rievaulx's *blome* of iron consisted of 24 stone (336lb - 53 kilograms). Awtry[14] states that 'Blast furnaces reached Bradford in 1592 when Thomas Proctor built a furnace at Shipley'. He notes that this was not successful, but the detail of a fine in 1567 refers to *'one strengharthe and two blome harthes for the making of irene, to which there be yerely worthe 120 l'*. The same account refers to *ockes* and *colyers* (charcoal burners or miners ?) and *colle*. He continued '*10 quarter or seame of colle wyll burne a blome of iron'*.[15] As noted in chapter one, the coal, which in Bradford dale is often associated with iron, crops out near the surface in many parts of our area, so that deep pits were not required, and shallow mining in bell pits was the common form of excavation in this early phase of mining. Mining during the 16th, 17th and early 18th centuries was widespread as the following list taken from deeds of transfer of land or mineral rights shows: reference to coal pit belonging to Tristram Tempest 1502, lease of coal mines to Robert Farrar on south side of Reevy Hill 1545, coal pit at Nethermore (Wibsey's turf ground) 1610. The freeholders of Bolton entered into an agreement to mine coal in 1699. Thomas Empson leased to John Dixon, yeoman of Bowling (sic) a coal pit and veins of coal on Wyke Common,1728.[16] In Outer Bradford there were workings at Wilsden, Cottingley and Riddlesden. Comyn, in his paper on the history of mining in Bingley, refers to an accident in 1594 when Thomas Illingworth of Cottingley 'died in a colepit with a damp'. There were also coal pits at New Holland and Harrop Edge.[17] There were pits at Morton and at Harden Park. Lakin speaks of coal worked there by David Leach, who in 1730 rented a mine on land adjacent to his own in which there was a complex of established pits. Morton Bank Colliery and Harden Park Colliery ceased production in 1854.[18]

## THE REGION'S ISOLATION

Ogilby's Itineraries 1675, indicate that Yorkshire was 'served' by a very open network of highways, none of which connected with Bradford. A road passed from Skipton to Huddersfield via Keighley and Denholme in our region and another from Rochdale via Littleborough, Liversedge, Birstall, Morley and Leeds. More importantly, the surface of the pre-turnpike roads was deeply rutted and badly maintained, so that they were often unusable. Contemporary accounts of the pre-turnpike state of the roads indicate their deplorable condition. Thoresby in his diary gives a vivid account of a journey he took on 13th August 1712.[18] It states how he lost his way due to the lack of signposts. The roads were flooded, and he had to circumvent them by riding across flooded fields, where the water was up to his saddle skirts; *the road was deeply rutted and snow and ice made it very troublesome* (Thoresby's diary edited by Hunter covers the period 1677-1724). His specific criticism was corroborated in more general terms by the petitioners for the improvement of the Aire and Calder navigation in 1698. Thus, from the Leeds petitioners: *'the petitioners having no convenience of water carriage within sixteen miles of them, which not only occasions great expense, but may cause great damage to their goods and sometimes the roads are impassable'*. The Wakefield petitioners stated that *'the towns of Leeds and Wakefield are the principal markets in the north for woollen cloths etc., that it will be to the great improvement of trade to all the towns of the north by reason of the convenience of water carriage, for want of which the petitioners send their goods 22 miles by land carriage (to Rawcliffe) the expense whereof is not only chargeable, but they are forced to stay two months sometimes while the roads are passable to market and many times the goods received considerable damage through the badness of the roads overturning'*.[19] The Leeds and Wakefield petitioners complained because they were cut off from navigable water by distances of 16 and 22 miles respectively, Bradford nine miles from Leeds, and places like Keighley, were even further away from navigable water at that time. The opening in 1700 of the improved navigation of the Aire and Calder from its confluence with the Ouse linking Leeds and Wakefield, was a major development from which towns of upper Airedale such as Bradford, Shipley, Baildon, Bingley and Keighley benefitted. The deepening of the water level of the rivers Aire and Calder by the improvement meant that merchandise could be carried the whole distance from Leeds to Wakefield and the Ouse at a cost of 16 shillings a ton during the winter months of October to May, and at ten shillings for the period May to October. This was for a single journey. Later improvements of these waterways in 1784 and 1785 enabled boats of 80 tons to reach Leeds from Goole.[20]

Before the construction of the turnpikes of the 18th century, the principal mode of transport of goods between Bradford and its neighbours was by packhorse. Trains of these animals traversed the narrow paths, the *'causeys'* of flagged footpaths and bridle tracks and crossed the streams by narrow bridges like those at Beckfoot Bingley and at Wycoller. The pack horse operators were common carriers. In 1613 they charged one and a half pence for each piece of cloth they carried. Carriage by packhorse was slow and limiting in the weight that could be carried. There could be no large-scale development of trade as long as it was dependent on such a slow, limited and costly form of transport of goods.

## POPULATION

The extravagant comment of Leland and others about the local economy and population are not supported by the low densities which may be derived from contemporary sources. For example an estimate based on the assessment for the maimed soldiers, made in 1602 put the population of Bradford Parish at 2,560 (the Parish was a larger area than the former Borough as it included parts of Airedale).[21] Parish registers such as those of Bradford and Ilkley show an excess of baptisms over burials (births over deaths) amounting to a slight increase over the period between 1600 and 1700, although there was a 'dip' in both births and deaths during the period of the Civil War which appeared almost to balance the lower growth revealed by the entries covering the years 1643 and 1666. A Commission reported that Keighley had a population of 1,704 in 1695,[22] and Bradford had an estimated population of 4,200 in 1780 but the parish had increased to 42,780 at the time of the first national census. Table 8 shows the populations of the three dales in 1801.

### Table 8 - The population of Airedale, Bradford-dale and Wharfedale in 1801

| Airedale ( included Bingley parish, Baildon, Esholt, Haworth, Keighley, Shipley, Silsden, Wilsden) | Bradford-dale | Wharfedale (included Addingham, Burley and Ilkley townships) |
|---|---|---|
| 23,902 | 42,780 | 3,467 |

Source: Census of Great Britain 1852

## REFERENCES
1  Cudworth, W. Bradford Glebe Lands. *Bradford Antiquary* vol. II. 1895 p.187.
2  Dodd, E.E. Bingley Chantry Endowments. *Bradford Antiquary* Vol.9 1952, p.293 and 296-97.
3  Dodd, op. cit. p.296-7.
4  Robertshaw, W Evidence of Enclosure in Keighley. *Bradford Antiquary* Pts. I and II p.45.
5  West Yorkshire Local Record Series, vol.II pt.II 1934 p.86.
6  Whone, C. The Manor of Harden *Bradford Antiquary* Vol.VII New Series and Vol.VI p. 273.
7  Richardson op. cit. p,35,
8  Richardson, ibid. Figure 9 Enclosures Bradford-dale p.36.
9.  Richardson, ibid. Table 7 Land Enclosure 1770-1888.
10 Pevsner, *N Buildings of England Yorkshire North and West Riding*, 1967.
11 Heaton, H *The Yorkshire Woollen Industries* 1965, p.330.
12 Jenkins, D.T. *The West Riding Woollen Textile Industry*, 1975.
13 Skaife, R.H. ibid.
14 Awtry, B.G. On iron industry, *Bradford Antiquary* Vol.X New Series, p.250.
15 Parker, J op. cit.
16 Richardson, ibid p.43.
17 Comyn, N.A, *Bingley: A Mining History*, 1986.
18 Sigsworth, E.M, *Bradford Textile Society Journal* 1951-52 p.61.
19 Lakin, W.G. A Footnote to Yorkshire Mining Industry - Coal and Mining and Iron and other mineral working in Mid-Airedale p.32-33 (In Bradford Central Reference Library).
20 Heaton, op. cit. quoting Thoresby's Diaries.
21 Turner, J.W. Bradford Piece Hall, *Bradford Antiquary* Vol I, 1884 p.135.
22 Judson, H.L.Keighley Chantry Lands. *Bradford Antiquary* Vol IIX 1952 p.57.

# CHAPTER FIVE

# THE INDUSTRIAL REVOLUTION
# TRANSPORT AND COMMUNICATIONS

## INTRODUCTION

Until the developments in transport and communications in the latter part of the 18th century the Bradford Region lacked links with the rest of the country and this had the effect of limiting early progress. The area's rapid growth in population and industrial production in the 19th century was based on its mineral wealth, but its riches lay dormant until a more effective transport and communication system was established. From 1774 Bradford became an inland port connected to its neighbours in Airedale by water, and the developing network of better surfaced roads. A number of transport undertakers were involved in these developments who competed with each other in turn and so helped to reduce transport costs for the industries which were springing up in Airedale and its tributary valleys. Bradford, in particular, was transformed from a relatively high-cost to a low-cost location. The remarkable change from its position as an economic backwater to that of a major manufacturing town owes much to its emergence as a man-made node, beginning with its position at the centre of a network of turnpikes. These were succeeded by important canal links with the Aire valley towns and later with the national waterway system and the ports of Liverpool and Hull. The impetus for the canal development was strongly based in Bradford, and at an early date towns in Airedale between Leeds and Skipton also benefitted as a result of the construction of the canal. Later, Bradford experienced the build up of a complex of rail routes in which it occupied a central position.

It may be noted that the Wharfedale towns and villages in our area did not 'take off' as early as the Airedale towns until the railway link with the Aire valley line was constructed in 1865. This is evident from the low average population increase of slightly over 1% per year in the combined area of Addingham, Burley and Ilkley between 1801 and 1851, compared with the 5.4% growth per year for the same period in the Airedale region, including Bradford. These changes in the communication net were brought about by the action of a succession of energetic, far-sighted, courageous men with capital to risk and invest in the local enterprises. Undoubtedly they had selfish motives in pursuit of their own interests but they transformed the economy of the Airedale region by putting it on the national communication map.

The canal and rail sides, the wharves and sidings were attractive sites for the owners of the many warehouses and factories which were built alongside, by reducing the unnecessary transportation and handling costs for the merchants and mill-owners. The permanent ways of the canal and rail system, the canal cuts, the embankments, the railway cuttings, stations, bridges and other works, imposed a skeletal framework on the towns to which other land users had to accommodate. This framework often has had a permanent effect on settlement morphology as the lines and structures of former routes continue to influence their shape long after the canals and railways had ceased to function. In the sections which follow we shall be tracing these developments.

## THE TURNPIKE ROADS

The state of the roads at the beginning of the 18th century has been mentioned. Movement of goods was difficult, limited and costly. Ancient roads did exist, as for example, the Roman road skirting the western part of Bradford-dale, and the road that carried salt from Colne to Otley. On the Moors there were green lanes - the drover routes, but they were of little use for wheeled vehicles. (See Raistrick A *'The Green Lanes of the Pennines'*.) The weavers and their families living on the Pennines were dependent on packhorse transport to carry their goods, notably the raw wool, and woven cloth on which their livelihood depended. The flagged footpaths and the narrow packhorse bridges, such as that at Beckfoot, or at Wycoller, are a picturesque reminder of that age. But the volume of goods that could be carried by this means was very limited.. Roads between towns and villages in the valleys were in a very poor state to the detriment of trade. An attempt had been made in 1555 when Thomas Cromwell introduced an *Act for the amending of Highways*. This required that each person should spend four working days a year on the roads. It was to be financed by a levy on the rates for *'Keeping in repair the Common Highways within this Nation'*. The Act was repealed after 1660, though parishes were still required by law to maintain the roads within their boundaries. As the records of court cases show, neglect continued in spite of the fines the courts imposed.

Leeds and Wakefield were on navigable waterways which linked them with the Ouse, Trent, Don and Humber river navigation. Bradford and the middle reaches of the Wharfe were dependent on a road and track system, the condition of which was described in the preamble to the Leeds Halifax Act of 1740. This stated that the roads: *'by reason of heavy carriages frequently passing the same, have become so deep and ruinous, that in winter and rainy seasons, many parts thereof are impassable for waggons, carts and other wheeled carriages, and very dangerous for travellers, and as the same cannot, by the ordinary course and method appointed by laws and statutes of the Realm now in being, be effectually mended and kept in good repair, therefore, to the intent the said Highways and roads may be effectually repaired, amended, enlarged and made passable from time to time kept in good repair etc. etc.*[1] James notes *"About this time (1745), commodious roads began to be formed in these parts, in the place of narrow pack-horse lanes. The turnpikes were, by the lower class, universally regarded as an obnoxious regulation - more adopted for the convenience of the wealthy portion of the community whose carriages could hardly pass on the old roads, than the benefit of such class".*[2]

During the period from 1727 into the 19th century, the national road system was largely managed by the turnpike trusts. Bradford's first turnpike Act was that of 1734 running from Leeds to Halifax, via Great Horton and Bradford, to which several branches were added. The initiative for the improvement of the roads in this area came from a wide cross section of moneyed interests. The trustees named in the Leeds-Halifax Trust Act of 1840, quoted above, included three peers, twelve knights, twelve clergy, sixty persons described as gentlemen, and twenty three who are named as merchants.[3]

It must not be assumed that the turnpike roads produced an immediate improvement. The trusts used the existing roads and the legislation was directed to their improvement. Arthur Young said the roads were *'execrably bad'*, and the Wakefield-Leeds turnpike was *'stony and ill-made'*[4]. Nevertheless, the turnpike trusts marked the beginning of the improvement of the local transport system. The turnpike roads of Bradford are mapped in figure 11. The key to that map shows that between 1734 and 1755, the main road links between Bradford and its neighbours,

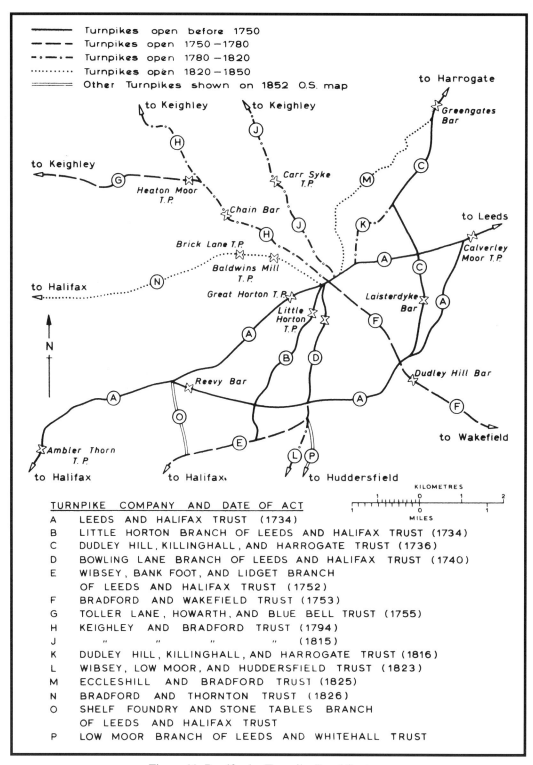

Figure 11. Bradford – Turnpike Road System

Leeds, Halifax, Wakefield, Harrogate, Shipley, and Keighley were under the management of turnpike trusts, to be further supplemented by the construction of turnpike roads to Shelf, Thornton, Wibsey, Brighouse, and Huddersfield after the latter date. There was a connection from the Dudley Hill-Harrogate turnpike to Ilkley. The convergence of the inner radial pattern in Bradford should be noted, together with the ring of toll bars around the centre.[5]. At each of these points tolls were levied, and in proceeding from town to town, travellers and goods were charged as they passed into each gated section. There were four toll bars to pass through between Bradford and Ilkley, the first at Eccleshill, followed by the Otley bars, and then the Burley bar which was about half a mile west of the village. However, market traffic in the area of Wharfedale would be largely oriented towards Otley. Nevertheless, we can see that a network of all-weather roads was evolving in the Bradford region.

The tolls varied from one trust to another. For example those on the busy Leeds-Bradford, Bradford-Halifax sections of the Leeds-Halifax trust were:

| | |
|---|---|
| Five horses or more | nine pence |
| Four horses | six pence |
| Two or three horses | four pence |
| One horse | threepence |
| Every extra draught horse was charged a | half pence |
| Every drove of oxen etc. | six pence |
| Calves, hogs | two and a half pence per score |

These rates were for the day, and there were exemptions from the payment of tolls for persons travelling to vote in parliamentary elections, vehicles carrying gravel, or road material for the turnpikes, vehicles carrying farm produce and implements in the normal course of husbandry, and churchgoers. The Toller Lane-Haworth-Keighley Turnpike Trust levied higher tolls:

| | |
|---|---|
| Six horses or more | twenty four pence |
| Five horses | fifteen pence |
| Reducing to:- | |
| One horse | three pence |
| For every additonal animal | two pence |
| Oxen | ten pence a score |
| Calves and hogs | five pence a score |

Between Keighley and Two Laws, the above tolls were halved.[6]

In 1825 the Dudley Hill-Killinghall Turnpike Trust realised £1,225, and the Bradford-Wakefield Trust £2,374 to rise to £3,362 in1845. The tolls ceased to be levied in 1853.

The cost of carrying goods on the turnpikes was considerable. John Hustler in developing his argument for the construction of the Leeds-Liverpool Canal, drew attention to the high costs of road transport for freight carriage. He calculated that in 1764, it cost £4 . 10s . 0d to take a ton of merchandise by road from Leeds to Liverpool and occupied three weeks by wagons. Using the published tolls in the Leeds and Liverpool Canal Act, he showed the economic benefits of canal over road transport which he stated were between 9 and 16 shillings per load (depending on its nature).[7] But apart from the high costs and the slowness of the road transport system, it was very limited in the kinds of loads it could handle. Bearing in mind the condition of the roads, loads of a ton would be near the limit of horse-drawn cart capacity, and should be compared with the 30 ton loads which the later canal boats were able to convey. Thus the effect of the turnpike roads on the development of Bradford has to be put in perspective. Undoubtedly, they helped to enhance the local commercial importance of Bradford in the Dale, but they were less useful in

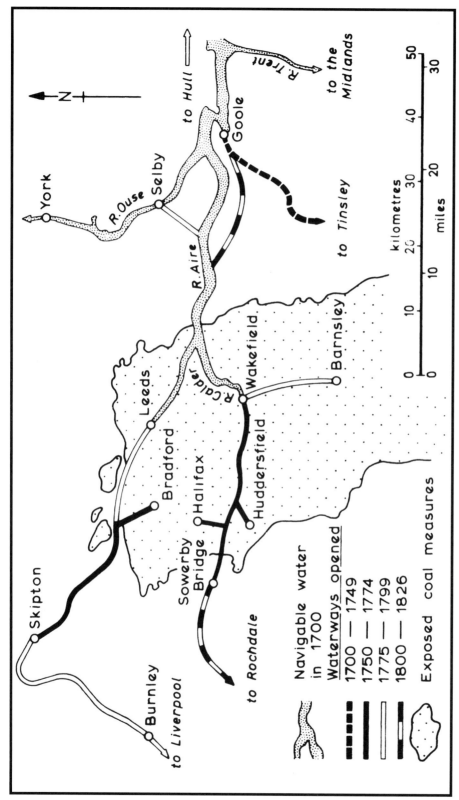

Figure 12. The Canal Systems of Airedale and Calderdale

the development of heavy goods transport. This had to await the construction of the canals and the railways.

## CANALS

1774 is a key date in the history of the Bradford region. It marks a watershed in the development of the Aire valley between Keighley and Leeds as a major industrial region in which Bradford played a leading part. It coincided approximately with a number of events affecting the whole of Britain. These included the widespread adoption of coke in the smelting of iron, the use of steam power to drive textile machinery, the changeover from a dispersed system of manufacturing based on workshop and cottage industries to large-scale factory organisation, and the re-organisation of the agrarian economy, which released huge amounts of surplus labour to work in the coal-based manufacturing sector. Associated with these changes were the revolutionary developments in transport technology, notably the construction of waterways.

In the case of Bradford it took the vision of one or two of its merchant class to recognise the potential of the new mode of transport and to act with others to promote a scheme to provide a water link crossing the Pennines giving the Airedale towns access to the eastern and western ports of Hull and Liverpool. The efforts of the merchants gave a new impetus to the growth of Bradford, which as the population tables show, also benefitted its neighbours in Airedale. The personal drive, tenacity and leadership manifested in individuals like John Hustler and his associates, was of vital importance in changing the geography of this part of the Bradford area. Not only did they see the commercial importance of the new transport facilities but it would seem they had the 'geographer's eye' in accepting the advice of the engineer that a route through the Pennines was technically and economically possible. These were Bradford's 18th century merchant adventurers. By creating a transpennine waterway they made Bradford into an inland port giving increased significance to the mineral wealth of the coalfield.

John Hustler was a wool stapler. He was joined in the enterprise by Abraham Balme, gentleman, and others, including the banking family of Hardcastle, but he seems to have grasped the technical and economic value of the canal transport which had been demonstrated by the Duke of Bridgewater in his canal from Worsley Mill to Manchester. It is suggested by Killick that John Longbotham, pupil and assistant of Smeaton of Halifax, who described the route through the Pennines, had some influence with Hustler. A paragraph appeared in the York 'Courant' on 7th August 1764 (four years after the opening of the Worsley Canal) which read: *'As the Rivers Aire and Ribble may be easily joined at different places and rendered navigable between Leeds and Preston at an expense which the gentlemen who have estates on their banks may readily supply, it is thought proper to mention it to the public at this juncture. No money can no otherwise be so well employed'.*[8] Out of this grew the proposal to construct a navigable cut joining Liverpool and Hull. The original scheme provided for a thirty foot wide by six feet deep channel capable of floating boats of sixty tons, with a journey time of three days, to carry goods across the Pennines at six shillings (30p) a ton.

Longbotham, together with Robert Whitworth, surveyed the route, and Brindley approved it. This was in 1768. On Brindley's death Longbotham became the engineer and Joseph Priestley, the clerk of works. Longbotham's scheme provided for a canal one hundred and eight and three quarters miles long, forty feet wide at the top, twenty seven feet wide at the bottom and five feet deep. It required ten acres (4 ha) per mile, and was to cost an estimated £259,777, one quarter of which was the cost of building the locks[9]. It was a major engineering feat, as can be seen at the five-rise locks at Bingley which involved a lift of 88 feet 8 inches (27m), the various aqueducts, the1640 yards (1500m) long tunnel at Foulridge and the system of reservoirs. It surmounted a summit level of 411 feet 4 inches (125m) above the Aire at Leeds. The canal which was eventually constructed, had a depth of 4 feet 9 inches (1.44m). Work began in July 1770 but the link to Liverpool was not completed until 1816, by which time it had cost £1.2 million.

Bradford was connected to the Leeds and Liverpool Canal by the three mile length of the Bradford Canal which was operating in 1774. It had ten locks and a rise of $86^{1}/_{4}$ feet (26.3m) above its junction with the Leeds and Liverpool Canal at Shipley. The canal basin was at Hoppy Bridge, in the vicinity of the present Foster Square.[10]

Table 9 shows the progress of the canal cutting between 1772 and 1777. It will be seen that long before the completion of the Leeds and Liverpool Canal, Bradford's geographical importance was transformed, for as figure 12 on page 50 indicates, Bradford stood on a waterway system linking the woollen textile region of West Yorkshire crossing and re-crossing the exposed coalfield, and gaining access at low cost, to the Humber and Mersey ports. The enormous advantage of the canal over the costlier road system which preceded it is all too obvious. This may be seen from table 10 which gives the freight and wharfage charges on the Leeds and Liverpool and the Bradford Canal systems.

The value of the waterway in moving low value bulky products such as coal, iron and lime, was of major importance, and its immediate effect is apparent from table 11, which shows how quickly the Yorkshire section was responding to this new low-cost facility. Even after the railways had begun to replace the canal as a means of bulk transport, the canal carried large quantities of coal and lime. There were wharves and stables along the Aire at Apperley Bridge, Shipley, Bingley, Stockbridge, Silsden and Kildwick to provide goods handling facilities for the towns in our study area. In 1868, the wharves at Apperley and Shipley were handling 33,840 tons, and in spite of difficulties which the Bradford Canal experienced in the1860's, causing it to close down temporarily in 1867, it was handling 102,000 tons in 1910. But by 1922, having served a vital purpose in the development of Bradford as a major industrial city, its link with the Leeds and Liverpool Canal had closed.

**Table 9 The progress in the cutting of the Leeds and Liverpool Canal**[11]

| A - Miles of cut in Yorkshire | |
| --- | --- |
| Date | miles |
| April 1772 | 14 |
| April 1773 | 16 |
| Oct 1774 | 23 |

| B. Dates of opening of local sections of the Canals | |
| --- | --- |
| Date | Section opened |
| 13th April 1773 | Bingley to Skipton |
| 22nd March 1774 | Skipton to Thackley |
| 28th June 1774 | Gargrave to Thackley |
| 22nd Oct 1774 | Bradford-Shipley-Leeds |

**Table 10 The Bradford Canal and Leeds and Liverpool Canal charges**[12]

Per ton mile (Under the Act the Leeds and Liverpool Canal 'ton' consisted of 30 cwts)

| Nature of goods | Bradford Canal Freight charges | Leeds and Liverpool Canal | |
|---|---|---|---|
| | | Freight Charges | Wharfage Charges |
| Clay, bricks, stone Lime, dung, and manure | 2d | 1d | 1$^{1}/_{2}$d |
| Timber, goods, wares merchandise | 3d | 1 $^{1}/_{2}$d | 3d |
| For soap, salt, scrow etc to be used for the manuring of lands of any person whose lands shall be cut through in the townships through which the canal passes | - | 1/4d | |

**Table 11 Coal carried on the Leeds and Liverpool Canal 1784-1834 Tons**[13]

| Year | Yorkshire section | Total including the Lancashire section |
|---|---|---|
| 1784 | 17,503 | 85,885 |
| 1794 | 32,800 | 252,494 |
| 1804 | 58,127 | 263,182 |
| 1814 | 106,314 | 357,428 |
| 1824 | 100,314 | 348,569 |
| 1834 | 100,726 | 418,685 |

## MINERAL WAGGON WAYS

Figure 15 in chapter six shows the mineral waggon ways which ran from the coal and iron fields in the southern part of Bradford-dale down to the centre of Bradford. These were of the 'Newcastle type'. They consisted of an inclined wooden track, later to have metal rails, on which large flanged wheeled trucks ran. These were drawn by an endless rope, and horses were used over certain sections. The rope passed round pulleys at each end. The Yorkshire waggons were varied in size between 38 cwts and 45 cwts capacity.[14] Parker gives the details (table 12) of these 'iron roads' as they later became.

**Table 12 Mineral Waggon Ways Bradford-dale**

| | |
|---|---|
| Royds Hall | to Little Horton staithes operating 1787 |
| Low Moor Company | to Old Black Horse Inn Little Horton operating 1785 |
| Low Moor Company | to Brigella Mills Little Horton and Bradford |
| Low Moor Works | to various iron stone pits |
| Low Moor | to Bierley Iron Works |
| Shelf | to Little Horton operating between 1793 and 1849 |
| Low Moor Iron Works | to Collier Gate-Well Street, Bradford |

Using the natural slope of Bradford-dale they enabled coal to be carried down to the staithes (loading platforms) in the centre of Bradford to supply the mills and deliver its surpluses to canal for export at prices which were only slightly higher than those asked at the pit head.

# RAILWAYS

The regional growth of the rail network is illustrated in figure 13. By the mid-1850's Bradford was beginning to occupy a central position as the focus of several rail routes, which linked it with the Aire valley towns, the West Yorkshire Woollen region and the national network.

West Yorkshire helped to pioneer railway construction in Britain. In 1778, a plateway from Middleton Colliery to Leeds township was in operation as early as 1802. The 'Leeds Mercury' carried a letter in its 16th January edition, signed 'Mercator', advocating a railway from Selby to Leeds. The first steam locomotive was operating on the Middleton Railway in 1818, one year before the *Stockton and Darlington Railway Act* of 1822, and landlords, merchants and manufacturers in Leeds were being asked *'to consider and adopt the safest, cheapest and most efficient conveyance of goods from and to Leeds and Hull.'* In 1834, the Leeds-Selby Railway was opened. The North Midland Railway Act of 1836 provided a line from Derby via Belper, Chesterfield, Rotherham, Barnsley, Wakefield and Leeds, and linked with London. In the following year the Manchester-Leeds line opened, by which time, links between Leeds and Newcastle and the north, together with an extension of the Selby line to Hull were completed.

Bradford was connected to this national network by 1846 via the Aire valley route. Once again, Bradford merchants and business men were instrumental in bringing this about, prominent amongst whom were John Rand and Abraham Balme, merchants of Bradford. The railway paralleled the Leeds and Liverpool Canal with which it competed.

The competitiveness of the railways lay in their increased speed, and to some degree in their capacity to travel over higher land. They influenced therefore, the location of industry and its spread to new sites away from the valley floors. The geometry of straight lines and speed curves, cuttings, bridges and embankments of the rail infrastructure however, produced a framework to which other users had to conform thus influencing the morphology of Bradford. The enhanced economy of rail over canal in moving goods was exemplified by the reduction in travel time and cost. For example the carriage of goods by waterway between Manchester and Hull took between five and seven days and cost 30 shillings per ton, the flyboats took four days and cost 40 shillings, and the overland route plus steam packet to Hull from Selby took three days and cost 50 shillings per ton. For passengers, the mail coach travelled at seven miles an hour and the ordinary coach took six and a half hours to travel from Manchester to Leeds, at a cost of fifteen shillings for passengers travelling inside and eight shillings for those outside.[16] The Manchester to Halifax Canal could claim that it was able to deliver goods the thirty two miles at two pence per mile, but more important, their railway competitors did the journey in two to three hours.

Figure 13 shows the development of the 19th century rail network from which it will be seen that the area of Bradford-dale was beginning to be integrated by the new form of transport as well as acquiring links with the national rail system. By 1846 Bradford and the Airedale towns of Keighley, Bingley and Shipley were linked to each other and to Leeds and the national network.

The link with Wharfedale was established in 1865, with the opening of the line from Apperley Bridge on the Skipton - Leeds line which joined the Skipton-Otley-Leeds line at Burley. These links are given in table 13.

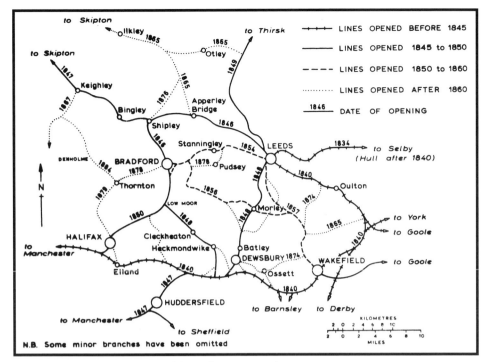

Figure 13. The development of the railway network

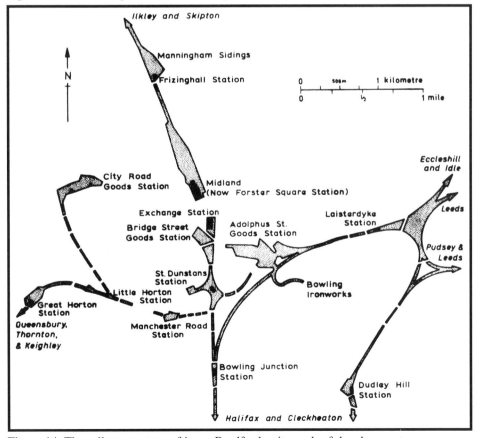

Figure 14. The railway system of inner Bradford at its peak of development.

## Table 13 The Development of the Rail System showing Inner Bradford's links with the Region[17]

| Date | Route | Railway Company |
|---|---|---|
| 30/5/1846 | Leeds-Aire valley | Leeds Bradford |
| 1/9/1847 | Skipton via Shipley | Midland |
| 18/7/1848 | Mirfield-Low Moor | Lancashire and Yorkshire |
| 7/8/1849 | Low Moor-Bradford | do. |
| 7/8/1850 | Halifax-Low Moor | do |
| 7/8/1854 | Leeds Central -Bowling Junction | Leeds-Bradford-Halifax Junction |
| 1/8/1854 | Leeds Central - Adolphus Street | Great Northern |
| 1/6/1855 | Bradford Exchange | do. |
| 16/7/1861 | Oakenshaw Branch - Wakefield | Lancashire and Yorkshre |
| 1/8/65 | Ilkley via Guiseley | Midland and North Eastern |
| 1/9/1870 | Halifax - Holmefield | Lancashire andYorkshire |
| 1875 | Bradford - Eccleshill - Idle | Great Northern |
| 14/10/1878 | Thornton - Queensbury | do. |
| 1/1/1884 | Thornton - Denholme | do. |
| 1/l/1884 | Bradford - Keighley via Thornton | do. |
| 22/4/1886 | Low Moor South Curve | Lancashire and Yorkshire |
| 1/12/1893 | Low Moor - Dudley Hill | Great Northern |

The Leeds-Bradford was a protege of the North Midland Company which had built the Leeds-Derby line, opened in 1840. It was later incorporated in the Midland Company. The Great Northern direct line to London went from Grantham and opened in the summer of 1852. It had connections with Leeds and the West Riding Junction Railway across the plateau between Leeds and Bradford, a distance of nine miles. The Aire valley route was thirteen miles via Shipley. Bradford, therefore, had by 1854, a choice of two routes to Leeds, which connected with the main national network, and was linked to Halifax and other Woollen Region towns.

The complexity of the concentration of rail lines is further illustrated in figure 14, which also shows the inner city spurs and the stations. It serves to emphasise how much the railways have left their stamp on the internal spatial organisation of the City. The two main line stations were sited where the Leeds line encountered the built up area of Bradford in 1846 and 1854. The City Road Goods Station was opened during the 1870's. These were connected by a complex of curves, and opened out into broad areas of sidings and engine sheds. They split the urban area into a number of divisions to form the major quadrants into which the city can be divided. The lines, rail heads and goods stations exercised strong locational pulls, exemplified by the grouping of industries, warehouse and wholesale markets in several areas.

## REFERENCES
1  Leeds Halifax Turnpike Act 1740.
2  James, J. *The History and Topography of Bradford*, Reprint of 1841 edition p.155.
3  Heaton, p.256.
4  Young, Arthur ibid. *Northern Tour* p.132 and p.575-7.
5  Parker, J *Illustrated History; From Hipperholme to Tong*, 1904 pp.100-101.
6  Leeds Halifax Turnpike Act 1740.
7  Killick, B.A.'The Leeds and Liverpool Canal' *Bradford Antiquary*, 1900 p.238.
8  Killick, op. cit.
9  Priestley, J. *Historical Account of the navigable rivers and waterways* p.386 f.

10  Killick ibid.
11  Priestley ibid. Bradford Canal p.84.  Leeds Liverpool  p.394-395.
12  Roberts  The Bradford Canal *Journal of the Bradford Textile Society*  p.146, 1962-63.
13  Report of the Select Committee of the House of Commons on the U.K. Coal Industry Vol  III, 1871.
14  Lewis, M.J.T. *Early Wooden Railways* p.188.
15  Parker, J.  op.cit.  p.34 and Lewis op. cit. p.130.
16  Marshall, J.  *The Lancashire and Yorkshire Railway* Vol  I, p.20.
17  Marshall, J. op. cit.  Vol 11, Appendix I.

# CHAPTER SIX

# THE INDUSTRIAL REVOLUTION
# COAL AND IRON INDUSTRIES

Coal was found in the Millstone Grit area of Outer Bradford. Comyns refers to several localities in the Aire valley region where coal was mined, but it was either in 'smuts' or thin seams measuring only a few inches in thickness. However, in the early years of the nineteenth century, it was of local importance for steam generation. The geological memoir records the presence of coal in the Middle Grit strata in the area extending from Oxenhope through Keighley, Snail Green and Bingley, but the seams were only a few inches thick. There was a Coal Measures outlier running from Denholme to Shipley and another at Baildon Moor. The main area of large scale coal mining was in the coal basin of Inner Bradford. This chapter therefore is largely devoted to that area.

The West Riding of Yorkshire produced 9.8 million tons of coal in 1866, and 1.9 million tons, over one fifth of that, was mined in Bradford's 46 collieries. That was a peak year.[1] Significantly, the increase in mining output and the associated development of metal manufacturing followed closely on the opening of the Leeds and Liverpool and Bradford Canals.

There was a spread of mine working in Bradford-dale during the 17th and 18th centuries. Thus, in addition to the continued working of the Shelf and Wibsey deposits from earlier times, Bolton, Bowling, and Heaton are mentioned during the 17th century, Wyke (1728), and Manningham and Four Lane Ends in 1750. The greatest changes, however, occurred during the last quarter of the 18th century, when the old technique of *bell pit* and shallow quarrying for coal, gave way to shaft mining in the dale. These operations were on a much larger scale and involved a number of coal-owning companies who utilised numerous sub-contractors or 'pit takers'. For example, Low Moor seemed to operate this way. They had 72 such pits in 1850; and 16 open workings at Wibsey Slack in 1860, together with another twenty pits and dayholes.[2]

The generalised section of figure 3 in chapter one shows the sequence of coal, iron and other useful minerals present in the Lower Coal Measures rocks of Bradford-dale. This assemblage of several coals, fireclays, ganister, and in some favoured areas, ironstone, made for considerable economy in working, making its coal industry highly competitive, and in particular, Bradford-dale an attractive location for coal-using industries.

Without doubt the most important of the coals were the Better Bed and Black Bed seams, because the latter occurred in association with ironstone. Table 14 gives the analyses of the Better Bed Coals. Together with their hardness, their high carbon content and freedom from impurities such as sulphur, these coals were specially useful for metal manufacturing up to 1860. By the latter date, however, a number of new iron smelting and steel-making techniques had been invented which enabled the phosphoric Jurassic ores of Cleveland and the East Midlands to be used. Green *et al* say of the Better Bed Coal, *'This seam is a 'bituminous' coal, dense, bright in colour and singularly free from sulphur, phosphorous and other impurities which unfit a coal for smelting purposes. It is chiefly used by the iron companies for the furnace the forge and it is to the purity of the coal that the bars known as Low Moor, Bowling and Farnley Iron is largely due.*[3]

The even consistency of the low sulphur content of this coal in Bradford-dale is borne out by table 14.

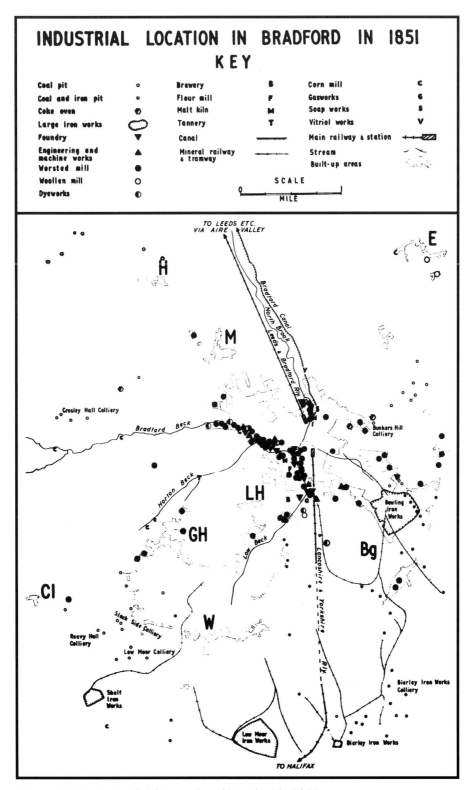

Figure 15. The Industrial Geography of Bradford in 1851.

**Table 14  Analyses of the Better Bed Hard and Soft Coals**[4]

|  | Hard Coals percent | Soft Coals percent |
|---|---|---|
| Fixed carbon | 83.45 | 84.03 |
| Sulphur | 0.41 | 1.41 |
| Ash | 1.08 | 1.75 |
| Moisture | 2.08 | 1.72 |
| Hydrogen | 5.35 | 4.98 |
| Oxygen and Nitrogen | 7.63 | 7.11 |
| Total | 100 | 100 |

**Table 15 Sulphur content of Better Bed Coal at various pits in Bradford-dale**[5]

|  | percent of sulphur |
|---|---|
| Sample from The Forge Bowling | 0.45 |
| 'Hunting' Coal Bowling | 0.38 |
| 'F' Pit Bowling | 1.42 |
| Holme Pit Bowling | 0.46 |
| Wibsey Pits of W  J Tordiffe & Co | 0.57 |
| Mean | 0.47 |

The Better Bed seams were worked mainly at depths of 240-285 feet (73.2-86.9m) in the east and 150-220 feet (45.7-67.1m) in the west of Bradford-dale. Over these, at a depth of between 30 feet (9.1m) and 100 feet (30.5m), was the Black Bed coal. This was too soft for metallurgical purposes, but it  was a good second class coal, having a high thermal value.  It yielded between 4,000 and 5,000 cubic feet (371.6-464.5 cu.m) of gas per ton. In addition to its industrial uses as an engine coal, the Black Bed sold as a fair quality house coal.

The seam thicknesses at various pits being worked in Bradford-dale in 1878 are given in Table16[6]. Bunkers Hill, which had coke ovens worked the Crow Coal, which was used locally as a gas coal (see figure 15). As well as giving the thicknesses of the coal seams, table 16 serves to show the effect of discontinuities resulting from faulting. This deprived some areas of the full suite of minerals. For example Great Horton pit had only the Black Bed Coal, whereas nearby Horton Bank Top had both Better Bed and Black Bed Coals.  The favoured localities which had both types of coal were Bowling, East Bierley, Bunkers Hill and Tong lying in the east, and Low Moor and parts of Wibsey in the south of the dale. The economic advantage of this vertical assembly of coals was enhanced by the presence of ironstone, (which formed the roof deposits of the Black Bed coal) and the valuable clays of the seat earths. Some of these were associated with ganister, a furnace lining material. Table 17 provides an analysis of samples of the local fireclays. These clays and refractories were of value in making firebricks, pipes and furnace linings. The bands measured  twelve inches (30.48 cm) thick at Horton Bank Top, between sixteen inches (40.6cm) and eighteen inches (45.7cm) at Mill Lane, but at Laisterdyke, where they were found in conjunction with ganister, they were two feet (70cm) thick  and the  ganister was four feet (121.9cm) thick.

## Table 16 Thicknesses of Better Bed and Black Bed Coals in Bradford-dale[9]

|  | Better Bed Seam depth (inches) | Black Bed Seam depth (inches) |
|---|---|---|
| Bowling | 29 | 22-29 |
| East Bierley | 19 | 24 |
| Bunkers Hill | 21-24 | 20 |
| Fagley | 29 | - |
| Great Horton | - | 37 |
| Calverley Moor | 29 | - |
| Horton Bank | 30 | 37 |
| Low Moor | 27 | 37 |
| Tong | 18 | 27 |
| Wyke | 22-26 | - |
| Wibsey | - | 37 |
| Cutler Heights | - | 28 |

## Table 17 Analysis of Fireclays of Bowling Iron Works[7]

|  | Sample A % | Sample B % |
|---|---|---|
| Silica | 81.25 | 68.12 |
| Alumina | 8.15 | 26.69 |
| Peroxide of Iron |  | 2 |
| Titanic Acid | 4.01 | 0.87 |
| Lime | 0.57 | 1.15 |
| Manganese | 0.46 | 0.59 |
| Potash | 1.9 | 1.17 |
| Water | 3.9 | 0.2 |
| Total | 100 | 100 |

The large undertakings held huge areas of land. Parts of their systems of collieries and their linking mineral lines and waggonways are shown on figure 15. The Low Moor system included twenty two miles of tramway in the Bradford area and in 1906 covered an area of 8,000 acres (1618.7 ha) lying in the district of Low Moor, Bierley, Cleckheaton, Scholes and several outlying hamlets.[8] Bowling Ironworks was dependent on places four miles from the main works, to which it was linked by narrow-gauge mineral lines.[9]

The productivity of the exposed coal-field in Bradford-dale in 1857, may be seen in table 18. Bradford had about 13% of the Yorkshire collieries and roughly 10% of the coal output in 1856-57. But by the 1860's Bradford had increased its output to a peak of 1,875,000 tons and it was second in volume of output after Leeds. Production fell off rapidly to 615,800 tons in 1869 out of a total tonnage of 10.8 millions. (See table 19). Ten of the 46 pits listed in the Select Committee's Report on the Coal industry in the U.K. were worked by Bowling Iron Company and another ten by the Low Moor Company. The coal was mined by the 'room and pillar' system, which was wasteful and inefficient because it left much of the coal in the ground. All

Bowling Ironworks' Better Bed pits were exhausted by 1896 and their Black Bed seams were worked out by 1913. Fifty three collieries were in operation in Bradford-dale in 1881, about 9% of the total of the 484 for the whole of Yorkshire. The changing fortunes of the local coal industry may be seen in the employment statistics in mining in table 20.

## 18 Coal Production in Yorkshire 1857[10]

| | Number of Collieries | Output (000's tons) |
|---|---|---|
| Leeds | 74 | 2,568 |
| Bradford | 48 | 976 |
| Huddersfield | 59 | 315 |
| Halifax | 50 | 2,521 |
| Barnsley | 30 | 410 |
| Wakefield | 36 | 740 |
| Rotherham | 18 | 458 |
| Sheffield | 26 | 490 |
| Dewsbury | 26 | ) |
| Penistone | 26 | ) |
| Pontefract | 5 | )  3 95 |
| Others | 7 | ) |
| Total | 374 | 8,875 |

## Table 19 Coal Production in Bradford, Leeds, Barnsley and Yorkshire 1860-1869[11]

| Year | Bradford (tons 000s) | Leeds and Normanton (tons 000s) | Barnsley (tons 000s) | Total Yorkshire (tons 000s) |
|---|---|---|---|---|
| 1860 | 1,250 | 2,459 | 2,430 | 9,284 |
| 1861 | 1,550 | 2,225 | 2,225 | 9,374 |
| 1862 | 1,525 | 2,195 | 2,195 | 9,255 |
| 1863 | 1,520 | 2,198 | 2,196 | 9,402 |
| 1864 | 1,425 | 2,120 | 1,435 | 8,809 |
| 1865 | 1,657 | 2,250 | 1,565 | 9,355 |
| 1866 | 1,875 | 2,215 | 1,550 | 9,714 |
| 1867 | 1,857 | 2,225 | 1,375 | 9,843 |
| 1868 | 1,157 | 2,505 | 1,799 | 9,740 |
| 1869 | 652 | 2,839 | 2,750 | 10,829 |

## Table 20 Employment in Mining in Bradford 1851-1891[12]

| | Bradford Borough | | Bradford Urban Sanitary District | | |
|---|---|---|---|---|---|
| | 1851 | 1861 | 1871 | 1881 | 1891 |
| Coal miners | 2,171 | 2,757 | 309 | 377 | 255 |
| Iron miners | 218 | 194 | 76 | 77 | 25 |
| Others not specified | 49 | 4 | 35 | 12 | |
| Total | 2,438 | 2,955 | 420 | 466 | 280 |

Note to table 20 -  *The areas covered by the above table vary at different dates*
1851-1861      *All ages Male and Female*
1871               *Persons aged 20 and over. As employment in this industry included only a few aged between 10 and 20, the figure may be compared with the 1881 - 1891 figures*
1881-1891      *Persons aged 10 and over*

Much of the coal was consumed locally[13]. The Smoke Prevention Committee of Bradford Corporation reported in 1867 that 2,500 tons were used per day in the city for manufacturing purposes and of this total, 1,200 tons was for steam engines and boilers. This gives an estimated 900,000 tons for the year[14]. A further 34,000 tons left the area by canal, and another 19,415 tons by rail[15]. In common with other coalfield areas, Bradford's coal prices were low. Horton and Wibsey coals sold for as little as 9d. per load in 1825-1831; and Haycliffe pits were charging 4$\frac{1}{2}$d. per cwt in 1825 (4s. 2d) per ton. These prices remained low as may be seen from table 21. The average price in 1849 was 8s. 0$\frac{1}{2}$d per ton compared with 21s. 6d in Bury St Edmunds; 22s. 6d in Oxford, 14s. 0d in Boston and 15s. 0d in Coventry[16]. The Yorkshire average pit-head price in 1857 was 4s. 10d. Table 21 gives the Bradford prices in 1870. At this time steam coal was 9s. 3d in Cardiff rising to 14s. 3d in 1875. These compared with U.K. averages of 5s. 0d in 1882, 5s. 2d in 1885, 8s. 3d in 1890 and 7s. 8d in 1903, indicating steady prices over a long period during the century. If the Better Bed is excluded, the comparable steam coal average price from table 21 was 6s.1d.

Bradford's fuel costs were therefore one third of those at places which lacked coal. This gave it a considerable competitive advantage. Coal prices in the west country in Cirencester, Brinscombe and Exeter were between 18s. 0d and 23s. 6d per ton at the beginning of the 19th century when coal was 3s. 2d per ton in Bradford. The London price for a chauldron (i.e. about 17.14 cwts), was 60s. 0d to 70s. 0d in 1800. Bradford's low prices were due partly to the accessibility of its coals, the economy of their working, and partly due to the low wages prevailing in the mining industry, 18s. 0d to 20s. 0d per week in Bradford and Halifax.[19] Coal could be delivered cheaply to Bradford, thanks to its network of mineral lines and waggon ways. The Bowling system consisted of twenty-two miles of 21 inch and 24 inch track which used a wire rope powered by a winding engine and gravity to pull the trucks. The line leading down to the coal staithe at the coal yard by the Golden Lion in Leeds Road may be seen in figure 15, but the town terminal of the Bowling line was the staithe near East Brook Lane (G.R 170330) and there was another staithe from Bowling Ironworks to the Duncan Street Staithe. The Low Moor system by 1906 included 95 miles of track, but by this time much of this was in its distant pits outside Bradford.

## Table 21  Coal Prices in Bradford in 1870[18]

|                  | Price per ton | |              | Price per ton | |
|------------------|------|------|------------------|------|------|
|                  | s.   | d    |                  | s.   | d.   |
| Bowling Best     | 9    | 0    | Shipley Moor     | 6    | 6    |
| Heaton (Shipley) | 7    | 6    | Shipley          | 6    | 0    |
| North Cliffe     | 3    | 8    | Wibsey           | 7    | 0    |

## IRON MINING AND IRON MANUFACTURING

The mineral wealth of Bradford included two vital raw materials, viz coking coal (the Better Bed) and the associated iron ore. These were found in close proximity to each other together with other coals suitable for gas, household fuel, or steam generating purposes.

Included amongst these were the Crow coal and Shertcliffe coal. The economy afforded by these varied resources together with the availability of cheap transport, especially water transport, gave the momentum to the growth of Bradford industries. Metal working was a major activity from the late 18th into the 20th century, though the mineral fields on which the industry was based were largely exhausted by 1900. Bowling's fields gave out in 1896 and the Low

Moor Company was having to depend on its collieries and ore supplies from pits at Beeston, Churwell, Hunslet, Osmondthorpe and other parts of the Leeds area at the turn of the century. The local metal resources gave rise to the establishment of important works at Low Moor (1791), Bowling (1788), Birkenshaw (1782), and Shelf (1794), all of which began their main operations in the late 18th century, only a few years after the opening of the canals; and the Bierley works began working in 1811. (For a historical note on these firms see note 31 at the end of this chapter). The development of large-scale plant depended on the invention of coke-making and its application to iron smelting following the work of the Darbys between 1710 and 1760. Their invention took some time before it was widely applied, but it is clear that by the end of the 18th century, favoured coal and iron producing areas were beginning to surpass the traditional metal manufacturing districts which had depended on plentiful supplies of charcoal. The Bradford area was one of the favoured locations. The total output of charcoal furnaces in England and Wales in 1788 was 13,100 tons compared with 48,200 tons of coke-smelted iron. By 1796 however, the total amount of coke pig-iron had risen to 167,322 tons, of which 21,984 tons was made in the twenty-two Yorkshire furnaces. Bradford's share of this was 4,390 tons (over 20%). Figure 15 on page 59 shows that coal and iron occur widely in a broad semi-circle along the eastern and southern edges of Bradford-dale and these extend eastwards. It was these beds that the Low Moor, Bowling, Bierley and Shelf iron companies exploited.

The clay ironstone is contained in carbonaceous shales forming the roof deposits of the Black Bed coal. They are partly in continuous layers, partly in bands of nodules and sometimes nodular beds, and these layers occur chiefly in the higher parts of this horizon. Their combined thickness never amounts to more than twenty two inches, but as is apparent in table 22, which shows a typical section through this stratum, generally they gave about ten inches of iron ore, diminishing in some cases to only two or three inches. On the Hunsworth side of Bowling Colliery they gave a pecentage of metalic iron ore ranging from 30.79 - 29.15%.

**Table 22  Section through the Black Bed ironstone at Bowling Ironworks Colliery[21]**

| Black Shale | 8 3/4 inches |
| Ironstone | 1 1/4 inches |
| Black Shale | 7 1/4 inches |
| Ironstone | 1 3/4 inches |
| Black Shale | 24 3/4 inches |
| Ironstone | 1 3/4 inches |
| Black Shale | 4 1/2 inches |
| Ironstone | 1 3/4 inches |
| Black Shale | 7 3/4 inches |
| Ironstone | 1 1/2 inches |
| Black Shale | 5 inches |
| Ironstone ('Flat stone') | 2 inches |
| Black Shale | 14 1/2 inches |
| Iron stone ('Middle ball) | 2 1/2 inches |
| Black Shale | 7 3/4 inches |
| Ironstone ('Rough stone') | 1 3/4 inches |
| Black Shale | 3 inches |
| Ironstone ('Coal head stone') | 1 inch |
| Black Shale | 7 inches |
| Black Bed Coal | |

Green *et al* stress that the *'Value of the Black Bed was much enhanced by the fact that the shale containing the ironstone (which) was largely worked for the supply of Low Moor, Bowling and Farnley furnaces, lies a little above it'*. (21A). Great care was taken to ensure the purity of the ore for the furnaces. The ironstone was picked over by hand to remove surplus clay and then left in flat heaps. These piles were regularly turned over and left to be cleaned by the weather. The extent of the largest ironworks can be seen in figures 16 and 17. They covered huge areas and, as is shown, had extensive buildings. But a good deal of land was used for storage and the dumping of waste from the pits and ironworks. Ibbetson's Directory for 1845 lists thirteen brass founders, and the first large scale Ordnance Survey sheet sixty inches to one mile for Bradford, dated 1852, shows that sixteen foundries existed in central Bradford in 1847-48 (see figure 15 on page 59). In the late 18th century the output of the largest works amounted to a substantial share of the Yorkshire total of iron. Table 23 gives details and provides an indication of the effect of the development of the canal system on this important industry.

## Table 23 Output of Pig-iron from Low Moor Ironworks 1773-1797[22]

| Year | Tons of Pig-iron | Year | Tons of Pig-iron |
|------|------------------|------|------------------|
| 1773 | 1,764 | 1795 | 2,573$\frac{1}{2}$ |
| 1793 | 2,196 $\frac{1}{2}$ | 1796 | 2,177 |
| 1794 | 2,152 $\frac{1}{2}$ | 1797 | 2,658 $\frac{3}{4}$ |

During the years 1795-98 Bowling produced 1,798 tons and Shelf ironworks 3,442 tons. The total for these three works alone, therefore, amounted to an estimated 4,390 tons in 1797, which was 20% of the Yorkshire total. By the 1880's Low Moor Ironworks was producing 60,000 tons a year. By modern standards these totals are small, but as proportions of the national and county totals they emphasise the relative importance of Bradford as a major iron manufacturing centre in terms of the scale of activity in the 19th century.[23]

The local pig-iron was of very high quality. Low Moor pig-iron had an iron content of 93.83%: their refined iron 95.0%, and their puddled iron 99.01%. (see table 24)

## Table 24 Analysis of Low Moor Iron Types[24]

|  | Pig-iron % | Refined iron % | Puddled iron % |
|------|------------|----------------|----------------|
| Combined carbon | 0.55 | 3.10 | 0.42 |
| Graphite | 3.06 | 0.40 | - |
| Silicon | 1.34 | 0.25 | 0.03 |
| Sulphur | 0.04 | 0.03 | 0.008 |
| Phosphorous | 0.37 | 0.22 | 0.24 |
| Manganese | 0.80 | 0.72 | 0.24 |
| Iron | 8.83 | 95.20 | |

From this high grade iron, the local ironworks produced a wide range of goods. The price list of Birkenshaw foundry dated 1792, included *various kinds of pots, pans, hearth grates, furnace frames and doors; a variety of tools for local industries: waggon, cart and chaise bushes, 'Newcastle waggon wheels', mortars, presses for dyers use, engine work, windmill shafts, gudgeons, spindles, cog wheels, pinions, sheaves, pulleys, malt rolls, paper screws, and all other castings in that way, for forges, boxes and rolls for rolling and slit mills, hammers, anvils, anvil blocks, legs, hursts and plates and all other castings'* [25].

The wars had the effect of further diversifying the iron industry as is evident from the Bowling records, beginning with domestic hardware in 1788. Soon after, the Company was making stationary steam engines, and during the Napoleonic Wars, heavy guns, carronades and howitzers, as well as shot. The comprehensiveness of Bowling Ironworks' production range is evident from the Deed of 1849 quoted by Hilary Long. This states that *'The object of the business of the said Company shall be the getting, producing and sale of iron, ironstone, iron and steel, and of smelting, working up manufacturing and vending of cast iron and steel of all engines, machines, machinery, articles, goods, wares and merchandise, wholly or principally made of iron and steel converting, selling of coal and other minerals in the form of coal, coke or cinders ...... dealer in ironstone and other mineral produce'*.[27] The Company produced boiler plates, angle- and T- iron sections, weldless metal tyres, weldless hoops for steam boilers, and sheet iron. Its engineering department made pumping engines, rolling mill engines, steam presses; and could handle castings of 30 tons. Forgings included: axles, shafts, piston rods, and cranks. The Crimean War created further demands for armaments from the local ironworks.

Low Moor also made guns and shot in the French and Crimean wars. Its advertising literature tells us that it *'made guns and shot, shells, guns, mortars'*. By the 1850's it was manufacturing steam engines, machine tools including lathes, boring and drilling machines, in addition to a variety of plates, metal sections and castings.

The aerial extent of the Bowling and Low Moor ironworks is shown on figures 16 and 17, reminding us that even in those early days this was a major space user. As is shown later, because of the dumping of large quantities of waste on their sites, large areas remained semi-derelict until the present time. In 1857 Bowling and Low Moor had between them 10 of the 25 blast furnaces of Yorkshire in blast, and of the 12 Yorkshire ironworks, three were located in the Bradford area as is evident from table 25. In 1869 these local works had 37% of the County's blast furnaces, 35% of its puddling furnaces and 30% of its rolling mills.[28]

**Table 25 The Main Bradford Ironworks in 1869 - Plant details**[29]

|  | No. of Ironworks | Blast furnaces built | Blast furnaces In blast | Tons of Pig-iron | Puddling furnaces | Rolling mills |
|---|---|---|---|---|---|---|
| Bowling Ironworks | 1 | 6 | 4 | detail | 26 | 6 |
| Low Moor Ironworks | 1 | 8 | 5 | not | 38 | 7 |
| J Parkins and Terry |  |  |  |  |  |  |
| Water Lane Bradford | 1 |  |  | available | 6 | 3 |
| Total ironworks in Yorkshire | 12 | 38 | 23 | 105,765 | 244 | 53 |

All the local ironworks used the cold blast process together with the hand puddling method of refining which had been developed by H. Cort between 1782 and 1784. By 1870 the rate of expansion of this type of iron in Britain slowed down because of its inefficiency compared with the new techniques which were beginning to replace it following the adoption of the Bessemer and later the Siemens-Martin and the Gilchrist-Thomas processes using the Jurassic ores in Cleveland and the East Midlands, thus the famous 'Yorkshire Irons' based on local Coal Measures ores became less competitive. The Emmett works at Birkenshaw closed in 1815, its stocks of iron being bought by the Low Moor Company. Work at Bierley ended in the early 1880's and the works were pulled down in 1889. Shelf ceased operation in 1849; and Bowling Iron Company went into liquidation in 1898. As well as having to compete with the new areas

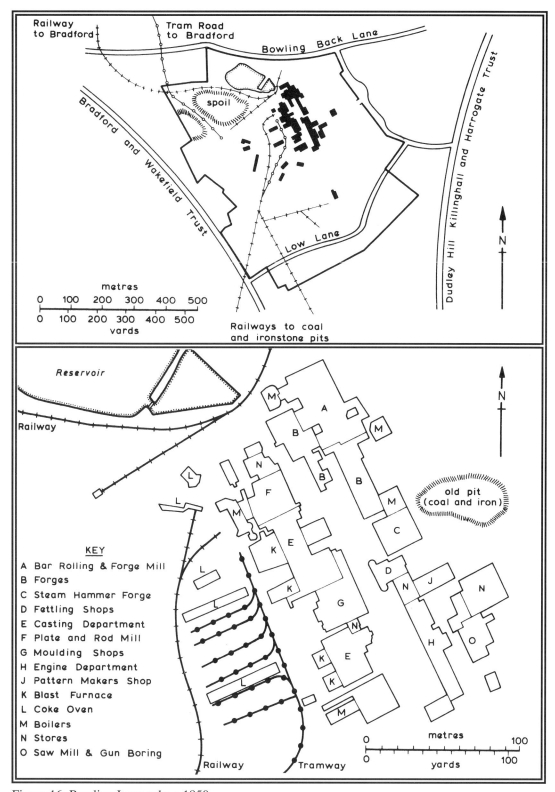

Figure 16. Bowling Ironworks c.1850

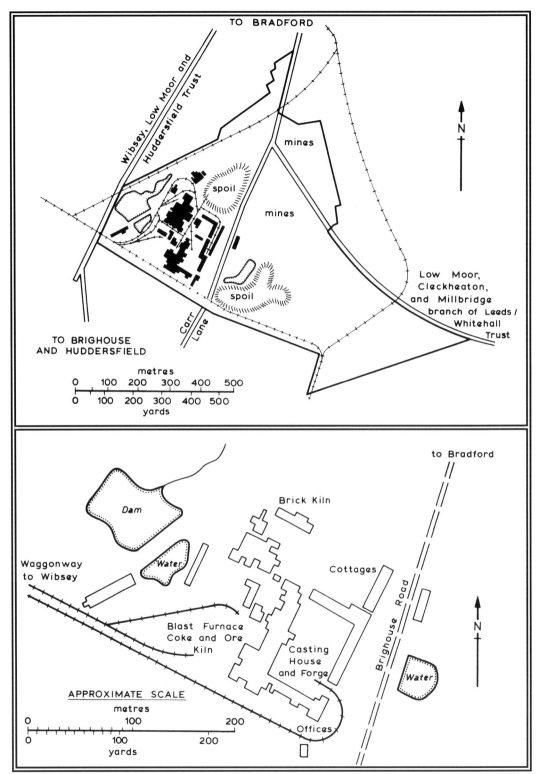

Figure 17. Low Moor Ironworks c.1850

in the Northeast and the Midlands, the Bradford iron industry suffered from the exhaustion of its coal and iron resources.

Table 26 indicates the scale of employment in metal manufacturing and its associated industries in Bradford. A large proportion of those referred to in the table were employed by the major iron companies. Low Moor for example, had 2,000 in its collieries alone in 1906. But the table is only an approximate indicator of growth in employment because of the complexities arising from the changes in the area to which the figures refer, and in the age categorisation at different census dates. It is useful however, in showing the importance of the industry and its growing diversification in Bradford between 1851 and 1891. In evaluating the position of iron manufacturing it should be remembered that the iron and coal industries were closely connected, as is evident from the Bowling deed of 1849 quoted earlier. Table 26 should therefore be related to the statistics of table 20.

**Table 26 Employment in Metal Manufacturing and Engineering in Bradford 1861-1899**[30]

| | Bradford Borough | Bradford Borough | Bradford Urban Sanitary District | | |
|---|---|---|---|---|---|
| Occupations | 1851 | 1861 | 1871 | 1881 | 1891 |
| Brass workers | 35 | 46 | 72 | | |
| Iron Manufacturers | 17 | 2,470(incl steel) | 1,420 | 1,549 | 1,572 |
| Nail Manufacturers | 14 | 25 | 16 | | |
| Anchor chain makers | | 3 | | | |
| Boiler makers | 101 | 144 | | 139 | 187 |
| Tool makers | 8 | | | 92 | 107 |
| Blacksmiths | 373 | | | 571 | 803 |
| Engine and machine makers | 1,014 | | 829 | 365 | 339 |
| Millwrights | 73 | 96 | 85 | 60 | 57 |
| Spinning and Weaving machine makers | | | 324 | 1,047 | 1,511 |
| Fitters and Turners | 13 | | | 484 | 813 |
| Tin and Tinplate | 63 | | | 180 | 297 |
| Other Metal | 126 | | | 186 | 275 |
| Total | 2,737 | 2,784 | 2,746 | 4,673 | 5,961 |

*Note on table 26 and note on table 20: The blanks in the columns do not necessarily mean that the trades did not exist, but that they have been included in one of the other categories. For example textile machine-making had become sufficiently important to merit separate categorisation by 1881, whereas the occupation this occupation is included in Engine and Machine-makers in the early years.*

In 1794 local pig iron was selling for £7. 10s. 0d per ton for cold blast iron, £7. 0s. 0d for first class iron and £6. 10s. 0d for second quality pig. These prices were also being charged in 1904. The large scale plans of figure 16 and 17, and the historical note show that the major companies of Bradford had achieved a high level of vertical integration by mid-century. Quite soon after beginning production they were manufacturing on the same site a wide range of products ranging from the preparation of ore to the manufacture of machines and engines.

Careful study of the layout of the buildings and other structures illustrated in figures16 and 17 shows that they were laid out to take advantage of the natural slope of the land and of gravity. This is apparent in the Bowling Ironworks, where the blast furnaces, which can still be seen on

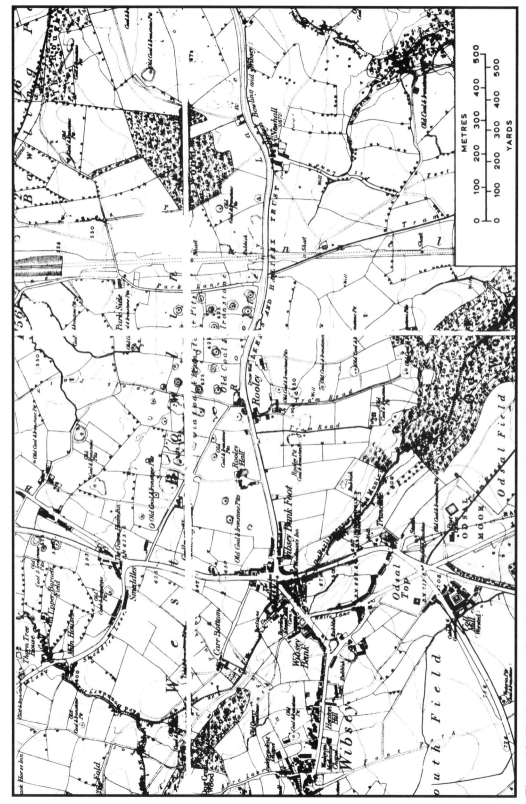

Figure 18. The landscape of a mined area – Workings at Bowling c.1847.

the site of Enfield Works, were located along the valley side and the main buildings on the floor of the valley. This meant that the cupolas could be charged from above the level of the valley side, and at least in the early days of the undertaking, the internal movement of material was largely operated, with great economy, by gravity. Later, as the firm grew in size it had to build on the higher land.

As may be seen from figures 15,16 and 17, the ironworks used large areas of land, which together with their coal and mined areas had an effect on the Bradford landscape that was both extensive and long-lasting. Devastated areas dating from the 18th century and 19th centuries can still be recognised. Iron manufacturing produced enormous amounts of *scoria,* the waste known as 'dross', which spread over huge areas, creating the desert landscapes of Bowling and parts of Low Moor. It was estimated in 1835 that the dross from the Low Moor foundry alone in that year amounted to 21,000 tons. This material was piled into heaps (see figures 16 and 17) of which it was said *'after forty years is quite extraordinary, those of the former having been set fire to are in substance like red tile; at this moment, supposing the whole were to form a cone in Grosvenor Square, I really believe its base would include all the houses.'*[31] The former greenfields and wooded slopes of 18th century Bradford were scored and scarred. As a consequence of the multiplicity of mined sites the surface is unstable in some areas. The 1852 six inch to one mile Ordnance Survey map of Bradford presents a picture of extensive areas, pock-marked by the small coal pits and ironstone pits with their aureoles of spoil suggestive of a moon landscape. (See figure 18). This is particularly evident in the south of the dale. But even today there are many coal spoil heaps to remind us of this period of Bradford's industrial history. To this must be added the dross tips. In spite of the fact that some of the material was sold off to build some of the turnpikes during the 1820's and 1830's, large amounts accumulated, creating tracts of sterile land in the area of the old Bowling ironworks. Neither the poisonous, free draining dross nor the acidic, unstable drought-stricken coal heaps would vegetate. They remained as ugly grey and brown monuments to this important phase of Bradford's industrial past though they are not without interest to the industrial archeologist.

## REFERENCES

1  Report of the Select Committee on Coal in the U.K. Vol III 1871 Appx 27 p.21 f
2  Parker, ibid. p.41-42.
3  Green, A.H, Russell, R., Dakyns, J.R. et al *The geology of the Yorkshire Coalfield,* 1878, p.132.
4  Low Moor Iron Company: *A Record of the origin and progress of the Low Moor Ironworks from 1791,* (1906).
5  Green, et al ibid. p.130.
6  Green, ibid. pp.151-152.
7  Green, et al ibid. p.131.
8  Low Moor Iron Company, ibid.
9  Dodsworth, C. 'Further observations on Bowling Ironworks' *Industrial Archeology,* Vol.6, No.2, May 1969.
10 Hunt, R. *Proceedings of the Yorkshire Geological Society* Vol.3, 1857 p.696.
11 Report of the Select Committee, loc. cit. p.89.
12 Registrar General: Census of Population for the years 1871,1881 and 1891 (see also note to table 20).
13 Maltby H.J. British Association for the Advancement of Science. *Handbook for Bradford,* 1924 p.99 et-seq.
14 Bradford Borough Council, *Annual Report* 1867.
15 Report of the Select Committee, ibid. p.95-97.
16 C.H.Wood Collection Books 1-199 Coal and iron mining XXVI of 1845, Folio A59 and A73, Located in Huddersfield University Library.
17 Galloway, R.I. *Annals of Coal-mining* 1898 p.460.

18 Parker, J ibid. Quoting the terms of a contract to deliver Best Bed coals.
19 Report of the Select Committee, ibid. p.212.
20 Dodsworth, ibid. p.117.
21 Green, et al ibid. p.155.
22 Report of the Select Committee, ibid. p.28.
23 Iron production in England and Wales 1788-1848 (tons):

|  | 1788 | 1796 | 1823 | 1830 | 1840 | 1848 |
|---|---|---|---|---|---|---|
| England & Wales | 48,200 | 167,322 | 442,066 | 652,417 | 1,396,000 | not known |
| Yorkshire | 4,500 | 21,984 | 27,311 | 28,926 | 56,000 | 66,650 |

From Report of Select Committee on coal in the UK, 1871.

24 Low Moor Iron Company, ibid.
25 Parker, J. ibid. p.296.
26 Long, Hilary. 'Bowling Ironworks' in *Industrial Archeology*, May 1968, p.176.
27 Hunt, R. ibid. p.696.
28 Report of Select Committee ibid Appendix table 140 p.140-145.
29 Parker, J ibid. p.294 quoting correspondence between Emmanuel Emmett of the Birkenshaw Foundry, and Richard Bradley of the Beargarden Foundry London in 1794.
30 Head, Sir George : *A Tour through the Manufacturing Districts of England in the Summer of 1835*, referring to Wibsey Iron Foundry' p.133.
31 A historical note on Low Moor, Bowling and Birkenshaw Ironworks Companies:

Low Moor Iron Company
    First ironmasters: Richard Hird, Joseph Dawson, John Hardy (originally included John Preston)
    First blast furnaces built 1789-1790

| Foundry | 1791 | a square furnace 50ft. high (making cannon, shells and shot) |
|---|---|---|
| Water wheel installed | 1800 | to feed cold blast furance |
| Forge | 1801 | (originally charcoal fired) |
| Slitting mill | 1802 | for nail and rod making |
| Forge hammer | 1803 | installed |
| Refinery and puddling mill | 1803 | this could handle charges of 30cwts of iron |
| Steam hammer | 1843 | installed |
| Forge | 1846 | |
| Plate mill | 1867 | |
| River machinery foundry | 1891 | could make stays, bolts and chain iron |

Bowling Iron Company
    First iron masters associated with Fall Ings Works, Wakefield: John Sturges of Sandal (Senior),
    John Sturges (Junior), William Sturges, Richard Paley of Leeds, John Sewell.

| First furnace built | 1788 | by Henry Leak initially producing domestic ironwork |
|---|---|---|
| Bar mill | c1790 | |
| Plate mill | | |
| Hammer shops | c1832 | |
| Boiler shop | | |
| Steel plant | c1850 | |

The map figure 16 shows the different departments of the works c 1847-48

| Emmetts of Birkenshaw | 1782 | |
|---|---|---|
| | | Was making steam engines in 1791 |

Foundry established John Emmett, Thomas Holden, William Bowlland and William Emmett, all of Halifax. After 1815 the Emmett family gave up their interest in the business.

# CHAPTER SEVEN

# THE GEOGRAPHY OF THE WORSTED INDUSTRY IN THE BRADFORD REGION

The area of the Bradford Region had a high level of specialisation in worsted manufacture even before the coal-based mechanisation of the industry. The tract of land between Halifax and Keighley was particularly important because of its abundant water-powered worsted mill sites. Textile manufacture using water power extended to other parts of the region including the Wharfedale area. However, Bradford as a water-power site was not so well resourced.

The peat-covered high moors behind Keighley, Addingham and Ilkley ensured a reliable flow of water to feed the streams which powered the water mills along their banks. Each village even in feudal times had its corn mill, which often also served as a fulling mill to beat the cloth. A. Raistrick, quoting from the 1379 Poll Tax returns refers *inter alia* to fulling mills at Ilkley, where there were two; at Addingham, Keighley, and Baildon which also had two mills. Bradford too, had its corn and fulling mill[1]. These early mills were often converted to cloth manufacture, first to make wool and then cotton, and later as worsted manufactories. There was therefore a major shift from the scattered distribution of the domestic system, to one based on water-powered mill sites, especially after the adoption of Kay's 'flying shuttle' and Revd. Edmund Cartwright's power loom, whose machines were widely used in the Bradford region from the 1830's onward. Table 30 on page 77 summarises the process of mechanisation in the Wool and Worsted manufacture.[2]

Figure 19 shows the distribution of the water-powered textile mill sites in Keighley in 1847-48. A number of these had been cotton mills, a few were silk, but most were converted to worsted-making by the beginning of the 19th century. An early example of a purpose built mill was Lister's at Addingham in 1787, and Aireworth Mill, Keighley. The latter, had been built as a cotton mill in 1790 and had become a worsted mill by 1808. Hodgson lists a number of worsted mills in Keighley that had been built for cotton manufacture in this early period, namely: Low Mill, Castle Mill, Screw Mill, Dalton, Low Bridge, West Greengate, Hope Mill, Damside Mill, Grove Mill, Damems, High Providence, Springhead, Ponden Higher and Lower Mills, Newsholme, Holme Mill, Brow End, Turkey Mill, North Brook Mill and Wood Mill. Apart from Low Bridge, Damside and Hope Mills, all of these were powered by water[2]. There were similar developments in Bingley, where in 1802 in Goit Stock, Timothy Horsfall and Charles Hartley were spinning cotton.[3]

Unlike mid-Airedale, Bradford as a water-power site was poorly endowed because it had an unreliable and inadequate local water supply. The Bradford Beck had only a small catchment and was short of water during drought periods. Proof of this may be deduced from the fact that the first mechanised mills in Bradford-dale were powered by horses i.e. at Fairweather Green, Little Horton and Bowling. Nevertheless stream side locations were still important as sources of water to store in mill ponds to supply the boilers for the steam engines, and as is noted later, they became open drains to the detriment of the health of many of Bradford's residents. The phenomenal growth of Bradford depended on coal rather than water energy, as did Foster's Black Dyke Mill, which worked pits at Clews Moor and Springhead. Waterside mills, served by canal and railway, proliferated. Though a canal had been proposed to link Keighley with the

Leeds and Liverpool Canal, it remained dependent on cart haulage until the rail link was constructed in 1846. In 1819, it was reported that 400 loads of coal per day were being delivered from the Canal to Keighley mills.[4]

With some justification, Bradford acquired the title of 'Worstedopolis' in the 19th century. Bradford had about 25% of the West Riding's production of worsted in 1810, and this branch of the industry employed 17% of the workforce of the town in 1881. The period spanned by these two dates saw a major re-distribution of the industry, not only nationally, but also locally within Bradford-dale. As has been noted, the industry was organised on the basis of the 'domestic system', which was a dispersed form of manufacturing carried on in the home of the cloth worker. By 1830's however, the industry was already showing signs of concentration on the mill sites in favoured power locations. Heaton noted that *'wool weaving might be either a person's staple occupation, or by members of his household, . . in Halifax and Bradford areas of cloth-making did not appear as an important means of livelihood, the cloths produced were made largely for home consumption'.*[5] It was not until 1468-69 that Bradford began to appear in the aulnage returns, though this exclusion may be largely due to the fact that the narrow coarse cloths which were made in the Bradford area were not covered by the Aulnage Statute which laid down standard sizes on which subsidies had to be paid. After 1393-94 the subsidy was applied to narrow cloths. The local cloths were about 14 yards in length by one yard two and a half inches broad. Wool-cloth making was a widely practised skill throughout Britain, since in the days of poor communications each settlement had to produce as much as possible of its own needs.

The cottage-based industry persisted in 19th century Bradford even in the warrens of narrow back-to-back streets, courts and alleys which were being erected in the growing town. By 1772 however, some regional specialisation was beginning to develop in West Yorkshire in which Bradford and its neighbours shared. The West Riding had surpassed the Norwich area in the value of its output in 1772. It had produced in that year cloth to the value of £1.4 millions compared with Norwich's £1.2 millions. By 1770 , the Pennine pastures were insufficient to satisfy the local demand for raw wool, and supplies had to come from places as far afield as Scotland and Ireland, even to keep the cottage industry supplied.

Bradford-dale, unlike its neighbour Halifax which had good water power resources, was poor in this form of industrial power. Halifax therefore was a more important producer until 1810, as is suggested by table 27. In interpreting the table, however, we must add that the some of the production on the moors between Airedale and Calderdale was traded in the Halifax and Bradford piece halls.

## Table 27 The Drawback on Soap in Bradford, Halifax and the West Riding[6]

| | £s Sterling | | | | | | | |
|---|---|---|---|---|---|---|---|---|
| Place | 1810 | 1815 | 1820 | 1825 | 1830 | 1835 | 1840 | 1850 |
| Bradford | 1,260 | 1,484 | 3,329 | 5,033 | 6,984 | 4,000 | 6,016 | 70,325 |
| Halifax | 1,264 | 1,419 | 2,699 | 3,294 | 4,148 | 3,449 | 5,214 | 5,777 |
| West Riding | 4,993 | 6,034 | 10,897 | 17,050 | 20,149 | 13,318 | 191,875 | 21,040 |

*Note on Table 27: The drawback was the amount that manufacturers could claim back on the duty they had paid on soap used in washing the wool. The duty paid was 2½ d a pound for hard soap and 1¼ d for soft soap, during the period 1783-1833 and after the latter date the duties were respectively 1½ d and 1d. Thus the figures after 1833 should be doubled to be comparable with those before 1833. In 1810, for the three areas of Haworth, Keighley and Bingley, drawback was £740, £1,111 in 1830, and £2,777 in 1850*[6].

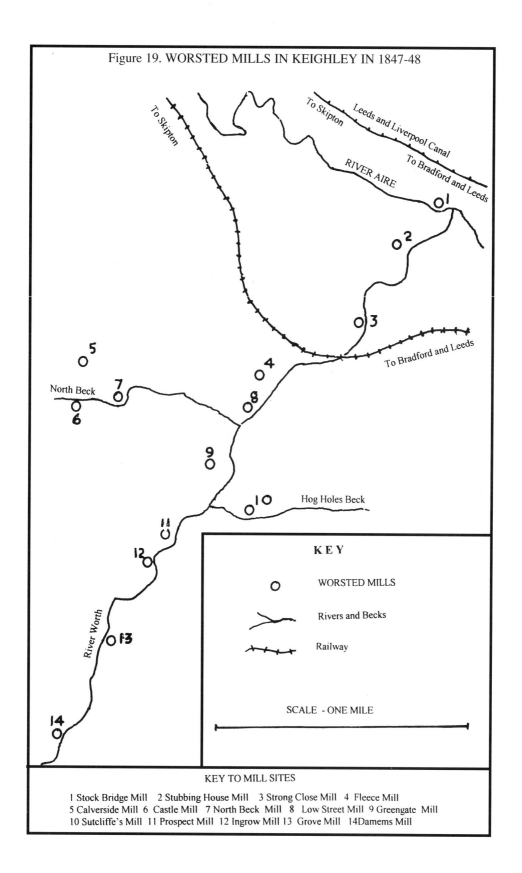

Figure 19. WORSTED MILLS IN KEIGHLEY IN 1847-48

To Skipton

To Skipton   Leeds and Liverpool Canal

To Bradford and Leeds

RIVER AIRE

To Skipton

1

2

3

To Bradford and Leeds

5

7

North Beck

6

4

8

9

10

Hog Holes Beck

11

12

River Worth

13

14

KEY

○   WORSTED MILLS

~   Rivers and Becks

—†—†—   Railway

SCALE  - ONE MILE

KEY TO MILL SITES

1 Stock Bridge Mill    2 Stubbing House Mill    3 Strong Close Mill   4  Fleece Mill
5 Calverside Mill  6 Castle Mill  7 North Beck  Mill  8  Low Street Mill  9 Greengate  Mill
10 Sutcliffe's Mill  11 Prospect Mill  12 Ingrow Mill 13  Grove Mill   14Damems Mill

As well as showing the growth of the worsted industry, the table also illustrates the extent to which the trade in West Yorkshire had come to be dominated by the two areas of Bradford and Halifax, which together, by 1810, account for 50% of the total West Riding production  based on the 'index' of the soap drawback.

**Table  28 Amount of wool consumed in Bradford and Keighley (1810-1853)**[7]

| Year | Bradford Million pounds | Keighley Million pounds | Year | Bradford Million pounds | Keighley Million pounds |
|------|------|------|------|------|------|
| 1810 |      | 0.38 | 1835 | 11.57 | 3.31 |
| 1815 | 2.14 | 0.98 | 1840 | 12.12 | 4.22 |
| 1820 | 4.63 | 1.63 | 1850 | 21.12 | 5.93 |
| 1825 | 6.38 | 2.28 | 1853 | 23.65 |      |
| 1830 | 10.1 | 3.58 |      |      |      |

## FABRIC DIVERSIFICATION - ALPACA, MOHAIR, SILKS AND VELVET

New fibres were introduced from about 1830 in the form first of alpaca, and later, mohair. The fabrication of alpaca into yarn and cloth presented considerable technical difficulties, but these were overcome, and when combined with cotton warps, a whole new range of fabrics was opened up, notably in the light fine figured cloths suitable for women's wear. Titus Salt shares the credit for these developments with other local manufacturers, but he seems to have exploited the innovations most effectively, because he had mastered the technique of producing an even and true thread by 1836.  Two or three producers dominated the alpaca mohair sector, namely John Foster's at Black Dyke Mills in Queensbury and Titus Salt's, in Bradford initially, and after 1853, at Saltaire. Another producer was Messrs Fisons of Greenholme Mill in Burley in Wharfedale who, interestingly, were using water power in 1853, and were still using water with steam at their mill in 1900.[8] Mohair is the fibre from the angora goat.  Its use in textiles was another innovation, and the Salt firm was using at its Bradford mills 37,513  pounds of this material in 1844, and 212,000 lbs in 1860, by which time it had moved all its production to Saltaire. These three producers are interesting in other respects.  The worsted mills were usually located alongside water to give access to a power source, and by a canal or a railway to minimise transport costs.  So they often occupied  the lower sections of the valleys.  Black Dyke Mill did not conform to this pattern and would seem to be at a locational disadvantage.  It is sited on the Pennine Plateau about 350 metres above sea level.  It had no direct rail connection to the works. The nearest rail link was 120 metres below in the valley on the Bradford to Keighley line via Thornton. Fosters had access to local coal from their own mines at Thornton in the valley of Bradford Beck and from the Clews Moor and Springhead pits on the plateau. They prospered nevertheless, chiefly it would seem, by innovating and by good management. Though originally sharing in the Pennine domestic worsted manufacturing system, they began to make special cloths using alpaca and mohair.  They also continued mining and their shop was an important part of the business.  But they gained economies by integrating cloth  production by concentrating all the processes at their large mill, thus achieving economies of scale. They were carrying stocks of 216,924 lbs of alpaca in 1850, 914,941 lbs in 1860 and peaked at 1,783,018 lbs in 1879. The corresponding stocks of mohair were 350,747 lbs (1850), 194,172 lbs (1860), and 2,189,476 lbs in 1890.[9]  For Salts it was a different story as far as location was concerned. In Saltaire they had a splendid site.  Initially, they were operating in a number of mill premises in central Bradford. In 1850 the firm's business was spread between four sites: Hollings Mill, Brick Lane Mill, Beecroft Mill and Union Street Mill. Earlier, they were apparently sharing mill accommodation in two factories alongside the Goit, one of which was Thomson's Mill.[10] In 1853 the firm moved into the newly built mill at Saltaire which had direct access to the canal and the railway for its coal and raw materials. Here again there were scale economies, as well as the advantage of carrying out all the production processes in one establishment. Like Fosters in Queensbury, Salts had their own gas works, which also supplied the workers' homes. To give an idea of the scale of the new production unit at Saltaire, the Mill was capable of producing 30,000 yards of cloth a day[11].

A further diversification began with the mass production of silks and velvets and plushes by E. Cunliffe Lister at his magnificent mill in Manningham. He too, was located in the Goit Side area of central Bradford at the same time as Salt was operating there.[10] By mid-century therefore, the Bradford region was established as a leading centre in the manufacture of worsted, wool-mix cloth as well as being a major producer of the new fabrics, to earn itself the title of 'the metropolis of the worsted industry'.

**Table 29   Number of worsted mills, engines, water wheels, and employees in the Bradford Region and in Halifax in 1850**[12]

|  | No. of mills | Steam No. of engines | Steam No. of horse power | Water No. of wheels | Water No. of horse power | Employees Total |
|---|---|---|---|---|---|---|
| Addingham | 3 | 1 | 8 | 3 | 21 | 104 |
| Bingley | 14 | 12 | 156$\frac{1}{2}$ | 8 | 66 | 788 |
| Bradford | 73 | 65 | 1,455 | 39 | 192 | 7,648 |
| Keighley | 22 | 9 | 107$\frac{1}{2}$ | 15 | 181 | 1,061 |
| Halifax | 45 | 84 | 750 | 25 | 201 | 3,606 |

The industrial geographer is concerned with plant location, industrial localisation, agglomeration and specialisation. The invention of the steam engine widened the choice of site as well as the scale of production. Users of steam were less dependent on the vagaries of the weather or the limitations of the water catchment. Bradford, with its abundant accessible coal deposits, was able to benefit from this, though as table 29 shows, there were 39 water wheels in operation in 1850 in the dale. At the same time the table demonstrates the continued importance of water power in Keighley, Halifax, Bingley and Addingham. Steam engines not only gave greater choice in the siting of mills, but were also generally more powerful than water wheels. The average h.p. generated by steam ranged from 8 to 22 in Addingham, Bingley and Bradford compared with 5 to 12 h.p for water power. Although the number of employers may be a rough indication of scale, the number of spindles and looms per establishment provide a better measure as table 30 shows.

**Table 30 The number of spindles and looms in use in the mills of Bradford, Bingley and Keighley in 1850**[13]

| Parish | No. of firms | Spinning spindles | No. of firms | Spinning spindles | Weaving looms |
|---|---|---|---|---|---|
| Bingley | 4 | 8,264 | 9 | 18,566 | 1,198 |
| Bradford | 67 | 150,986 | 74 | 231,348 | 10,107 |
| Keighley | 13 | 28,642 | 14 | 27,844 | 1,484 |

The mills of Bingley and Keighley had an average of about 2,000 spindles per firm, and those of Bradford had 3,126, though there was little difference in the average number of looms per firm, however, we can see a beginning here of the integration of processes in the worsted industry.

**Table 31  The sequence of processes in Worsted Manufacturing Technique and the phasing of their mechanisation during the 19th century**[2]

| Process | | |
|---|---|---|
| Sorting | A hand operation involving the separation of the various parts of the fleece categories for the wool industry. | |
| Combing | The wool is first washed in soap and hot water and then wrung out to dry, initially a hand operation. In the hand combing the cleansed wool was oiled and then combed using one, two or three-pitched combs (a) to separate the long fibres from the short strands and (b) to align them ready for later processing prior to spinning. This stage required warm combs and a warm atmosphere, and the stock in trade of the hand comber was the comb, the pot and the brazier. | Arkwright invented a mechanised comb in 1792, and a combing machine was installed in a horse mill in Bradford in 1794. Platt and Collier patented a combing machine in 1827, but the main development was the Lister-Donnisthorpe combing machine, with modifications to prevent snarling (1842-1849). These were "pretty extensively used in 1842-44". Crabtree produced an improved combing machine in 1854. |
| Carding | The separation and aligning of the wool fibres for spinning. Was used in both wool and worsted fibre preparation. | Carding machine for use in worsted yarn preparation as used in Idle in 1820. An improved machine was invented by G. Anderton of Cleckheaton in 1829. |
| Drawing | The preparation of the fibres prior to making the sliver ready for the spinners, it involves the placing of the fibres in line, so that they overlap, the fibres being stretched, laid straight and cleared of knots. | Machines appear to have been invented contemporaneously with the combing machine. |
| Roving | A further stage, in which the threads are given a slight twist to fit them for spinning. | |
| Spinning | The rovings are twisted and drawn into yarn ready for weaving. | In worsted manufacture the spinning machine was known as a throstle. Wyatt invented a machine in 1741, Highs later, but Arkwright took up the idea and patented a spinning machine, the first being used in Preston in 1768. Hargreaves' "Spinning Jenny" appears in 1780, and was "early applied to worsted manufacture". The Arkwright machine was used locally (Halifax) in 1757. Hargreaves' machine was driven by water, hence his "Water frame". Bradford mills were using mechanical spinners c 1801. |
| Weaving | This remained a hand operation, hand looms being used into the late 1830's. There were 10,000 hand-weavers in 1838, by which time they were reduced to a state of near pauperdom. | Wool power looms were introduced into the Bradford area c. 1822 (James Warbrick of Shipley, and Messrs. Horsfall Bradford 1825). Introduction of cotton warps in 1836 must be treated as major weaving innovation. |
| Dyeing | Involves the dyeing of either yarn or finished cloth. Worsted is made with coloured yarn. The fibres have to be treated chemically before immersion in the dyevats. The industrial group includes scourers and bleachers. | Bradford stuff was formerly dyed in Wakefield or Leeds, but was doing its own by 1797 when there were two dyehouses in the town (Bowling Dyeworks and Peel's of Thornton Road). Bradford Dyers established c. 1843. By 1871 this industry employed 1,829. |

## LOCATIONAL PATTERNS, DIVERSIFICATION AND LINKAGES

Table 31 summarises the changes in the technology of wool and worsted textile manufacture and the progress of its adoption in the Bradford region. Wool sorting remained a hand operation with increased dependence on foreign sources for both wool and mohair. The mohair came from areas where anthrax was endemic, and the woolsorters were exposed to this disease to such an extent that the disease was known locally as the 'Bradford Disease' or the 'woolsorters' disease'. Although Arkwright had invented a mechanised comb, combing remained a hand operation until the 1840's. Home based combing was carried on in the centre of Bradford in the homes of the hand-combers, some of which was concentrated in the crowded unhealthy area known as Thompson's Buildings, which were no doubt built to serve the adjacent Thompson's Mill at Goit Side in central Bradford (see figure 24 on page 98).

The object of combing was to separate the long fibres, used in worsted manufacture, from the short fibres used in wool manufacturing. Spinning mechanisation came earlier, especially after the adoption of Hargreaves' 'Spinning Jenny'in 1780, and came into general use in the worsted region before the widespread application of steam power by the worsted manufacturers. Hand weaving continued to be important until the mid-1820's chiefly because of the difficulty in using machine-made worsted warps. This problem was overcome with the introduction of cotton warps in 1836, after which hand-combing became a depressed industry.

The movement of dyeing to Bradford in the late 18th century was not without its environmental consequences, especially as this branch of the industry included scouring and bleaching, and it contributed to the pollution of the Bradford Beck and the Canal Basin. The soft water collected on the local moors was an important resource, not just for water power. It was much sought after by the cloth mill owners who needed it to supply their steam engines, and by the dyers, bleachers and wool scourers, for whom it was an essential raw material. It is noticeable that the dyeworks were located upstream in order to obtain the cleanest water. But the local water had properties which were especially attractive to the wool textile trade. It was collected on the coal measures and the gritstone peat-covered moors of the Pennines. The water, therefore, was soft and suited to the treatment of textiles. Equally important, the soft water did not fur up the boilers of the steam engines, economised in the use of soaps and detergents, and so reduced the maintenance costs on the steam boilers. Unfortunately, as a result of the concentration of dyeworks alongside the Bradford Beck, it came to be used as a drain, effluent from which found its way into the Canal Basin.

The most fundamental consequence of the changes in textile manufacture set out in table 31 was that they enabled the re-distribution of the industry from a dispersed to a concentrated form, which is also evident from figure 15 on page 59, where we can see mills located on the higher parts of the Bradford Beck valley east of the town centre. Table 32 also summarises this movement. However, where handwork continued alongside the mechanised mill, as it did with wool-combing in central Bradford, for example, the houses of the hand combers near the mill became an extension of the factory. Unlike the hand loom weavers on their small-holdings in the rural areas of the Pennines where they could produce some of their food needs, the urban handcombers were particularly hard hit by the move to the mechanisation of the industry. As figure 15 shows, the mills and other industrial establishements are clustered alongside the Beck on the valley floor, which was the most accessible area for their coal and water needs. In Bradford the natural slope favoured gravity systems of local transport, in the form of waggon ways, and cheap coal was readily accessible, so reducing production costs. Technology, especially by using more powerful machines, was making large-scale production possible, so that scale economies could be made. Integration of the production processes e.g. the combination of spinning and weaving on the same site, as revealed in table 31, was already taking effect in 1850. But there were also developments in associated industries such as dyeing and the manufacture of textile machinery, both of which had close technical links with their cloth-making customers, leading to the kind of agglomeration seen in figure 15. These contributed to the development of industrial complexes revealed in the map.

**Table 32 The increase of Mills and their spread in Bradford-dale 1834-50**[14]

| Place | No. of mills 1834 | No of mills 1841 | No of mills 1851 |
|---|---|---|---|
| Eccleshill | 1 | 1 | |
| Shipley | 2 | 5 | 3 |
| Thornton | 2 | 4 | 9 |
| Bowling | 2 | 4 | 18 |
| Little Horton | 7 | 13 | 36 |
| Great Horton | 4 | 9 | 13 |
| Bradford centre | 21 | 38 | 59 |
| Allerton | | 1 | 3 |
| Bierley | | 1 | 4 |
| Clayton | | 4 | 2 |
| Manningham | 3 | 3 | |
| TOTAL | 39 | 83 | 153 |

In addition, the valley floor sites were also easier to develop because they provided flat land for building development and easy gradients for transport.

The mills also clustered alongside the canals and the railways. In fact the railway released industrial location from water side sites and the valley bottoms as is evident from figure 15 and table 32, but this was largely after Bradford had begun to augment its water supply from areas outside the dale.

Table 33 shows the changes in the size of worsted undertakings in Bradford between 1835 and 1850. As can be seen it suggests that the mills combining both spinning and weaving were larger than the single-function establishments.

**Table 33 Changes in the size of worsted undertakings in Bradford 1835-50**[15]

| Year | Average number of employees |
|---|---|
| 1835 | 103 |
| 1841 | 124 |
| 1850 | |
| Spinning only | 53 |
| Weaving only | 67 |
| Spinning and weaving | 192 |

The census returns show the importance of the textile industry in 1871-1911, summarised in table 34. Bradford had 21% of the worsted factories in 1871 and 25% of the national labour force in that industry, indicating a degree of localisation, and the importance of Bradford in the manufacture of worsted cloth.

## Table 34  Employment in Textiles in Bradford 1871-1911[16]

| Industry | 1871 Aged 20 + | 1881 Aged 10+ | 1911 |
|---|---|---|---|
| Total Textiles | 13,944 | 37,878 | 64,000 |
| Worsted | 13,944 | 26,711 | 49,036 (including wool) |
| Dyeing, Bleaching Scouring and printing of cloth | 843 | 1,829 | 6,288 |
| Cotton | 1,288 | 1,801 | ) |
| Silk | 286 | 1,604 | ) 8,947 |
| Woollen cloth and other textiles | | 2,098 | ) |

This chapter has dealt with the progress of the Bradford region as the most important production area for worsted manufacture in Britain. The industry was localised, as evidenced by the large number engaged in the industry in the Bradford area in 1871. The wool textile industry continued to dominate the local industrial economy into the closing decades of the 20th century. This emphasis, however, should not lead us to under-rate the importance of the iron and engineering industries discussed in the last chapter. But the concentration of textile manufacturing in the area exerted a strong gravitational effect on those industries discussed in the last chapter, especially textile machine makers, amongst which should be included Keighley firms like George Hattersleys and Sons, Prince Smith and Son, and Dracups in Bradford. The Directory of 1884 also includes several machine tool makers, and brass and iron founders in Keighley. While textiles clearly dominated the economy, the trade directories also include other industries, notably the washing and wringer machine manufacturers of which there was a concentration in Keighley.

## REFERENCES

1  Raistrick, A 'The Yorkshire Monastic Wool Trade' *Bradford Textile Society Journal*, 1947-48 p.24.
2  James, J. ibid. Ch. XIV.
3  Hodgson, J *Manufacturing and other Industries in Keighley in 1879* p.18.
4  Dewhirst, I *A History of Keighley* 1974 p.14.
5  Heaton, J. ibid. p.273.
6  James, J. ibid. Ch. 10.
7  James, ibid. p.604.
8  James, ibid. Ch.11.
9  Sigsworth, E. *Black Dyke Mills* Tables IV and V, 1958, pp.276- 279.
10  Balgarnie, Sir Titus Salt 1874 p.12 and plan in Bradford Central Library Archive showing riparian tenants bordering Bradford Beck and the Goit (included Salt's and Listers).
11  Balgarnie, op. cit.
12  James, J. ibid. p.152.
13  James, J. ibid. p.512.
14  James, J. ibid. pp. 606-609.
15  James, J. ibid. Derived from the tables p.607,608 and 609.
16  The Registrar General: Decennial Census Tables. It should be noted that the areas referred to are slightly different in different years, and the age categories are not strictly comparable. But these differences do not alter the argument that growth occurred, nor the relative importance of each sector of the industry in each of the years indicated.

# CHAPTER EIGHT
# 19TH CENTURY POPULATION GEOGRAPHY

Since 1801 a full census of the population of Britain has been carried out at ten year intervals except for the war year 1941. At first these decennial surveys were simple counts of the numbers of people and houses in the administrative areas the surveys covered. Refinements have been introduced from time to time so that today the census constitutes an increasingly important social document, recording peoples' circumstances, including: occupations, social class, ethnicity, educational attainment, work journey, car ownership, and quantitative and qualitative data on housing. The censuses are therefore valuable sources giving periodic snapshot views of the communities and neighbourhoods in the three dales over the years. The previous chapters have included estimates of the population at different times living in the various centres and districts in Greater Bradford. Because the 'counts' on which they were based were made for different purposes, not directly connected with assessing the size of a particular population, they present difficulties in making comparisons between one period, and one place, and another. For example, they were concerned with such matters as the collection of a tax; like the poll tax of the 14th century. Sometimes they only included males, or referred to the number of families, so that assumptions have had to be made about the size of families in estimating the total size of the population. The Domesday Book for example, was intended primarily to assess the value of William the Conqueror's newly won possession. Since all the former Saxon manors were recorded as waste, it is generally concluded that there was no one living in the vills of our region in 1086, though we may reasonably ask how the areas were eventually re-populated. But the Poll Tax of the 14th century is still a useful source of demographic information. Thomas Cromwell's instruction to the parish clergy to maintain registers of births, marriages and deaths, enables us to learn more about population dynamics during the period to 1801. The visitations of the Archbishop (not necessarily in person) tell us something about the state of the English Church in England, but incidentally, about the numbers living in the parishes. But here again the figures are about families rather than individuals As can be seen the areas covered by these statistics may relate to manors, vills, townships or parishes, each with different acreages. With these reservations in mind table 35 presents a summary of the estimated population of settlements in the three dales between the 14th and the 18th century.

**Table 35 Estimates of population in the settlements in the Bradford region from the 14th to the 18th century (Years are shown in brackets)**

| Area | 14th century | 16th century | 17th century | 18th century |
|---|---|---|---|---|
| Baildon[1] | 150 Poll tax (1378) | 300-500 (1548) | | 1603 (1798) |
| Bingley[2] | 300 Poll Tax | 1500 (1601) | | 2900 (1751) |
| Bradford[3] | 344 Poll Tax | | | 4500 Archbishop Herring's visitation |
| Keighley[4] | | | 1330 (1623) | 2160 (1730)  4645 (1769) |
| Ilkley[5] | | 240 (1540) | | c 400 (1743) |

Population change consists of two elements, natural increase or decrease (the difference between births and deaths in a population) and migration (immigration or emigration). From table 35 we can see that population increased slowly during the five centuries covered by the table in spite of the periodic visitations of the plague and the impact of the Civil War. The parish register for Bradford showed a sharp rise of 300 in burials in the year 1643 which was the the start of the Civil War, but it was also a plague year, and in 31 of the 56 years between 1644 and 1700 the number of burials exceeded births by a total of 221, yet as we see, the parish population had increased to 4,500 by the 18th century, probably due to inward migration. On the other hand, in Ilkley, between 1600 and 1654 baptisms exceeded burials for all but 11 of the 54 years, and in Bingley the registers show that there were only 3 years when burials exceeded baptisms, indicating steady growth between 1590 and 1800.

**Table 36          Population of the Bradford region 1801-1901**[6]

| Year | 1801 | 1811 | 1821 | 1831 | 1841 | 1851 | 1861 | 1871 | 1881 | 1891 | 1901 |
|------|------|------|------|------|------|------|------|------|------|------|------|
| Baildon | 2214 | 2659 | 3357 | 3775 | 4072 | 3760 | 3895 | 4784 | 5486 | 5430 | 5797 |
| Bingley | 4938 | 5769 | 7375 | 9255 | 11850 | 15339 | 13254 | 15955 | 9465 | 10465 | 18449 |
| Bradford | 13264 | 16012 | 26309 | 43527 | 66715 | 103778 | 106218 | 147101 | 194495 | 216361 | 279767 |
| Burley | 842 | 1175 | 1200 | 1448 | 1736 | 1894 | 2136 | 2271 | 2550 | 2661 | 3310 |
| Denholme | | | | | | | | 3469 | 3549 | 3237 | 2913 |
| Haworth | 3164 | 3971 | 4668 | 5835 | 6303 | 6848 | 5966 | 5655 | 5366 | 8395 | 7492 |
| Ilkley | 426 | 459 | 496 | 691 | 778 | 811 | 1043 | 2511 | 4736 | 5767 | 7455 |
| Keighley | 5745 | 6864 | 9223 | 11176 | 13413 | 18279 | 15005 | 19775 | 30663 | 44566 | 41564 |
| Oakworth | | | | | | | | 5683 | 5762 | 5880 | 4261 |
| Oxenhope | | | | | | | | | 2443 | 2475 | 2727 |
| Queensbury | | | | | | | | 6012 | 6824 | 6740 | 6416 |
| Shipley | 1959 | 2302 | 2823 | 3358 | 3986 | 4929 | 7100 | 11757 | 15093 | 23387 | 25573 |
| Silsden | 1323 | 1608 | 1904 | 2137 | 2346 | 2508 | 2582 | 2714 | 3329 | 3860 | 4304 |

Between 1801 and 1851 the population of the combined area covered by table 36 increased from 33,875 in 1801 to158,146, and it had a total of 410,028 in1901. The Wharfedale townships of Ilkley and Burley together had a  population of 1,268 in 1801 and 2,705 in 1851, but Ilkley showed  a large increase of 7,455 inhabitants by 1901 from the low figure of 811 in 1851, and Burley 3,310 in 1901 against the 1851 figure of 1,894. The discovery of the mineral springs in Ilkley early in the 19th century, led to the establishment of hydropathic centres at  Ben Rhydding near the hamlet of Wheatley in 1844, and a further centre at Wells House in 1856.  A number of lodging houses were opened in this part of Wharfedale, and later, following the construction of the rail link with Leeds and Bradford, Ilkley developed as a health resort and a preferred residential location for business men escaping from the unhealthy industrial centres of the coalfield areas.[7]  From a much higher base, the population of Airedale grew from 19,343 in 1801 to 51,663 in 1851, averaging 646 (13.3% a year), and growth continued in this area for the remainder of the century, reaching a total of 113,080 in 1901 (equivalent to an annual average increase of 1,228,  2.4 % per annum over the 50 year period).  It was in Bradford-dale that the most dramatic increase took place. It had a population of  13,264 in 1801 and 103,778 in1851. That amounted to an eightfold increase, or an annual average growth rate of 1,810 (13.6%), and it continued to grow by an average of 3,648 a year to 279,767 in 1901.  Natural increase, the excess of births over deaths undoubtedly accounted for a part of the increase discussed above, but the evidence of the census enumeration books shows that immigration accounted for a significant proportion of this growth.

Paralleling the better data collection of the decennial censuses, from about the middle of the century, the reports of the medical officers of the townships give details of births and deaths, as well as the mortality, morbidity and sanitary conditions. The adoption of the Public Health Act by the local town authorities resulted in the appointment of local Medical Officers of Health who produced annual reports. In the early 1840s the Health of Towns Commission reported on the conditions in the townships of this study, reporting inter alia on mortality, and sanitation. Their work resulted in the appointment of Medical Officers of Health and Sanitary Inspectors for the larger towns and for the groups of smaller places in the sanitary unions. Their reports revealed high death rates in all the areas covered by this study. In spite of these high rates, as we noted earlier, populations continued to grow throughout the 19th century in all the centres, partly because birth rates were high, and natural increase was positive, and partly because of inward migration. For example Bingley in 1830 had a birth rate of 28.2 per thousand births, against a death rate of 17.2 per thousand[11], and Bradford in 1840 there were 31.2 births per thousand of population with a death rate of 25.7/1,000[12]. While in Keighley, the birth rate was 28.3/1,000, exceeding the death rate by 3.1/1000[13]. When Shipley petitioned for the application of the Public Health Act in the township in 1848, there had been 298 deaths in the previous two years, giving a death rate of 35/1000[14]. Town Commissions had been established under local Improvement Acts in Bradford (1803), and Keighley was governed under the terms of a Lighting and Improvement Act by a Commission, and it also had a Board of Guardians. It is noteworthy that these established authorities resisted the implementation of the recommendations of the Commission's inspectors. For example, the Keighley Improvement Act Commissioners at their meeting of 16th November 1855, resolved *'that the establishment of the Public Health Act in this town as recommended by Mr Ranger (the inspector) be opposed'*.[15]

Child deaths accounted for the high crude death rates, and the infant mortality rates (I.M.R., i.e. the number of deaths of children aged under five per thousand births) were reported separately. They were the chief victims largely due to the very poor environmental conditions which existed in the older crowded, unsanitary parts of the developing towns. The Infant Mortality Rate (I.M.R.) for Bradford in 1840 was estimated at 140/1000 and remained high through the century, reaching 201/1000 in 1880, and peaked at 203/1000 in 1895. In Keighley in 1849 there were 134 deaths of children under five, rising to 182 in 1852 when there were also 42 deaths of children aged 5-15, giving an I.M.R. 136/1000.

There were visitations of cholera and typhus in both Bradford and Keighley during the 1840's, in the areas where most of the Irish immigrants congregated after fleeing from the potato famine. But consumption and fevers were the most frequently recorded causes of death. Fever deaths, the zymotic diseases, i.e. those pertaining to, or causing infection, chiefly affecting children, were high. In Shipley they accounted for 98 of the 298 deaths recorded in the years 1848-51, and in Keighley there were 253 deaths of which 134 were of children under five.[16] Bradford showed a similar pattern with an I.M.R of 176/1000 in 1870 and things were little better there by the end of the century when, in 1895, the I.M.R peaked at 203/1000.[17]

The 1841 Census of Population for Bradford recorded that 7,903 (12 percent of the population of Bradford Borough) were born outside Yorkshire. The figure included a small but influential number of foreigners amounting to 244, who were mostly from north Germany. Bradford had already become a major industrial centre and was attracting large numbers of people seeking work. Migrants came from all parts of the British Isles, as can be seen from figure 20.[8] Some counties appear more prominently than others on the map, from which it is possible to identify three migration routes: first one via Lancashire; then a second route following a line running from Norfolk and Suffolk, through Lincolnshire and Nottinghamshire;

and a third string of counties extending from Devon, through Somerset, Gloucestershire, Worcestershire, Staffordshire and Cheshire. By 1851 the former cloth-making areas were suffering from the competition of the areas of machine-based textile manufacturing like Bradford and Keighley, and significantly, East Anglia and the West Country appear to be the starting point of these routes, strongly suggesting that some of the migration originated from these former cloth-making towns. But as is shown later, there were other causes producing the flow, particularly amongst those who were born in Ireland. The most numerous county contingent born outside Yorkshire, was from Lancashire, which lay on the most direct route from Dublin to the worsted region. There were 801 who were born in Scotland and 98 Welsh-born in the 1851 recorded in table 37, the census enumeration for Bradford. Those born outside Yorkshire, and the Irish migrants are defined as 'long distance migrants'. It should be remembered, however, that there were significant numbers arriving from a shorter distance, so that a considerable proportion could be treated as 'short distance migration' coming as they did from within our study region and from the rest of Yorkshire. If the numbers coming from the Bradford Region we have defined are excluded, then those coming from the rest of Yorkshire were 277(9.1%) in Baildon; and 693(15.7%) and 539(17.0%) respectively, in Bingley and Shipley.

Of the 244 foreigners who began to settle in Bradford in the 1830's, most were from north Germany. They were merchants and were quickly absorbed into the Bradford 'Establishment', playing an important part in its commercial, cultural and civic life. In 1851 the German residents were important in founding the Bradford Chamber of Commerce, 50 of them made up one quarter of its total subscribers between 1851 and 1881. By 1902, 23 of the 36 yarn merchants, and 31 of the 63 piece merchants were German. The German, Jacob Behrens, who came to live in Frizinghall, and later Whetley Hill, opened his warehouse in Thornton Road in 1838. Another German, Charles Simon, became mayor, and Frederic Delius's father, Rudolph, came from Bielfeld in Westphalia in 1874. With his brother, he established the firm of D. and R. Delius. Moritz Rothenstein moved to Bradford in 1859 and established a warehouse in Hall Ing. His son, William, the painter, was born in Bradford in 1872. This small German group included Evangelicals, Catholics, and Jews. They left their mark in the cultural buildings, places of worship and in the names of some of Bradford's streets. The area where many of them had their warehouses is still known as 'Little Germany'.

In contrast to the small number of foreigners recorded in the 1851 enumeration, the Irish formed the largest ethnic group, constituting distinctive minorities in 19th century Bradford and Keighley. Table 37 includes figures of Irish settlers taken from the studies by the author on Bradford[9] and from the work of R.A. Schofield on the Keighley migrants.[10] From table 37, it will be noted, the Irish migrant settlement was mainly in Bradford and Keighley and there were very few in the other Aire Valley towns. As far as we can talk of Irish settlement with such small numbers, the enumeration sheets show that in Baildon it was confined to the Brooks Hill and Lane End area; in Bingley there were one or two families in Burrage Street and Chapel Yard; but in Shipley they were more widely scattered in the older streets of the town, but still only numbered 12.

**Table 37 'Long Distance' Migration into Bradford Borough and the Airedale Towns**[18]

|  | Baildon Township | Bingley Township | Bradford Borough | Keighley Parish | Shipley Tonwship |
|---|---|---|---|---|---|
| Township etc Population | 3,028 | 4,425 | 103,778 | 12,644 | 3,173 |
| 'Long Distance'Migration' | 66 (2.2%) | 303 (6.8%) | 7903 (7.6%) | 862 (6.8%) | 100 (3.2%) |
| Population born in Ireland | 51 (1.2%) | 37 (0.8%) | 8677 (8.4%) | 870 (6.9%) | 12 (0.4%) |

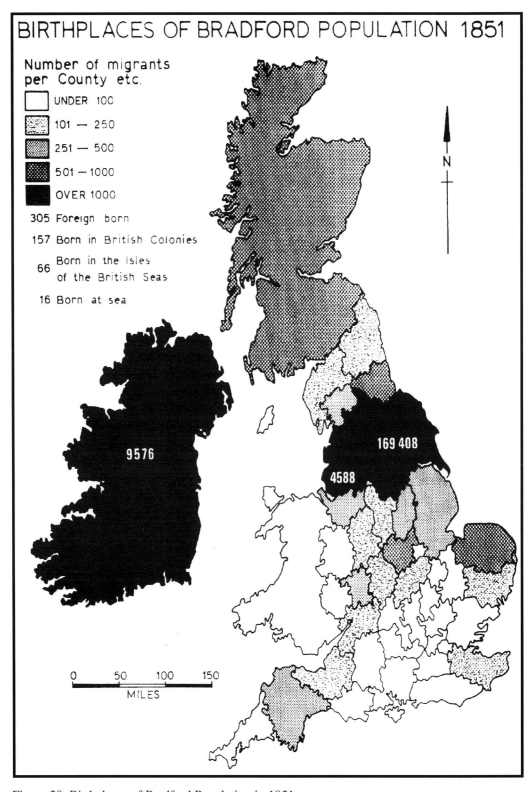

Figure 20. Birthplaces of Bradford Population in 1851.

Migratory pressures resulting from the technological changes in cloth-making were shifting production from the Pennine areas, as was noted earlier, and the hand weavers were amongst the first to suffer as their livelihoods were threatened, and machine production competed with the former cloth making areas in the southwest and in East Anglia. Also the so-called agricultural revoluton was releasing labourers and small-holders from rural areas. However, in Ireland there were other pressures. Changes in the franchise, based on the size of holdings, from £2 to £10, encouraged landlords in Ireland to amalgamate the small holdings to form larger holdings, and to evict the tenants. These added to the misery of the Irish peasants, culminating in the failure of the potato crop on which they depended. There were 'local' famines in Ireland before the Great Hunger of '45, which precipitated some migration. On the other hand the textile towns on both sides of the Pennines were major work places, and work meant food, shelter and survival. They attracted population which flocked to the textile manufacturing centres. As table 37 shows, Bradford and Keighley were the chief reception areas of this population movement. In Bradford parish in 1851 the Irish numbered 9,581 equal to 26% of the Irish-born population of West Yorkshire. In the same year 8,677 of the Irish-born lived in the newly formed Borough.

Irish settlement became significant in the 1820's. The settlers were nearly all Catholics, and the number of Catholics had increased sufficiently to justify the construction of a church at Stott Hill, just east of the present Cathedral. The name evidence of the Registers of Births, Marriages and Burials of St Mary's Catholic Church shows that between two thirds and three quarters of the Catholic congregation were Irish. The priest of St Mary's, the Revd. M. Kaye, stated in 1837 that his congregation was between 2,000 and 3,000[19] and the 1841 Census recorded 1,868 living in the township (i.e. 5% of its population) were born in Ireland[20] There was a small Catholic population in Keighley in the 1830's who attended the mission in Myddleton Lodge, Ilkley, later, after the arrival of the priest, the Revd George Hampson, in 1835, they rented premises in Queen's Street which was used until the opening of St. Ann's Church in 1841.

Migration from Ireland to Bradford under pressure of eviction began before 1830, but following the changes in the Irish electoral laws in 1829, this speeded up, reaching a peak in 1841-1854. It did not begin to diminish until 1851-1861 as can be seen from table 38.

**Table 38 First generation Irish migrants in Bradford Borough 1851-1901**[18]

| Year | Number | Percent |
|------|--------|---------|
| 1851 | 8,677 | 8.3 |
| 1861 | 6,761 | 5.9 |
| 1871 | 8,371 | 6.2 |
| 1881 | 7,864 | 4.3 |
| 1891 | 5,352 | 2.5 |
| 1901 | 4,294 | 1.5 |

Table 39 shows that the greatest proportion of Irish migrant families,16%, came during the period 1841-1851. If allowance is made for the probability that the families of those referred to in the table had dispersed, and some had died, it is clear that large scale movement from Ireland to Bradford was greatest during the 10 years before the Great Famine of 1845-46. R.A.Schofield, in his study of migration in Keighley, noted that 2.8% of the population of Keighley parish numbered in the 1841 Census were Irish migrants. The number increased from 284 in 1841 to 870 in 1851, but began to fall proportionally in 1861 671 (4.1%), rising again to 1239(5.7%) in 1871 and falling to 141(4.1%) in 1881.

**Table 39  Estimates of the phasing of the migration of Irish Families in Bradford before 1861**[21]

| Year of migration | No of Irish Families in Bradford | Percent of total | Note: numbers before 1851 shown as living in Bradford in 1851 |
|---|---|---|---|
| Prior to 1830 | 46 | 2.5 | ] |
| 1830-1834 | 94 | 5.2 | ] |
| 1835-1841 | 187 | 10.4 | ] |
| 1846-1845 | 294 | 16.4 | ] |
| 1846-1850 | 1236 | 13 | ] |
| 1851-1855 | 31 | 1.2 | Shown as living in Bradford in 1861 |
| 1856-1861 | 36 | 2 | ditto |

Table 38 suggests there was a slight renewal of migration between 1861 and 1871 in Bradford during the 'boom' years of the late 1860's, but as the table shows there was a further proportionate fall during the decade 1871-1881, matching the general slowing of the growth rate in the town. Both the Richardson and the Schofield studies showed a high proportion of the migrants came from the western Irish counties of Sligo and Mayo. The census enumeration sheets for Keighley do not always show the county of origin of the migrants from Ireland. However where this information is available it may be noted that 205(24%) of the total Irish in the town in 1851 were from Sligo, and 86 (10%) were from Mayo. Schofield, covering the period 1841-1881 noted that 80% of the total first generation Irish were from these two western counties.[19] The percentage was rather less for Bradford, where they made up 37% of the Irish in the Borough in 1861.

The map, figure 21, shows the main Irish localities in Bradford Borough in 1851,[23] and their numbers are given in table 40. The largest concentration was in Goit Side, Adelaide Street, Wapping and Bedford Street areas. In Keighley, the numbers of first-generation Irish migrants were smaller, but as table 40 shows, there were significant clusters in certain parts of that town.

It should be noted that the Irish coming into Bradford and Keighley were a youthful population, 42.7% of Bradford's Irish population were children, and many were born in Great Britain, and were therefore counted as 'non-Irish'. Schofield labelled this 'co-resident population'. It amounted to an average addition to the recording of 'Irish', of between one and four percent to the total based on the place of birth criterion.[22]

The Irish came mostly from peasant backgrounds, evidence exists that some could not read or write, and a number were Irish monoglots, more significantly, most were Roman Catholics. They were not welcome in 19th century Bradford which was predominently Protestant. This could have been one of the factors contributing to their congregating in the established Irish quarters of the town. But their income status also gave them little choice where to live. As table 40 shows, they occupied the lowest-paid occupational groups. In Bradford, hawkers and pedlars occupied about 81% of Bradford's total in this group, and 25% of the town's charwomen and washerwomen. With 62%, the Irish men had a disproportionate share of the labourer group. The most numerous employment group was in the woollen and worsted sector, occupying nearly 40% of the Irish population and 10% of Bradford's total were in that category. Many were in the woolcombing and weaving group which, by 1851, had become very poorly paid, due to the development of machine manufacture (which displaced most of hand labour in these two sectors). In contrast there were no Irish house proprietors, bankers or agents, and they had only

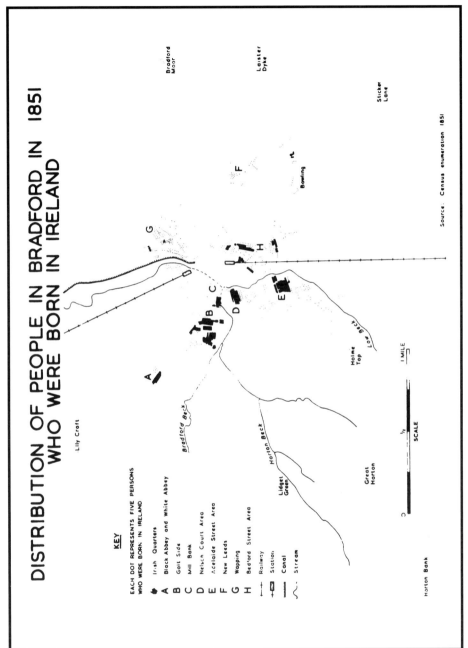

Figure 21. Main Irish Localities in Bradford Borough in 1851.

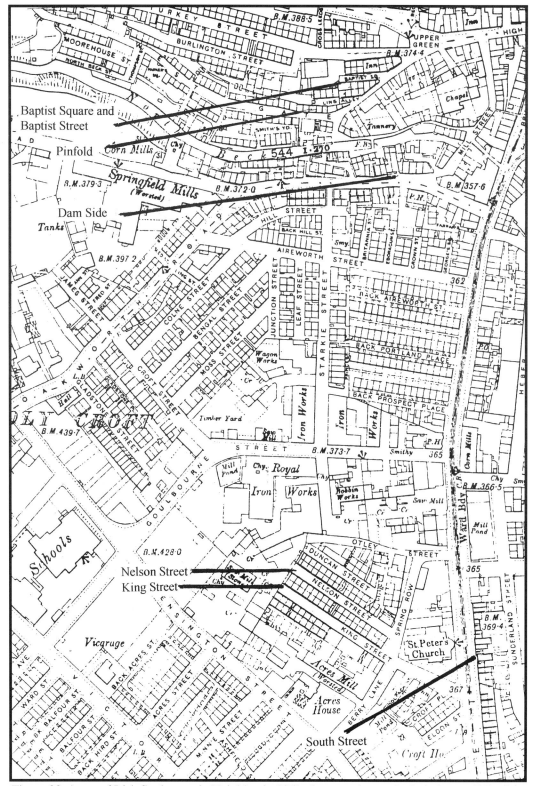

Figure 22. Areas of Irish Settlement in Keighley in 1851, the named areas included over 60% of the residents in that year who were born in Ireland.

three-eighths of their 'share' of the shop-keeping group. Low pay meant they had little choice of residence and tended to crowd together in the cheapest property. Crowding was therefore, more or less a necessity, when rents were relatively high at two to four shillings per week for a worker's cottage, while the woolcombers' pay for a sixty hour week was only 6s. 8d, which was little better than what was paid to people on outdoor parish relief.

## Table 40 The Distribution of Irish in the Irish Quarters of Bradford 1841-1861[23]

| Map Key Figure 22 | Name of the quarter | 1841 | | | 1851 | | | 1861 | |
| | | Pop. | Streets | | Pop. | | Streets | | Pop. |
| | | % | No | No | % | No | No | % |
| A | Black Abbey and White Abby | 8 | 21 | 409 | 5 | 19 | 381 | 6 |
| B | Goit Side | 26 | 17 | 2,334 | 27 | 18 | 1,237 | 21 |
| C | Mill Bank | 2 | 7 | 315 | 4 | 6 | 162 | 3 |
| D | Nelson Court | 21 | 4 | 535 | 6 | 5 | 336 | 6 |
| E | Adelaide Street | - | 17 | 1,170 | 14 | 10 | 624 | 10 |
| F | New Leeds | - | 8 | 193 | 2 | 4 | 44 | 1 |
| G | Wapping | 17 | 18 | 849 | 10 | 28 | 854 | 14 |
| H | Bedford Street | - | 21 | 1,025 | 12 | 38 | 1,162 | 19 |
| Total A-H | | 74 | 118 | 6,830 | 79 | 128 | 4,800 | 80 |
| | Total streets in which all the Irish lived | 100 | 356 | 8,687 | 100 | 384 | 6,025 | 100 |

## Table 41 The main areas of Irish Settlement in Keighley in 1851[24]

| Street | Number | Percent | Street | Number | Percent |
|---|---|---|---|---|---|
| Baptist Square & Baptist Street | 177 | 20.6 | Beck Side | 7 | 0.8 |
| Brick Lane | 52 | 0.8 | Carrudus Street | 49 | 5.7 |
| Dam Side | 49 | 5.7 | Fell Lane | 33 | 3.8 |
| Goose Eye | 48 | 5.5 | Gunnell | 38 | 4.4 |
| King Street | 100 | 11.6 | Mill Hill | 13 | 1.5 |
| Nelson Street | 24 | 2.8 | Pinfold | 163 | 18 |
| South Street | 76 | 8.8 | Rest of Town | 37 | 4.3 |

*See the map figure 22*

Room occupancy was high in the Irish areas in both towns. The Woolcombers Report on Bradford in 1845 showed an average of 5.5 persons per room, and the Bradford Medical Officer reported a figure of 6 per room, the reason being that there was a large number of lodger families. He reported that 22% of the 8,687 Irish in Bradford in 1851 were in two-or-more family households. A similar situation existed in Keighley, for example, in the Baptist Square and Baptist Street area the four houses numbered 23, 24, 25, and 26 contained 130 people of whom 76 were returned as lodgers, and in number 37 Pinfold there were 16, comprising one family of six from Sligo and one of eight from Mayo.

# Table 42 The Occupational Structure of the Bradford Borough and of Bradford Irish Population in 1851[25]

| Occupation | Bradford Brough | Bradford Borough | Bradford Irish | Bradford Irish | Bradford Irish as percent of Bradford |
|---|---|---|---|---|---|
| | No. | % | No. | % | % |
| Total | 103,788 | 100 | 8,687 | 100 | 8 |
| Teachers | 240 | 0.2 | 19 | 0.2 | 8 |
| Servants, Nurses and Midwives | 2,108 | 2.2 | 268 | 3.1 | 12 |
| Charwomen and Washerwomen | 894 | 0.7 | 199 | 2.3 | 25 |
| Tailors | 816 | 0.1 | 143 | 1.7 | 18 |
| Other Needle Trades | 2,078 | 2.9 | 222 | 2.6 | 11 |
| Boot, Shoe, Footwear | 1,069 | 1 | 52 | 0.6 | 5 |
| House Proprietors bankers, Agents, etc. | 200 | 0.2 | | | |
| Food and other Shopkeepers | 2,347 | 2.3 | 66 | 0.8 | 3 |
| Hawkers and Pedlars | 413 | 0.4 | 334 | 3.9 | 81 |
| Agriculture and Horticulture | 1,020 | 1 | 73 | 0.8 | 3 |
| Machine-making Millwrights etc | 1,113 | 1.1 | 4 | 0.1 | 0 |
| Building Crafts | 2,628 | 2.6 | 72 | 0.8 | 3 |
| Dyers a and Bleachers | 539 | 0.5 | 18 | 0.2 | 3 |
| Stuff, Woollen and Worsted | 33,142 | 32 | 3,377 | 38.9 | 10 |
| Woolstaplers | 136 | 0.1 | 1 | 0 | 1 |
| Other Textiles | 1,520 | 1.2 | 30 | 0.3 | 2 |
| Coal Mining | 1,049 | 1.1 | 10 | 0.1 | 1 |
| Iron Mining | 76 | 0.1 | 1 | 0 | 1 |
| Railway Labourers | 139 | 0.1 | 60 | 0.7 | 43 |
| Other Labourers | 997 | 1 | 584 | 6.7 | 62 |
| Iron Manufacture | 870 | 0.8 | 17 | 0.2 | 3 |
| Boiler Manufacture | 101 | 0.2 | 3 | 0 | 3 |
| Other Metal | 761 | 0.7 | 20 | 0.2 | 3 |
| Other Occupations | 5,473 | 5 | 172 | 2 | 3 |
| Children etc | 44,349 | 42.7 | 2,942 | 33.8 | 7 |

Table 43 shows a pattern for Keighley similar to that of Bradford, where the most numerous occupational groups were the textile, agricultural and other labourers, and among women, the spinners. If unspecified textile machine employees are included, most were employed in the worsted cloth-making sector.

**Table 43 The main occupational structure of the Irish Population in Keighley in 1851**[26]

| Occcupation | No. | Percent |
|---|---|---|
| Agricultural Labourers | 74 | 13.2 |
| Other Labourers | 57 | 10.2 |
| Woolcombers | 18 | 3.2 |
| Weavers | 14 | 2.5 |
| Spinners | 122 | 21.8 |
| Other Textiles Unspecified | 189 | 33.8 |
| Charwomen and Washerwomen Servants | 15 | 2.6 |
| Hawkers | 30 | 5.4 |
| Rag cutters ,sorters, and paper makers | 13 | 5.4 |
| Tailors , milliners,  shoemakers | 6 | 1.1 |
| Metal Manufacture | 4 | 0.7 |
| Professional, Clergy, Teachers | 5 | 0.9 |
| Other | 13 | 2.3 |

Agricultural and other labourers were the next most numerous group, occupying 131 (23.4%) followed by spinners with 122 (21.8%). All the textile employees whose particular task was not specified, were worsted millworkers. Hawkers constituted a significant proportion. It is noticeable however, that the professional group totalled only five, of which two were teachers, and a curate.

Mortality rates were generally higher in the Irish neighbourhoods than in other parts of Bradford. As late as 1900 the western end of the 'Goit Side' area had a crude death rate of 45/1000, which was more than twice the Bradford rate. In the non-Irish parts of the town, the infant mortality rates of 100/1000 (Allerton), 135/1000 (Bolton) and 149/1000(Great Horton), compared with rates of 329/1000 in the West Ward which contained the 'Goit Side' quarter, and 386/1000 in South Ward, which included Nelson Court and Bedford Street areas. As will be shown in the next chapter, these vital statistical differences bear a strong relationship to very poor environmental conditions, but they also reflect the high mortality risks confronting the poorest citizens of Bradford in the 19th century.

The German merchants initially settled in the area known as Bermondsey, which is the site of the present Midland Hotel, and significantly near the Piece Hall and the Wool Exchange which replaced it, not far from the canal and rail heads. Unlike the poverty-stricken Irish however, the wealthy could afford to move away from the centre of the town. The better residential areas of the town were Manningham, St Paul's Road, Wilmer Road, Spring Bank, Oak Lane and Manningham Lane; and in Little Horton: Claremont, Ash Grove and Trinity Terrace. Some went further afield, and after the development of the rail connections were able to commute to Bradford and Keighley. Some built their mansions in the surrounding country, examples being Titus Salt, who not only moved his mill and work-force to a healthier area in Shipley, but also moved house to Lightcliff near Halifax in 1869. His son Titus, went to live at Milner Field, Gilstead in 1867; William Murgatroyd, worsted spinner of Bradford, moved to Bankfield, Cottingley in 1848; J.T. Hemingway, wool merchant to Heathcote, Ilkley in 1906; James Padgett, woollen merchant to Menston Hall in 1876; Sir Swire Smith, worsted spinner of Keighley to Steeton Manor 1895; and Henry Isaac Butterfield, worsted manufacturer, built Cliffe Castle on an existing site in 1874-78. Many others are mentioned by George Sheeran in his book *Brass Castles* dealing with the architecture of the local mansions. These anticipated the modern function of the more rural parts of outer Bradford as commuter territory.

This chapter has dealt with the modest growth of population in the settlements of the

Bradford Region in the pre-industrial era and its huge population increase during the 19th century. It has been noted that this growth consisted of two aspects, natural increase and migration. Migration drew people from all parts of the British Isles, and a small number of merchants from Germany. The thousands of migrants included a large contingent from Ireland especially during the peak period of the 1840's. They were desperately poor and had little to offer except their labour. Although they were to be found in other centres, the main concentrations were in Bradford and Keighley. Both Germans and Irish left their mark on the city. The next two chapters deal with the unhealthy environment the poor endured.

## REFERENCES

1   Baildon, W.P. ibid. Vol I .
2   Dodds, E.E. Ibid. p.248 .
3   Letter of the Revd.B Kennett, Vicar of Bradford, dated 20 June 1843, addressed to Archbishop Herring on his visitation to the Parish of Bradford.
4   Keighley, William. *Keighley Past and Present* 1879 p.14.
5   Bradford Art Gallery and Museums: Pamphlet *A Brief History of Ilkley*.
6   *Note: Between 1801 and 1851 the totals for Baildon, and Shipley are parish populations, (Keighley parish had 8,387 in 1801 and 23,716 in 1851, when it included Beckfoot, Cross Flatts, Cross Roads, Cullingworth, Eldwick, Faweather, Gilstead, Hainworth, Harden, Priesthorpe, Riddlesden and Rushworth). The area covered by Bradford during the same period corresponded to the Borough as constituted in 1847, Bolton was added in 1871, and Allerton, Heaton and Tyersal townships were added in 1881. Silsden was returned with Keighley until the creation of the urban and rural districts in 1894. The figures for Ilkley between 1801 and 1871 are for the township at that time, Ilkley parish had 2641 inhabitants. The urban district of Queensbury had previously been part of Northowram which had a population of 6012 in 1801 and 8223 in 1841*
7   Hunter, Adam *An Essay on two Mineral Springs at Harrogate, and on springs at Thorpe Arch and Ilkley*, and Shuttleworth John *A Guide to Ilkley (Olicana)* p.9.
8   Richardson, C. *A Geography of Bradford* Figure 20 p.93.
9   Richardson, C. "Irish Settlement in 19th Century Bradford", in *Yorkshire Bulletin*. Vol. 20, No. 1, 1968.
10  Schofield, R.A. *A Peculiar Tramping* ( OU Ph D Thesis 1990) p.71.
11  Dodd, E.E ibid. Table III p.248.
12  Cudworth, W. Quoting W.H. Hudson, The Town Clerk of Bradford Borough.
13  Ranger, William. *Report to the General Board of Health*, 1853.
14  *Bradford Observer*, 9 December 1852, report "The Sanitary Condition of Shipley".
15  Keighley Improvement Act Commissioners - Minute of meeting dated 16. 11.1855.
16  Ranger, William. Report op. cit. p.47.
17  Bradford M.O.H. Report for 1870 and 1895.
18  Compiled from the Census Enumeration Sheets for 1851.
19  *Bradford Observer* dated 26 November, 1837.
20  Census of Ireland 1841 p.LXXXVIII.
21  The table is based on the ages and birthplace of children given in the Census Enumeration Books for Bradford in 1851 and 1861. It gives minimal figures of migration and the dates are approximate. For example the statistics exclude childless families and those whose chlldren had dispersed. Also a time lapse must be considered between the the birth of the children and the migration. Prior to 1840 the estimate of family movement has been based on the age of the youngest child born in Ireland and the next youngest child born in England, the period between being the assumed date of migration. For the period 1841-61 the age of the youngest child born outside Ireland was taken, the assumption being that the family had moved shortly before that date.
22  Schofield, R.A. Op. cit.
23  Richardson, C. *Yorkshire Bulletin* vol.20 No.l May, 1968.
24  Census Enumeration Sheets Keighley, 1851.
25  The Occupational Structure of the Bradford Borough and of Bradford Irish in 1851 Census, 1851.
26  Census 1851.

## CHAPTER NINE

# THE BUILT ENVIRONMENT I – House and Town layouts

In earlier chapters the medieval origins of the settlements of the region were discussed. We now turn to the Bradford region's built environment, and the accommodation and living conditions of its people in the 19th century. At an early date, places like Bingley and Keighley had their local commercial function while Bradford assumed a central role. The reason for Bradford's central position lay especially in its possession of the accessible resources of coal and iron, and in the physical links that developed between it and other areas by the building of the turnpikes and the canals, to which was added, the rail connection in Airedale in the 1840s, and Wharfedale by the late 1860s. But it was the cloth trade, particularly worsted, which established the critical link. Each settlement had its church, and its market place. In Bradford the shopping streets of Kirkgate, Market Street and Westgate existed from medieval times, but it was the Piece Hall, built in 1773, which symbolised the central regional function of Bradford in the worsted trade. At the beginning of the 19th century, 3,000 pieces of cloth were traded at the Hall. Later the Piece Hall was replaced by the Victorian Gothic Wool Exchange in1863. The public buildings, mills, other structures and streets serving the central function of Bradford, constituted a framework into which the houses of its inhabitants were crammed. This framework included the canal and its basin (1777), Forster Square Railway Station (1846) and the Exchange Station (1854), which were located on the edge of the existing built-up area of the town in the middle years of the 19th century. By 1853 its cultural life was enhanced by the construction of St Georges Hall, and the Mechanics Institute, to be succeeded by the Bradford Technical College (1875), which foreshadowed the City's development as an educational centre. The little band of German merchants had their meeting place and their own places of worship. The small chapel of St Mary On The Hill (1825) close by the late medieval Anglican Church, preceded the building of a number of Catholic churches, beginning with St Patricks (1853), and non-conformist chapels were proliferating. To these cultural structures must be added the mills, the foundries and the dyeworks, often side by side with the clustering of the dwellings of the poorer inhabitants of the rapidly growing town. Extending outwards from the centre of Bradford, like tentacles, ribbons of houses were reaching towards the old manorial centres of Bradford-dale. This development can be seen in Figure 23 overleaf.

All the settlements in the study area had been agricultural villages, and in spite of the build-up of people and houses, well into the 19th century, they continued to possess many of the characteristics of the rural village as they grew into towns. The reports of the Medical Officers of Health and the Sanitary Inspectors make frequent reference to the presence of animals, pig styes and middens in the cramped streets of the crowded towns. The need to limit the clustering of houses and people in the rural village did not seem to be the urgent health hazard to the developers in those early years that it became in the conditions of rapid urban growth. The rural backgrounds and the experience of the creators of the 19th century industrial towns must have influenced their approach to such matters as public health. Many of the industrialists of the late 17th and early 18th centuries combined farming with their mining and cloth-making pursuits, so it is not unreasonable to assume that that would influence their priorities when it came to providing housing for their employees. The way workers' houses were constructed, serviced and laid out, would not be seen as urgent to them as the conditions in the towns required. The influx

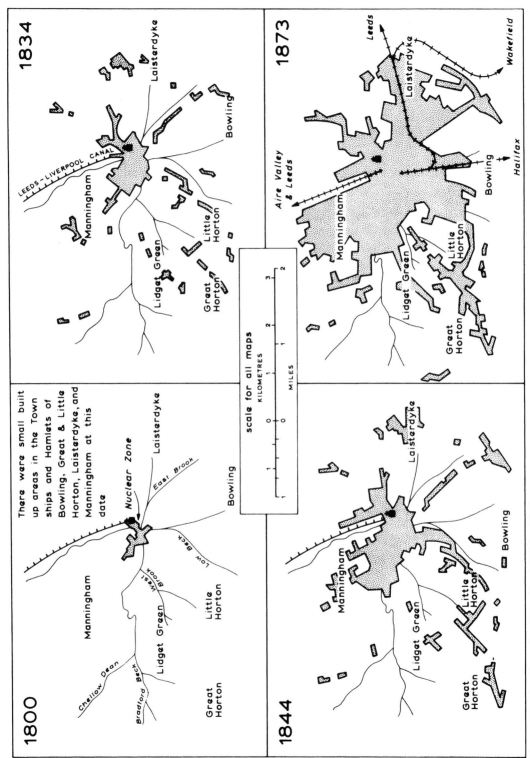

**1800**

Manningham

There were small built up areas in the Town ships and Hamlets of Bowling, Great & Little Horton, Laisterdyke, and Manningham at this date

*Nuclear Zone*

Chellow Dean

Bradford Beck

WEST BROOK

Lidget Green

LOW BECK

Great Horton

Little Horton

East Brook

Laisterdyke

Bowling

**1834**

LEEDS - LIVERPOOL CANAL

Manningham

Lidget Green

Great Horton

Little Horton

Laisterdyke

Bowling

scale for all maps

KILOMETRES

MILES

**1844**

Manningham

Lidget Green

Great Horton

Little Horton

Laisterdyke

Bowling

**1873**

*Leeds*

*Aire Valley & Leeds*

Laisterdyke

*Wakefield*

Manningham

*Halifax*

Bowling

Lidget Green

Little Horton

Great Horton

Figure 23. The Growth of Bradford 1800 - 1873.

of poor people, and their congregation in the cramped streets, courts, yards and alleys of places like Bradford and Keighley, would challenge the expertise, resources and powers of modern local government. As the next chapter shows, early 19th century town administrations were barely able to cope with the management of the unhealthy environments that were being created. The relationship between dirt and disease was not properly understood until the middle of the century. But more than anything, the prevailing philosophy of *laissez faire* gave great freedom to the developers to pursue their own economic interest rather than the welfare of their 'hands'. Therefore even when administrations to regulate and manage the growing urban agglomerations were created, the ignorance and the indifference of the town developers to the condition of their employee inhabitants, meant that insufficient was done to deal with the unhealthiness of the evolving unsanitary urban environments.

This chapter examines the growth of the built-up area of the towns, their evolving structure, of housing, street layout, and mills. The associated pollution and its control, waste disposal, sanitation and water supply will be discussed in chapter ten. Maps are useful in showing the extent of housing congestion, and, where the scale is large enough, some of the communal facilities that did, or did not exist. The maps, though useful, give only a two dimensional view of the town, caught in time. Early town planners paid special attention to the visual aspect and the spatial characteristics of urban development but initially, they were mainly concerned with the creation of healthy living places.

Later, examples of what might be called the 'social dimension' are discussed. Saltaire provides a good example of the social and aesthetic benefits of the planned, compared with the un-planned town development so typical of 19th century urbanisation. During the 1840's, leading national figures such as Edwin Chadwick, were responsible for producing reports on the heavily populated towns, and these, together with the reports of the Health of Towns Commission and the pressures exerted by the sanitary movements, focussed attention on the unhealthy environments that were being created. In support of their arguments they drew on the way that human life was shortened and the economic loss that resulted from disease and early death, which were so prevalent in the badly managed free-for-all development of the industrial towns. Locally, the *Bradford Observer* carried a report of a meeting of the Bradford Sanitary Movement in June 1845 in which its chairman, the Revd. Scoresby, noted that the '*general mortality rate of Bradford was 5% above the national average'*, which he attributed revealingly, to '*overcrowding and the low state of morals'*.

The map, figure 24, typifies conditions in the older parts of Bradford. It shows a section of the Goit Side area of Bradford as it was at the time of the survey in 1847-48.[5] It reveals a clutter of back to back houses and courts packed tightly into narrow streets, where little light or air could penetrate. Closer examination of the map reveals the absence of privies. Contemporary accounts, such as those of the Woolcombers' Report[1] or the writings of J Burnley,[2] give vivid descriptions of the conditions in that area of Bradford, adding to the detail of the map. The usual street sanitation was the midden or the shared privy. Contemporary writings provide the 'human dimension' the map cannot give. For example, Burnley spoke of the lack of lighting and paving, and the Bradford Medical Officer's Reports tell us of the totally inadequate drainage. The local Board of Surveyors of the Town Commission reported that '*The drains of the town emptied into the Beck, principally above the flood gates of the canal'* and, as for the drains themselves, the Borough surveyor stated that '*Experience proves that for the purpose of carrying away sullage water from the houses, the square rubble drains are worse than useless'*. Cellar dwellings were common and occasionally flooded by water, which was already heavily contaminated. P.

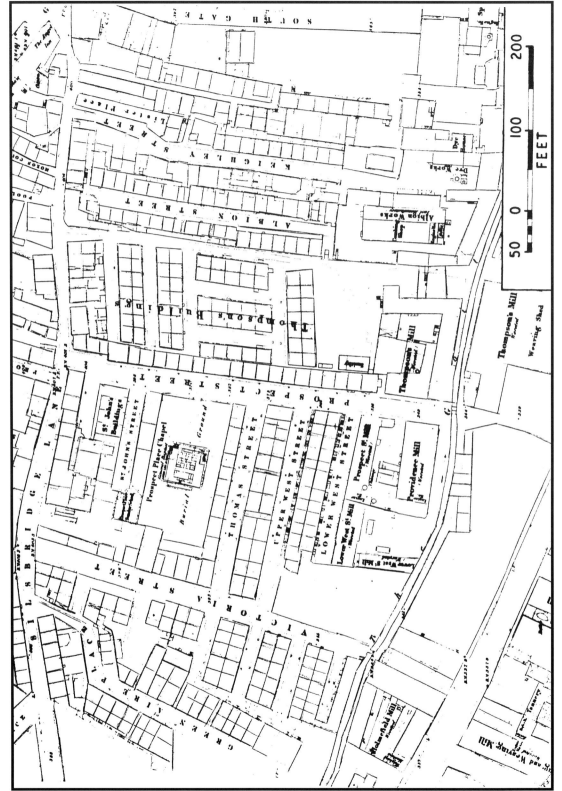

Figure 24. Thompson's Mill and Thompson's Buildings – Goit Side c.1850.

A. Brady, writing in the *Bradford Observer,* spoke of the water of the Bradford Canal, which was fed by the Beck and the Goit waters, being a *'fermenting mass of corruption and putridity'*. As was seen in table 40 on page 91, Goit Side housed 2,334 Irish immigrants in 1851, of whom a number lived in Thompson's Buildings, which as the map shows, lay close by Thompson's Mill, suggesting that the mill-builder was also responsible for the adjacent housing property. The entry of the Woolcombers' Report describing conditions in Thompson's Buildings reads: *'A stream impregnated with refuse of dyehouses, manufactories and dwellings contiguous to it. Its streets are narrow and filthy and the general arrangement of dwellings is unfavourable to the health. The inhabitants uniformly complain of ill health. In 12 cases taken in rotation the figures showed that the dwellings are inhabited by 95 persons who have only 23 apartments for all purposes, and 24 beds, making an average of four individuals to each and eight persons to one bedroom, of which the average size is 17ft by 15ft.'* [1] In additon it should be noted that there were no sewers, except the Beck, and after leaving the Bradford Canal Basin its sewage-laden waters flowed northward to join the Aire at Shipley where extremely unhealthy conditions existed.

When the Shipley petitioners asked for the application of the Public Health Act in 1852, they gave the crude rates of mortality for the town as 35/1000 in 1850 and 33/1000 in 1851, to which they added that 98 of the 298 deaths during the years 1849-51 were from the zymotic diseases, 77 of which were from fevers, including smallpox, cholera, diarrhoea, and four fifths of these were of children.

Turning to Keighley, figure 22 (page 90) and the contemporary O.S. map show that in the oldest part of the town the clustering of houses, yards, and narrow streets flanking the North Beck, can be identified. The map shows in its easterly extension, the characteristic features of closely packed back-to-backs wrapping around the church, squeezed between the Beck and the iron works, and the whole arranged in the right-angle made by the Beck and the River Worth. This high density massing of houses, mills and foundries forms an inner zone, beyond which there are more back-to-backs along West Lane and on either side of North Street. Further from the old centre the more regular lines of the terraced streets can be seen. It may be noted that the area, included the streets where the Irish and other migrants lived. It included Baptist Square, Pinfold, Damside, Adelaide Street, Low Street, Wellington Street and Wellington Square, and Greengates, and it was here that many of the woolcombers dwelt. The Report of John Hopkinson, the Inspector of Nuisances of Keighley, which was presented to the Board of Guardians in 1854, vividly described the appallingly unhealthy state of this inner area of the mix of manufactories, pigstyes and houses. His report listed nearly 300 cases, itemising instances of dirty unpaved streets, pigcotes, cellar dwellings and properties *'lacking the proper conveniences'*.[6] His report detailed the existence of cellar dwellings in which sewage leaked. For example he stated that at the end of the house occupied by Mr James Romley was *'a foul, stinking, and nauseous nuisance, a sumphole or tank which receives the contents of Mr Romley's privy, slops and water from cottages which leaks and runs into the road leading to Beckside Road'*. From his report we learn that Adelaide Street was un-paved. Reporting on Springhead Clubhouses he stated that *'the refuse from Mr J Robinson's property drains itself into a cottage'*. Again at Brickhouses he refers to a cellar *'used as a cottage where there are two beds in a dark room'*. The cellar was in *'a yard where there were open drains and filthy choked drains'*. This description was replicated at Church Green, Fell Lane, Back Wellington Street, Sun Street and Low Street and several pigstyes are also mentioned. Of a house in Back Eastwood Square, Mr Hopkinson commented, *'This is one of the most disgraceful affairs in the whole district'*, later he goes on, *'there is (at Eastwood Square) a living room over a privy where the stench from the privy below was suffocating'*.

J. Milligan, the Keighley Union surgeon, in 1838 reported 427 deaths which, with a population of 11,176, gave a rate of 38/1000, and William Ranger reported to the Keighley Board of Health that in 1853 there were 347 deaths, 161 of whom were under five years old.[7] J Milligan in a lecture on *'Poverty and the Source of Disease'*, given in the Keighley Mechanics Institute, quoting the Health of Towns Commission, said that the average size of families in each house was 5.57 and the average number of beds 2.16. The causes of death identified were consumption (17% of total), convulsions (10.5%), smallpox (2.6%), measles (3.2%) scarlatina (3.3%), whooping cough (2.8%) and typhus (2.6%). The family size of the woolcombers was high. The Ranger Report recorded examples of family size, weekly earnings and rents. In the cases on which he reported, the earnings of the heads of households ranged from 6s.4d to 8s.6d per week and rents were from 1s.6d to 2s.2d per week, highlighting the low pay, and the relatively high rented, poor houses of this particular class of workers. Even with the earnings of other members of the household the total income for one of the families cited was as low as 15s. for a family of eight, and their rent was 1s.6d.[8]

Some community buildings existed from early in the century, amongst which may be included the Parish Church of St Andrews (the present building was built in 1846 on the same site as an earlier church); and St Anne's Roman Catholic Church which was built in 1840. Roman Catholics had worshipped in an upper room of a building in Queen Street until the building of Pugin's church in 1840. The 1852 ordnance map shows a National School (now demolished and the health centre is on the same site) and a Wesleyan school as well as a Mechanics' Institute (founded 1825) to be replaced by a building designed by Lockwood and Mawson, the architects for Saltaire and many public and commercial buildings in the Bradford region. The Baptist Chapel (built 1819) which gave its name to the Square which was identified earlier as the 'Irish area', just north of Pinfold and Damside. By 1847 the town had its railway station (1847). Other important public buildings came later in the century with the opening of the Victoria Hospital in 1876, the Queens Theatre, and the Opera House (the latter re-built in 1880, seated 1800), to name but a few.

Old settlements such as Baildon and Bingley, which by the first decade of the 19th century had populations of 2,659 and 5,769 respectively, had their crowded unhealthy areas. For example in Angel Street, Perseverance Street and the area west of St John's and south of Westgate in Baildon, and in Bingley the 1852 ordnance survey shows concentrations of back-to-backs in several streets, including Ireland Street, Kings Court, Market Street, Queens Street, Waddington Street, Russell Street, and Lime Street extending to the northeast of Bowling Green Mill.

## MILL VILLAGES

Against the squalor of these older localities we may set places like the mill villages of Queensbury and Saltaire. Queensbury was built to serve John Foster's Black Dyke Mill in its hilltop location, and Salt's Saltaire was located in the Aire valley. Queensbury's development was not the outcome of a pre-determined plan, as the pattern of its growth demonstrates. Its housing content and layout exhibited many of the poor environmental features of its large urban neighbours. In contrast, Saltaire was a pioneering experiment in town planning, embodying the aesthetic and social ideals of its founder. Both settlements started from 'scratch'. Queensbury was a very tiny hamlet in 1800. Saltaire was constructed on the green-field site on land belonging to Lady Rosse which formed part of the Esholt Estate of the Crompton Stansfields. In both instances the growth was motivated by the utilitarian need to provide housing for their workforces, but it would be fair to say that both entrepreneurs' business aims were mixed with

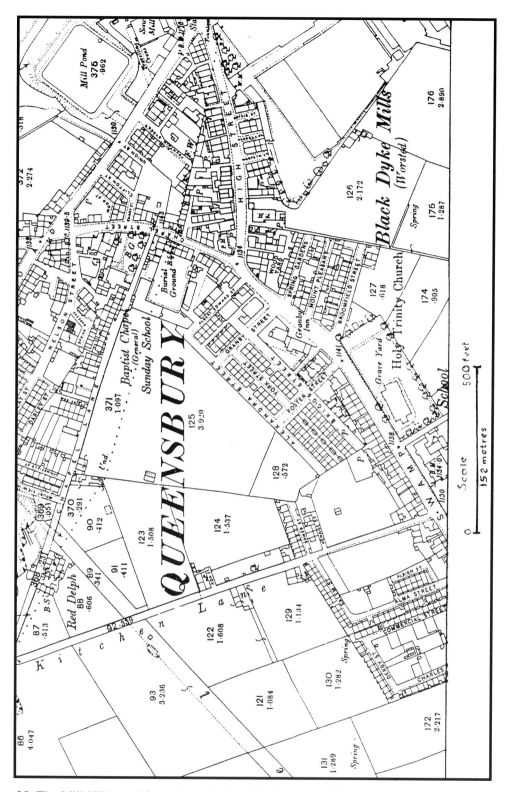

Figure 25. The Mill Village of Queensbury in the 19th Century – Note the random arrangement of its high density housing, and back-to-backs of different design and period e.g. in York Street.

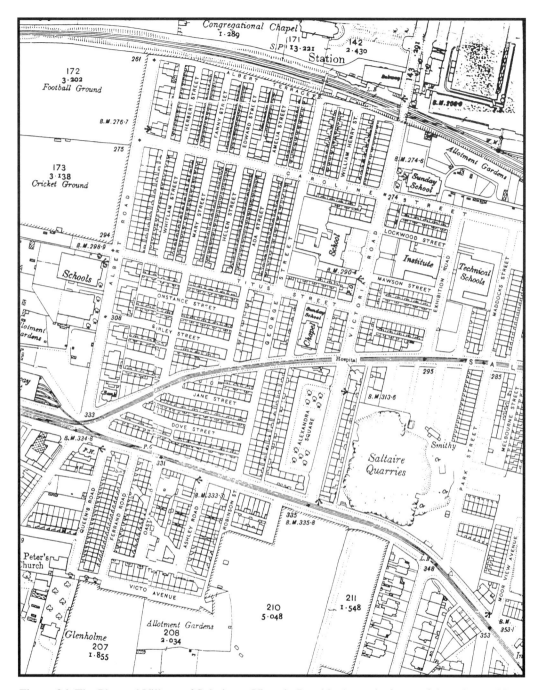

Figure 26. The Planned Village of Saltaire – Victoria Road is the main focus of the scheme. Note its squares and open spaces (off the map is Roberts Park), the park-like setting of the Congregational Church (opposite the mill), the Allotment Gardens, the school and institute, and Alexandra Square, which included almshouses, a chapel and a hospital. The scheme was built between 1853 and 1871 and Lockwood and Mawson of Bradford were the architects.

identifiable benevolence, as was evidenced in John Foster's generosity towards the hard-hit handloom weavers in the 1820's, and the more widely publicised philanthropy of Titus Salt.

The spatial outcome of these different approaches to the development of these two villages can be seen in Figures 25 and 26. The map, figure 25, shows that Queensbury was to a large extent linear, spreading conveniently along the lines of the existing turnpike, from which 'spine' there are lateral blocks of back-to-back housing served by narrow streets, whereas Saltaire was a comprehensively planned, one might say, regimented, ordering of living space, but with important elements of style and social content. Saltaire's houses were spacious, each house was provided with its own yard, privy, ashpit and was served by a back street so that the italianate frontage would not be impaired. Each house had its well-lit airy rooms with high ceilings. As for the mills, both village developers were innovative, not only in the cloth they produced, but also in adopting the new technology. According to one 19th century source it seems that Foster's were their own architects for both the mill building and the houses[10]. Both sites were developed away from the polluted squalor of the older industrial centres; Fosters' on the airy Pennine upland where they already had mining interests, and Salt on a virgin site in the Aire valley.

Queensbury began as a hamlet consisting of 39 blocks of houses and isolated dwellings, centering on the Queenshead Inn from which the village at one time drew its name of Queenshead. Previously it had been known as Causewayend. Cudworth, the 19th century historian of Bradford and district, estimated there would be about 250 inhabitants in the Queenshead area at the beginning of the century.[11] It acquired the name of Queensbury in 1863. There were other mills in the area before the building of Black Dyke Mills in 1835, e.g. John Ambler's at Mountain. Jonas Foster, father of the founder John Foster, was a farmer who owned and worked pits at Clews Moor and Springhead, and he had pits in Thornton, as well as renting Cannon Mill in Great Horton. Foster built and owned some 400 of the cottages in Queensbury by mid-century.[12] The 1851 census recorded 485 houses in the part of Northowram covering the Queenshead district. Mention has already been made of the benevolence of John Foster and Sons. They provided a number of amenities in the village, including the library, its institute, as well as the swimming baths and the village gas supply. They also donated land for the Sunday School (1825). The symbiotic relationship of Queensbury and the Black Dyke Mills may be summed up in the words of E. M. Sigsworth, the historian of the firm of John Fosters and Son. Of the mills and the village he wrote *'The growth of the village and its prosperity, were a function of the firm's growth and prosperity'.* [13]

Daniel Salt, father of Titus, was a woolstapler and farmer. Titus Salt was born in 1803 and worked in his father's business. As was noted in an earlier chapter, the firm set up business in Bradford in the Goit Side area in one of the worst slums of the town. So Titus was familiar with the evil effects of the industrial environment, which it can be assumed, clearly influenced his thinking on how Saltaire should develop. He was a Congregationalist, an idealist with a strong paternal streak. His ideology is reflected in the village he created. He asked Lockwood and Mawson, the architects who were responsible for his great scheme, *'to use every precaution to prevent the pollution of the air by smoke, or the water by want of sewerage, or other impurity'.* And *'nothing should be spared to render the dwellings of the operatives a pattern to the country',* showing that he was sensitive to the visual impact of the bad housing usually associated with the industrial environment.

The site depicted in figure 26 took twenty years to develop and covered a total of 46 acres (18.6 ha), of which 6½ acres (2.63 ha) were for the factory, 25½ acres (10.3 ha) for the houses, streets, squares and public buildings and 14 acres (5.7 ha) for the Park. Developed on a grid

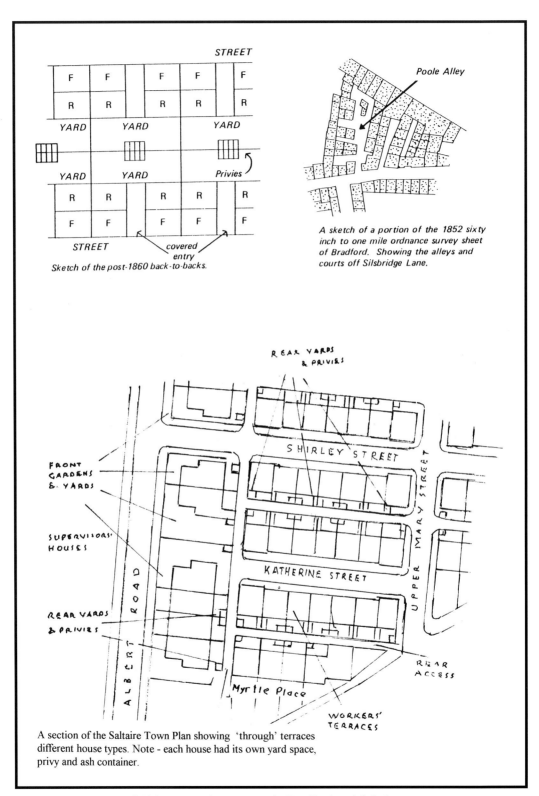

STREET

F | F | F | F | F
R | R | R | R | R

YARD | YARD | YARD

YARD | YARD | Privies

R | R | R | R | R
F | F | F | F | F

STREET | covered entry

*Sketch of the post-1860 back-to-backs.*

Poole Alley

*A sketch of a portion of the 1852 sixty inch to one mile ordnance survey sheet of Bradford. Showing the alleys and courts off Silsbridge Lane.*

REAR YARDS & PRIVIES

SHIRLEY STREET

UPPER MARY STREET

FRONT GARDENS & YARDS

SUPERVISORS' HOUSES

ROAD

KATHERINE STREET

REAR YARDS & PRIVIES

ALBERT

REAR ACCESS

Myrtle Place

WORKERS' TERRACES

A section of the Saltaire Town Plan showing 'through' terraces different house types. Note - each house had its own yard space, privy and ash container.

Figure 27. Examples of 19th century house types in Bradford and Saltaire

pattern, it has as its main spine, Victoria Road, along which are grouped a number of small squares accommodating the main urban amenities of the village. These include the palatial mill with its 250 ft chimney disguised as an Italian campanile, and opposite the mill, the elegant Corinthian style Congregational church in its own green setting. This main thoroughfare opens out in a square accommodating the school (750 boys and girls) on the west side, and on the east the institute and club which was intended to *provide the convivial advantages of the public house without its evils'*. The Institute satisfied a variety of the needs of the inhabitants and fulfilled a 'further educational function'. The 45 almshouses together with the hospital are grouped around Alexandra Square. By 1870 the Wesleyan Church, situated on land donated by Sir Titus, had been added. The bath and washhouse was an important amenity, and the Park with its sports ground and arboretum was completed by 1873, and allotments were also included in the scheme. It had access to the canal, and its own railway station and village gas supply. Not least, when Shipley was adding its sewage to the already heavily polluted Bradford Beck, Saltaire had its own sewerage system. The main streets were paved and the rest had a hard surface of packed ash and stones.

Figure 27 C and D shows two examples of house types in Saltaire. When the whole scheme was completed, the village had 750 houses, including 21 large dwellings intended for Salt's managers and overlookers, 114 four-bedroomed houses, 550 two-and three-bedroomed houses, 45 almshouses and 45 lodging houses. It is said that before the start of the scheme Salt had carried out a survey of his workpeople to assess their housing needs.[14] Each house had back street access to its own paved yard, privy and ashpit so as to preserve the appearance of the street at the front. The buildings were stone-faced with the simple decoration of string courses, and round arches to doorways and windows replicating the italianate theme of the major buildings. The lowest rents were 2s.4d for a five room house, including the kitchen, and 7s.6d for the large houses. There was no skimping of standards as the building of the village progressed.

## ILKLEY - SPA RESORT

The section of the large-scale ordnance survey map illustrated in Figure 28 shows Ilkley as it was in 1890. It will be seen that in contrast to the high density housing environments discussed so far, Ilkley's townscape is generously open and spacious. As befitted its function as an inland resort and watering place, there is abundant provision of both private and public landscaped open space. The map also reveals the resort's educational as well as its health functions. As was pointed out earlier, the full potential of its local spa water resource was not fully exploited until the construction of the rail link in 1865. The rail connection also served the growing number of commuters from Leeds and Bradford, as well as linking the town with a wider leisure-seeking public. But the key to its 19th century town development lay in its mineral wells, one of which, the Canker Well, can be seen on the map. Others were at White Wells and Ben Rhydding. The wells influenced the location in the town of hydropathic establishments and hospitals, some of which are shown on the map. There were also smaller hydros such as Craiglands and Troutbeck. In addition, its growing importance as a holiday centre led to the building of hotels. The original spring is on the moorland edge at White Wells and its plunge pool is still open. It was there that the first house and bath seems to have been built in the early 18th century.

Although water power was used to drive the cloth mill, it was the mineral waters that helped to make the modern town, especially after the construction of the railway, which gave it access

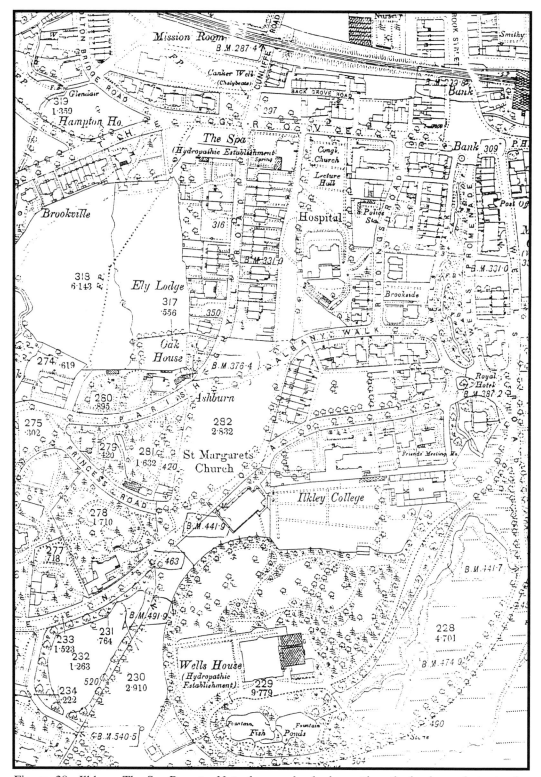

Figure 28. Ilkley – The Spa Resort – Note the moorland-edge setting, the landscaped streets, the large houses, many detached; the hydropathic establishments, hospital and the generous provision of open space both public and private.

to the fine scenery of Wharfedale and the adjacent moors, which became so important in the development of the spa resort. Even so, the town had its black spots, as the Medical Officer's Reports revealed. J Netton Radcliffe, who enquired into the sanitary state of Ilkley in 1871, reported on nuisances arising from poor drains which he stated *'had wide interstices'* allowing leaks and from which *'stench is given off'*. Later he referred to *'cottages having no connection with a sewer. An open ditch emptied its foul contents into a stream and into the Wharfe'*. (15) Neverthless Ilkley was a healthier place, as the Medical Officer of Health's Report of 1896 revealed. He gave details of deaths in the area. During a period of the previous 23 years they ranged from a low level of 54 to a maximum of 101 persons per annum, and the infant mortality rate of 10.5 per thousand births in 1895, compared with Bradford's 203/1000.

This chapter has focussed on the man-made geography of the 19th century town, where houses were located, the kind of accommodation they provided, and their spatial arrangement. It has touched on the extent to which the community's wider cultural and spiritual needs were met. It has also discussed the common features present in the housing environments of the labour force in the growing textile towns, notably the pattern of narrow streets, yards, courts and alleys of the poorly serviced houses. The exceptions were Saltaire and, later, Ilkley. The randomness of the street organisation in the oldest parts of the main textile towns reflected their organic growth, echoing the 'agricultural phase' of their earlier development, often manifesting itself in the mixing of animals and their shelters with the human habitations. Consistently high housing- and population-densities characterised these unhealthy environments. A sequence of house types which is illustrated in figure 27 can be recognised, and in general they follow a broadly concentric urban structural arrangement, as can be seen in the sequence of back-to-backs and crowded courts, and then a linear pattern of back-to-back streets lacking the most basic sanitary necessities, followed by the by-law back-to-backs, but still grouped in straight lines and still depriving their occupants of privacy and good ventilation; and beyond them further from the the ancient core, the closely packed terraces. The explanation of the resultant unhealthy urban agglomerations of the early years of the 19th century lies in the *laissez faire* philosophy of the urban developers of the period and their indiferrence to the welfare needs of their occupants. The urban spatial patterns were the result of locational decisions in which the owners and builders had almost unlimited freedom in the siting and the construction of the dwellings and the living space of the work-seeking poor residents. The occupants had little choice of where they could live because of their low incomes and the relatively high house rents they had to pay. It is against this squalid background that Saltaire may be judged. Amongst model mill villages built in the 19th century of which New Lanark in Scotland, Tremadoc in North Wales, Mellor in Cheshire and Bessborough in Northern Ireland are examples, Saltaire still stands out as an important social experiment. Though philanthropically motivated, it was still the outcome of the self-interested decision of its industrialist creator. Nevertheless it is against the lack of order of the 19th century industrial slum, that Salt's model village can be judged. Salt constructed an environment which occupies a special place in the history of town planning, pre-dating by about fifty years, the work of the Cadburys, the Levers, and the ideals of Ebenezer Howard and the national town planning movement.

# REFERENCES

1   *Report of the Woolcombers' Sanitary Committee* 1845.
2   Burnley, J. *Phases of Bradford Life* 1871.
3   Report on 'The Sanitary Condition of Shipley' in *Bradford Observer*, 9 September 1852.
4   Richardson, C. op. cit. p.104.
5   Richardson, C. ibid. p.84.
6   Report Book of John Hopkinson, Inspector of Nuisances, presented to the Board of Guardians in 1854 pages 52-66.
7   William Ranger *Report to the Keighley Board of Health* 1854.
8   Ranger Report ibid. p.47.
9   For a comprehensive history of Keighley see I. Dewhirst *A History of Keighley*, 1974.
10  Cudworth, W. *Roundabout Bradford* 1876 p.113.
11  Offprint in pamphlet form on John Foster and Son, from the *Fortunes made in Industry* 1884 page 30.
12  Cudworth, W op. cit. p.113.
13  Sigsworth, E.M. *Black Dyke Mills* 1958. Introduction p.xi. Sigsworth's book is 'the bible' on the origin and development of the mills, and is revealing about the involvement of the firm of John Foster and Son in the local community.
14  Dewhirst, R.K. In the *Town Planning Review*, July 1960.
15  Ilkley Medical Officer of Health Report 1896.

# CHAPTER TEN

# THE BUILT ENVIRONMENT – II
## Towards its Public Management

From the beginning of the 19th century, Bradford, by its Improvement Act of 1803, had a town administration, and a similar body was established in Keighley by that town's Improvement Act of 1824. Here the legislative and other processes which led to the better management of the towns are considered. It can be said, however, to a certain extent all the local town authorities lacked the administrative skills, public health expertise, legal powers, finance, and not least, the political inclination to control the actions of the developers, and to manage the lethal environments that were being created. In addition, the membership of these bodies included people who had a vested interest not to deal with the worst instances of neglect and bad practice. For, as can be seen later, even when elected town government was introduced, those who were making the bye-laws, who were responsible for their enforcement, and who, as justices of the peace, had to adjudicate when the laws were broken, were found to be the same people. Nevertheless, there were people and movements that recognised the increasing dangers to public health of the uncontrolled development of the industrial towns, and they called for measures to improve their sanitary condition.

The administrative structures of Bradford were created in order to manage, and partly to shape, the industrial environments. Their origins and effectiveness are examined with particular reference to the health environment, focussing largely on Bradford. The Borough's experience exemplifies in many respects the conditions to be found in other towns of Airedale and Wharfedale. The truth is that in spite of the existence throughout the 19th century of town governments operating under improvement acts, mortality rates remained high. Mortality rates, particularly of infants, and for specific diseases, provide a measure of the unhealthy conditions resulting from rapid urban growth as well as exposing the ineffectiveness of the local administrations in improving the health environnment. To illustrate this figures 29 and 30 show population growth, infant mortality, the chronology of measures to improve the environment, and other relevant events for Bradford Borough. The rise in infant mortality in Bradford between 1841 and 1901 is the more remarkable because it covered the years when the town had an elected administration with considerable legal powers. A number of public health acts had given local urban authorities general powers to manage and improve the sanitary conditions of their urban environments. But as the graph (figure 30)and table 44 on page 114 show, in Bradford, infant mortality, one of the most sensitive of environmental indicators, remained high in the town, even into the 20th century. No single cause can be identified to explain the depressing mortality statistics. Initially, attention dwelt on the provision of a clean and reliable water supply, and better sewage disposal, but air pollution, and the appalling overcrowding in bad housing, malnutrition, poor standards of hygiene, child-and maternal-care, also contributed. Until the second half of the 19th century the connection between poverty, malnutrition, dirt, and disease and death were only partly understood. But air pollution was a major enviromental problem. Official mortality statistics singled out the zymotic diseases for special attention. This category included: scarlatina, diarrhoea, typhus, whooping cough, and diphtheria, and children were the chief victims. But consumption (phthisis) accounted for about 11% of the deaths for

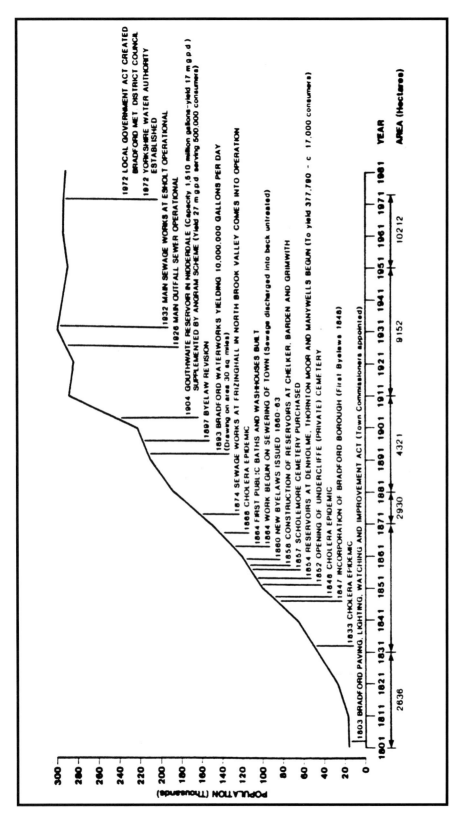

Figure 29. The population growth of Bradford 1801 to 1981. It should be noted that some of the increase was due to the extension of the Borough area.

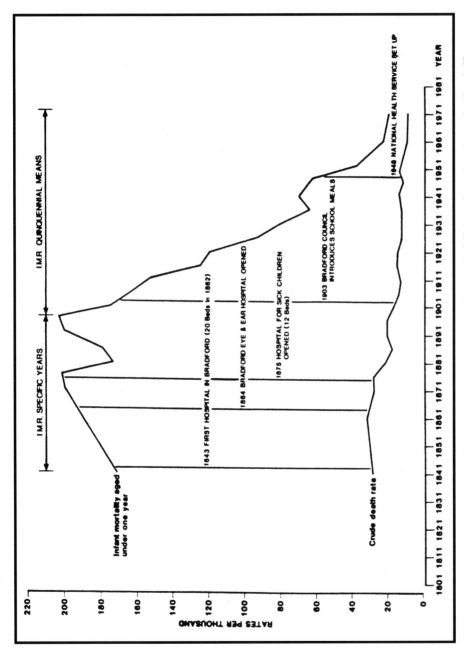

Figure 30. Mortality in Bradford. Crude death rates between 1841 and 1862 but since then have declined. However, infant mortality rose until 1872, falling slightly in the following decade, to reach a peak in 1895, since when it has dropped.

most of the years, and respiratory diseases, no doubt associated with overcrowding and a smoke-laden atmosphere, also were important killers. Leading national figures, such as Edwin Chadwick, who was responsible *inter alia* for many of the public health enquiries during the 1840's, looked upon the zymotic diseases as preventable. Expert opinion at that time believed that infectious diseases resulted from the poisoning of the atmosphere by *'exhalations'* given off by decaying and fermenting human and animal wastes, domestic refuse and other organic substances i.e, the so-called 'miasmatic' explanation. It was not until the discoveries of the germ theory and the development of the science of bacteriology in the later years of the century that a truer understanding of the nature of disease, its causes and prevention, emerged. Thus Chadwick's advocacy of an *'arterial-veinous'* system of sanitation was considered to be a main corrective measure. This called for a water-borne sewerage system to flush away solid and liquid human and industrial wastes. It was good in theory, but without leak-proof sewers, an adequate supply of clean water, and an appropriate treatment plant, the sanitary problems could not be remedied satisfactorily. Bradford and other areas lacked these essentials until well into the second half of the 19th century. Chadwick's proposed remedies and recommendations were taken up by local sanitary groups, but there were also strong forces working against their implementation. In any event, municipal engineering was in a rudimentary state of development. It was not merely a question of providing clean water and better methods of sewage disposal.

The herding of desperately poor people into back-to-back, high density housing, much of which included cellar dwellings lacking the most elementary sanitary facilities, grouped in unpaved, ill-drained streets, courts and alleys, created conditions for the ready transmission of air-borne and contagious diseases.

The Bradford Region's rapid industrial growth was accompanied by the outpourings of numerous coal-burning steam engines and the smelteries of its metal-working establishments, as well as the emissions of thousands of house chimneys, which earned Bradford in particular, the reputation as one of the smokiest places in the country. Its citizens paid a high price for this notoriety, in the high incidence of bronchial and pulmonary disorders arising from its heavily polluted atmosphere. Until the wholesale adaptation of machine woolcombing, this process was carried on in the living rooms of the hand woolcombers. The raw fibres were separated over the heat of a coke brazier, which filled the rooms with sulphurous fumes. Small wonder that chest complaints were common.

Economic necessity and custom obliged young children and women to work, which contributed to child neglect. Deaths from premature births and infantile convulsions in 1859, a typical year, accounted for 13% of Bradford's total mortality.

Household waste collection and street cleansing were carried out by private contractors at the ratepayers' expense. The overflowing churchyards and chapel cemeteries in the midst of Bradford's slums produced a health hazard, which was not relieved until the 1860's, when cemeteries were opened outside the old town centre.

Poverty and expensive water put even minimal standards of personal hygiene beyond the reach of the poorest sections of the population.

The worst overcrowding, and the highest infant mortality rates as we have shown, occurred in the reception areas of the immigrant population from other parts of Britain and from Ireland.

Town government in Bradford prior to its incorporation, was a confusion of separate authorities. These included the parish vestry, an institution going back many centuries. It fixed the poor rate and was responsible for appointing constables to maintain public order, surveyors to supervise road and other works, and it administered the poor law. Next there was the lord of the manor, an office having its origins in feudal times. Under the lord's jurisdiction were the courts baron, which tried civil cases, and the court leet, which tried criminal cases and appointed two constables. The justices of the peace too, had their fingers in the administrative pie. Lastly, under the Local Act of 1803, an improvement commission was established. Its responsibilities included street cleansing, lighting, road works, nuisance control and police duties. The Commission did not supersede the vestry surveyors, hence a conflict of interest followed. This state of administrative affairs continued until 1847, and for certain functions, after the granting of the Borough charter.

The preamble to the Bradford Local Act of 1803[1] throws light on the state of the environment and its management in the early years of the 19th century. It refers to the lack of street paving, lighting, cleansing and policing. The Commission had the duty to contract for persons to act as surveyors, ' *who shall twice in each week. . . cause to be brought a cart, or carts, into all the streets, lanes, entries, public passageways, and places where such cart, or carts, can pass, and shall at and before this approach, by sound of bell, loud voice, or otherwise, give notice to the inhabitants of his or their coming . . . so that the inhabitants thereof may bring forth their (except from ashes) rubbish, dirt, dung and filth from any privy or necessary house, to the doors of their respective houses and there to deliver the same to the scavengers etc. . . . .*' The 1803 Act also dealt with night soil disposal, and it required owners of engines to '*destroy and consume smoke arising therefrom . . .* '[2]

The outbreak of Asian cholera in 1832 aroused public awareness. It alarmed both local and national authorities, and a local Board of Health was set up under Order in Council dated 11th March 1832. Provision was made to isolate the town's victims at a house in the Wapping area, north east of the town centre.[3] The Board of Health was an *ad hoc* single-functional body, which was disbanded once the cholera epidemic had passed, but the experience gave the basis of arguments which led to the important administrative changes in the late forties.

Edwin Chadwick wrote that disease prevention lay in removing substances which caused foul odours. He argued that the remedy lay in disposing of solid refuse and sewage from the streets and privies by suspension in water, conveyed in glazed bored drains. A plentiful, reliable, clean water supply was an essential pre-requisite, but Bradford sadly lacked this. This vital service was in the hands of a private company whose water source was totally inadequate. Some mills drew water from wells. Together with its tributaries and such water channels as the mill goit and the Bradford Canal, the Beck served as an open drain, into which domestic and industrial wastes, as well as the run-off and seepages from the streets were poured. Streets were fouled by the droppings of horses and domestic animals, including pigs.

The sanitary argument figured strongly in the campaign to incorporate the town. Local entrepreneurs had an interest in satisfying the huge water demands of their mills, dyeworks, and metal manufacturing establishments, and this too provided an incentive to increase the water supply, although real progress did not come until the second half of the century after the incorporation of the Borough. In 1844, at the time of the first petition to Parliament to grant Bradford its charter of incorporation, there were 80 steam-driven worsted mills, 16 dyeworks, and a number of large iron works and foundries.[4] All were large consumers of water. But non-technical appeals were advanced in support of improved water supply and drainage. For example, during the cholera epidemic, it was noted that '*the wealthier classes could not escape scot free from contagion and disease*', or, the cost of treating epidemic diseases was justified by the argument that '*when the head of the family was carried off by disease the poor family falls a burden on the rates.*'[5] Again, in 1837, William Byles, the editor of the newly established

Bradford Observer, wrote *'It is to everybody's advantage to promote the habits of cleanliness among the poor'*.[6] At the time of incorporation, 46,395 individuals were being served by the Bradford Water Company, i.e. less than half the 107,778 inhabitants enumerated in the 1851 census for the central townships of Bradford parish. The town's crude mortality rate was 25.7/1000 and infant mortality stood at 170/1000.[7] As table 44 shows, infant mortality remained high until the end of the century. There were serious cholera epidemics in 1848 and 1866, and diseases such as scarlatina, infantile diorrhoea and dysentry were endemic.

**Table 44 Death rates in Bradford at selected dates between 1840 and 1900**[8]

| Year | Crude death rates per 1000 population | Infant mortality rates per 1000 aged under 1 year |
|------|---------------------------------------|---------------------------------------------------|
| 1840 | 25.7 | 170 |
| 1855 | 24.2 | no data |
| 1860 | 21.0 | no data |
| 1870 | 27.5 | 176 |
| 1880 | 17.7 | 176 |
| 1890 | 23.0 | 201 |
| 1895 | 20.0 | 203 |
| 1900 | 20.0 | 141 |

Little serious effort to improve the health environment of Bradford was made until the formation of the Borough in 1847. On 29th December 1847 power was transferred from the various authorities described earlier. But between incorporation and the passage of the Bradford Improvement Act 1850 the town was governed under the byelaws of the Municipal Corporation Act. The local Act transferred the control of the Board of Surveyors to the Corporation. Clauses gave extensive powers to purchase waterworks, gasworks and the manorial rights. It set limits on rate levies in any one year, which reminds us that a major constraint on improving the physical environment of the town was that it had to be financed out of rates levied on property. A supplementary Act of 1855 empowered the Corporation to borrow money and levy a rate for the waterworks.

The first officials of the corporation consisted of one head of police, three inspectors, six sergeants and sixty one policemen, together costing £3,156 per year; a clerk, an assistant clerk and an accountant whose combined salaries amounted to £340. The meat inspector received £80 annually, which was £10 more than the surveyor of streets; and the nuisance inspector together with nine other employees cost the council £700 a year. The differences in the remuneration of these officials may be seen as an indication of the priorities of the newly created town government. These few officials had the enormous task of monitoring, reporting on and enforcing the byelaws passed by the elected administrators of a rapidly growing town of over 100,000 inhabitants. The succession of Council Reports through the century demonstrates the zeal of the council's officers, but it also reveals the weakness on the part of the elected council in fulfilling its responsibilities. Councillors were anxious to keep down the costs to the rate-payers, and were soft on those who were committing environmental offences in breach of their own byelaws.

The first reports of the Council tell us a lot about the environmental legacy the Council had inherited and the scope of the work carried out by its tiny staff. Thus the 1854 Report of Council records that it had approved 4,311 house plans, 138 warehouse and mill plans, the construction of 15 churches and chapels, and 246 new streets during the three years 1852-54. During the same period 202 privies had been provided to serve 608 houses, but the surveyors complained that *'Builders do not always adhere to the plans'*. Although byelaws had been drawn up, the surveyor noted that *'notwithstanding the efforts of your committee, great numbers of the dwellings for the labouring classes are still being built back-to-back in courts, with a semi-cellar dwelling beneath, circumstances very much to be regretted, as it must be evident that proper and effective provision of a sanitary character cannot be maintained under these conditions'*. *'As to the condition of the drains,'* he said *'the custom was common to lay square rubble drains (which were) . . . not permeable'*.[9]

The usual form of sanitary 'provision' was the midden, and the shared privy. Later in the century, Dr Hime the Medical Officer of Bradford in 1884, stated *'The use of middens in a large populous town . . . is a violation of the fundamental principles of sanitary science'*.[10] Commonly householders kept a slop pail in the house, and its contents of excrement and urine were carried out to be tipped on the midden. Night soil was collected from the middens, removed by contractors, and taken away in carts. It was not unknown for sewage to be tipped into disused coal pits.

Bradford Corporation purchased the works of the private Bradford Waterworks Company in 1855, when official returns showed there were 15,792 consumers. The first waterworks management consisted of a partnership formed in 1744. Until the Manywells scheme described later came into operation, water was drawn from a coal drain in the Haycliffe area of Horton, from which it was conveyed in wood and lead pipes and a conduit, to a tank in Westgate. The partnership was converted to a private company in 1790 and in 1837 this company supplied 344 of the 6,063 houses in the central built up area, and 58 mills and other premises.[11] Distribution was by means of twenty two carts, and water was sold at one penny for three gallons. Manufacturers were charged one shilling per thousand gallons.[12] This was the main public supply until the middle of the 1850's. Up to 1855 very little had been done by the Water Company to secure an adequate reliable supply. The main development had been the abstraction of water from a spring at Manywells in Wilsden, yielding 500,000 gallons a day, from where it was piped to a reservoir at Chellow Dene. Although a private act had given the Corporation the power to borrow money to buy the assets of the Water Company, it had no power to levy rates until 1855. During periods of drought, there were serious water shortages, in spite of the fact that by 1857 the reservoirs at Stubden and Doe Park had increased the storage capacity to 70 million gallons.

By 1866 Bradford was drawing on a catchment covering large sections of the Aire and Wharfe valleys, with reservoirs at Chelker House, Barden Broad Park, Grimwith, Hartlington and Appletreewick. As well as supplying the villages of Bradford-dale, Bradford Water Works served places in Wharfedale and areas south of Bradford town, and consumption had increased from half a million gallons in 1855 to 7 million in 1870.[13] In spite of this extra capacity it was still insufficient to meet the demands of the mill and domestic users. By 1880 it had to seek legal powers to extend the system, this time by drawing on the Nidd valley catchment where reservoirs at Angram, Haden Carr and Wooddale, with a compensation reservoir at Gouthwaite, were constructed. By 1901 water was conveyed to Bradford by a main which was $31^1/_2$ miles (50.4 km) long. There were further developments of the system during the 1920's, including covering the storage reservoirs and the installing of water treatment plant. Figure 31 shows the extent of the system in the 1990's. During the 19th century there was a close relationship between the water supply, mortality and disease. This was especially the case during periods

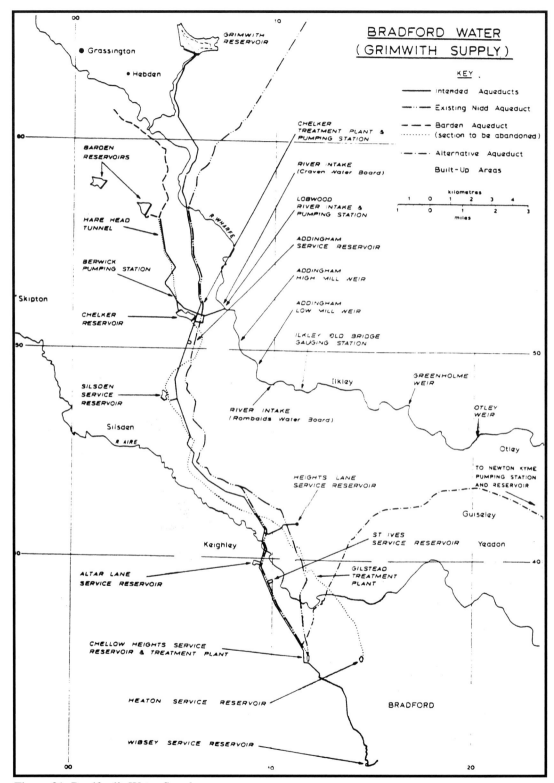

Figure 31. Bradford's Water Supply.

of drought when the mortality rates increased. But the  mortality rates remained high, well into the 20th century.

In the worst housing areas the dwellings lacked the most elemental sanitary facilities. Careful examination of the large scale map of Thompson's Buildings shown in chapter nine (page 98), is of sufficient scale to reveal cellar steps, and there is no indication on it of  privy outbuildings. The reports such as that of the Woolcombers, and those of the Medical Officers of Bradford and the other towns, add detail to the maps. As was indicated in the previous chapter, the drains were of ummortared rubble, square in section so that sewage seeped into the adjacent cellar dwellings. The Bradford inspector's report stated that *'Sewage of the inferior streets ran into open channels'*.  The byelaws of Bradford were updated in 1860.  Byelaw xiii  specified that house drains should be by glazed stoneware pipes in fireclay, and pipes below houses should be embedded in puddled clay. Right angle junctions were forbidden.[15]  This byelaw is revealing as to usual practice. Further amendments to the byelaws in 1897 stipulated that privies and ashpits should be further than ten feet from the doors and windows of dwellings.[16] In spite of the byelaws and the extensive powers granted to the authority by its charter and the Bradford Improvement Act 1850, the Borough surveyor often complained of the failure of builders to conform to the plans they had deposited. In extolling the beneficial effects of the 1862 byelaw revision, the Surveyor wrote revealingly that they would replace *'the long rows of back-to-backs, one half having no prospect but a narrow yard crowded with privies and ashpits, no access but through a covered passage 3 $^1$/$_2$ feet wide, and having no ventilation beyond what can be obtained at one side of the house, from the atmosphere of the yard, tainted by the emanations from a cluster of privies and ashpits immediately before the door'*. . . the new byelaws would ensure *'in every instance a frontage on the street, and at the side and rear, an open space appropriated as a separate yard for the use of the house having at two sides  from which ventilation can be secured.'*

The map 'figure 32'  shows the street location of deaths from zymotic diseases during the period 1876-1885, from which it will be seen that the Goit Side and similar areas of poorly serviced housing, suffered high specific disease mortality, and this continued until late in the century.

Two court cases reported in the Bradford Observer may be cited to illustrate the attitude of the local establishment towards those who breached the byelaws, as well as revealing the complacency and irresponsibility of the speculative builders. On 11th September 1875, E. Hodgson, property owner, was charged with not having provided a privy to a house he had built in  Barkerend. He was fined five shillings with eight shillings costs. On October 23rd 1875, J. Beanland, builder, was prosecuted for having built a row of houses and allowing them to be occupied before receiving a certificate of habitation from the surveyor. This he could not obtain because he had not provided any lavatories. He was fined a maximum of forty shillings per day of occupation per house. But on his refusal to turn out the tenant until sanitation had been provided and after promising to *'build lavatories as soon as it was convenient'*, his punishment was reduced to a ten shillings fine, and eight shillings costs.

Although a model form of sewer construction had been described by Edwin Chadwick in the early forties, and the  byelaws were specific on the house drain design, it was not until the 1860's that a start was made on the main sewering of Bradford. And the construction of the defoecation plant  had to wait until the 1870's. The sewerage scheme began in 1863 with the construction of a main outfall sewer along Valley Road.  The Borough surveyor proposed *'in the design to make provision in the sewers for the whole of the storm water, which from its situation must pass*

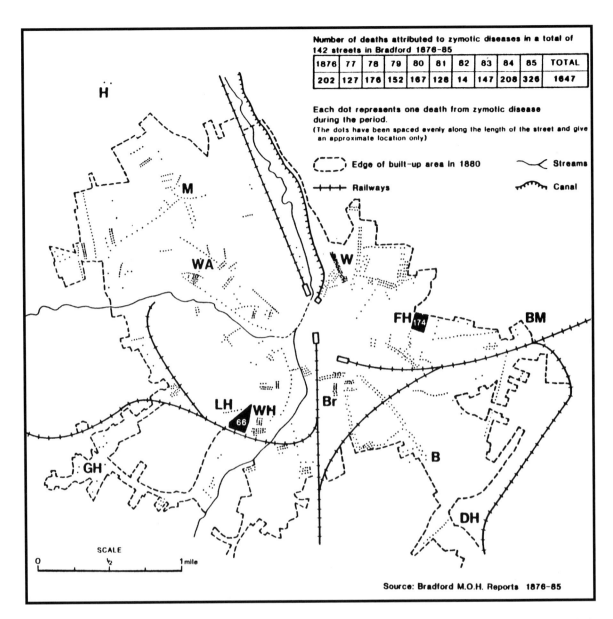

Figure 32. Deaths from zymotic diseases in Bradford during the period 1876-1885. These diseases included: scarlatina, typhus, smallpox, diphtheria and diorrhoeal diseases. The clustering of these deaths occurred where there was a high degree of overcrowding in the least sanitary areas of the town.

KEY TO PLACES: B Bowling, Br Broomfields, BM Bradford Moor, DH Dudley Hill, FH Fever Hospital, GH Great Horton, H Heaton, LH Little Horton, M Manningham, W Wapping, WA White Abbey.

*through the town. This can only be done by the Bradford Beck and its tributaries. The only way to sewer the town permanently against floods is to entirely re-construct the Beck for about a mile in its length . . . . . removing the walls, pillars etc. from the course of the Beck . . . the buildings which stand over the Beck could be carried on strong girders. . . . None of the old existing sewers are of such a character as to render it desirable to incorporate them in the new general system.*[17] The surveyor's report on the encroachment of the property owners on the Beck provides further evidence of the lack of control over buildings, structures and effluents by the town governors.

## SEWAGE PURIFICATION 1871-1932

The County Rivers Pollution Committee, which investigated the state of the local watercourses in 1866, had severely criticised Bradford's sanitary condition. Polluted river water passed through the estate of William Rookes Crompton Stansfield, owner of the Esholt Estate, which in 1868 took the Borough Council to court to stop the nuisance. The Court of Chancery ruled initially that a limit should be set on the nuisance by prohibiting the opening of additional sewers in Bradford. This decision was annulled after the Corporation constructed a works at Frizinghall downstream from Manningham Station, and in 1871, the Authority gave a contract to a private company to treat the sewage without charge. The firm failed, and the Corporation took over the works in 1874.[18] The main filtering process involved passing liquid through peat charcoal. In addition to the normal domestic effluent, the industrial waste complicated the operation of the works because it contained the large quantities of grease or lanolin, mainly produced by the scouring or washing of wool from the bleachers and the dyeworks. This caused the effluent to run acid at times and sometimes it was strongly alkaline, making effective treatment difficult. The Frizinghall plant, covering 38 acres (15.4 ha), was too small to cope with the volume of sewage it was receiving and there was serious river pollution. The West Riding Rivers Board which was formed in 1893, pressed the Bradford Corporation to remedy the pollution and the Borough Council had to look for a site downstream that was less restrictive in area, and it bought the 1700 acre (688 ha) Esholt Estate in 1904, with possession in 1906. A 2¼ mile tunnel was constructed between the North Brook and the Aire Valley, which was completed in 1924. Another tunnel linked the Idle and Eccleshill areas with the Esholt Works. The biological filter beds covered 53½ acres (22.7 ha). It was not until 1932 however, that a comprehensive system of sewerage and sewage treatment was operating. Included in the scheme was a plant to recover wool fat.

## AIR POLLUTION

That air pollution was an issue of public concern at an early date is evident from the clauses in the Bradford Act of 1803, which stipulated that *'Engine chimneys be erected of sufficient height as not to create a nuisance by the emission of smoke. All owners of engines etc. are to construct fireplaces thereof in such a manner as to destroy and consume smoke arising therefrom'*. Pollution got steadily worse as the mills multiplied and thousands of domestic chimneys poured forth huge volumes of smoke and other pollutants into Bradford's atmosphere. There was a sharp rise in the number of deaths from chest complaints, both in absolute and relative terms, between 1859 and 1876. For example there were 363 deaths from these causes in 1859, rising to 962 deaths in 1876 giving a rate of 4.5/1000, and the mean five-yearly rate 1891-1895 was 4.23/1000, but since 1900 there has been a steady fall to 1.52/1000 in 1971.[19]

# THE EFFECTIVENESS OF LOCAL LEGISLATION

The local byelaws specified a chimney height of at least 30 ft (10.8 m) and time limits on smoke emissions.[20] In 1859 the Council's officers reported on their survey of all mill chimneys which were below the minimum height. This issue was raised again in their reports of 1861 and 1863, when they recorded that *'several owners have introduced* (smoke reduction*) appliances'*. But subsequent reports show how little was done to alleviate the main problem in the town. A separate smoke committee existed in 1867, and from its report of 1867 we have something of an 'industrial domesday book of Bradford'. The report stated that there were: 591 boilers consuming 1200 tons of coal a day; coal used in other establishments amounted to 1300 tons per day; the surveyors had examined 264 works and they had delivered 693 smoke prevention notices. The Council's response to the nuisance inspector's reports on these breaches of the smoke prevention byelaws was to advocate that the *'problem be tackled in a spirit of conciliation'*.[21]

Dr Hime, the Bradford M.O.H. in 1884, drew attention to the two aspects which accounted for the lack of remedial action on the part of the mill owners. Firstly, he noted the widespread belief that because factories provided work, the employers should not be pressed too hard, and secondly, the low fines which were being imposed by the local justices of the peace, which did little to discourage law-breakers. It should be noted that the Public Health Act of 1875 limited maximum fines for smoke nuisance offences to ten shillings per offence. But in many case even these derisory punishments were not levied. For example in 1900, 103 notices were served on local owners of steam engines, of which 71 cases reached the courts. Of these 49 were fined an average of ten shillings and sixpence, with eighteen pence costs.[22] The use of crushed low-grade coal know as 'smudge'or 'slack' exacerbated the problem by producing large amounts of atmospheric grit as well as black smoke. In 1904 there were 714 deaths from respiratory diseases, more than a quarter of which were children under five years of age.[23] Figure 33 shows air pollution and deaths from respiratory diseases other than pthisis in Bradford. By 1921 there were 351 large factory chimneys in Bradford, ranging in height from 45 feet (16.45m) to 345 feet (88.5 m). The report also listed 521 Lancashire boilers, 67 Cornish, 34 vertical, 29 Babcock & Wilkinson boilers, and 31 other types of steam boiler. From these it was calculated that in a ten hour day, 53,732,500 lbs of water were evaporated and a total of 1.6 million tons of coal went into the plants in Bradford. It also noted that 1921 was a year of depressed trade.[24] Figure 33 shows the correlation between the reduction of air pollution represented by the volume of air-borne solids in the main industrial centre of Bradford and the drop in the number of deaths from respiratory diseases from the peak of 318 deaths in the peak year of the 1890's and 993 in 1900.

The real attack on air pollution came with the clean air programmes, following the passage of the Clean Air Act 1956. The Bradford Local Act empowered the Borough Council to create smokeless zones in which all smoke emissons, both domestic and industrial, could be controlled. The City's Clean Air programme was completed in 1974 when there was a reduction in fall out from an average of 292.3 mg of smoke per cubic metre in 1959 to 73.4 mg per cubic metre in 1971, and the associated mortality rate for respiratory diseases was down to 1.52 per thousand of population.[25]

# SLUM CLEARANCE - COUNCIL HOUSING

Areas of exceptionally bad housing persisted into the 20th century. Reform began in Bradford when the Council was being pressed to use the newly passed Housing of the Working Classes Act 1890. The Act gave councils the powers of compulsory acquisition of slum property to be cleared,

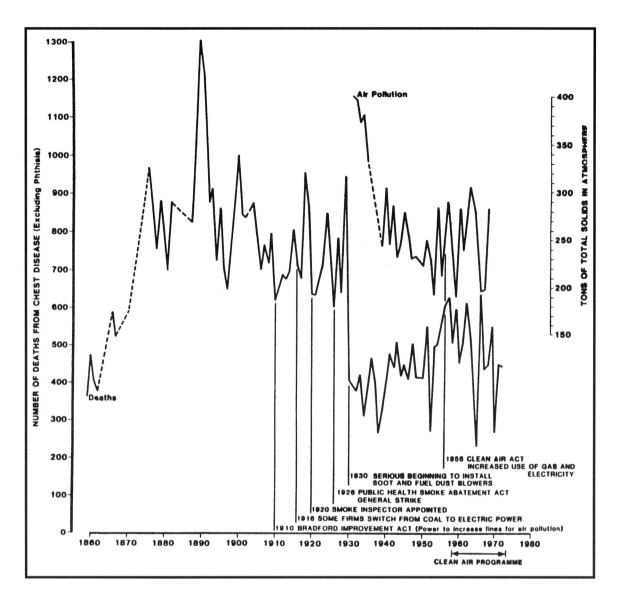

Figure 33. Air pollution and death rates from respiratory diseases other than phthisis. The peak in 1890 was due to an influenza epidemic.

and provided for compensastion of house owners, the cost of which was borne out of rates. Under the Act Bradford carried out a major clearance of the Longlands area. This was a cluster of back-to-backs which still depended on middens for the disposal of human wastes. It consisted of 280 houses having about 1,500 occupants in 1894. Its crude death rate was 45.6/1000 compared with 19.8/1000 for Bradford Borough. The resistance of the property owners caused a delay in the replacement of the houses by the Council. It was estimated that the rate charges would amount to 3/8ths. of a penny in the pound.[26] When the Council finally gave its approval, 1,357 people were re-housed, 432 in the Longlands area, and 925 on the Faxfleet site in the south of the town.

Further phases of slum clearance occurred in the 1920's and 1930's to relieve overcrowding and remove people from insanitary premises Table 45 gives details of infant deaths in the years 1925-1937 in the four inner city wards of Bradford containing the areas designated for clearance. These show that pockets of housing with appalling health records existed well into the 20th century. The Medical Officer reported on the city's morbidity in 1934 that scarlet fever cases amounted to 1,588, with ten deaths, diphtheria 846 cases with 43 deaths, measles 3,215 cases and 15 deaths, and there were 110 deaths from bronchitis and 201 from pneumonia, and 237 cases of tuberculosis with no deaths, but 30 deaths from diorrhoeal diseases. The people covered by the table were re-housed in the Canterbury Avenue estate.

**Table 45 Proportion of crowded houses in the Wapping and Broomfields clearance areas in 1933**

| No of persons per room | Wapping area % of houses | Broomfields area % of houses |
|---|---|---|
| 5 | 11.7 | 12.4 |
| 6 | 6.1 | 7.1 |
| 7 | 3.8 | 4.7 |
| 8 | 3.7 | 2.4 |
| 9 | 0.9 | 0.4 |
| 10 | 0.1 | 0.9 |
| 11 | 0.1 | 0.6 |
| Total with over 5 persons per house | 26.4 | 28.4 |

Source: Bradford Medical Officer of Health Report 1937 p 146

## THE MOTIVES, INTERESTS AND ATTITUDES OF BRADFORD'S CIVIC LEADERS IN THE 19TH CENTURY

To understand the slow progress in improving the health environment of Bradford in the 19th century it is appropriate to examine the interests, motives and attitudes of the council members. In addition it is necessary to look at the cross-functional nature of the civic establishment as council byelaw makers, policy makers and executives, also as judges in their own cause (since aldermen were also magistrates as well as being predominantly in business). The oligarchic nature of the establishment had its roots in the limited franchise, confined as it was to the wealthiest property owning classes of the town. There was also the prevailing philosophy of opposition to public intervention which conflicted with the interests of the owners of wealth. Not least, public works had to be paid for out of local rates on property. Wealthy individuals, including those serving on the Council, satisfied their civic pride by building hospitals, establishing clinics, and until the 1870 Education Act, providing denominational schools.

Between 1847 and 1880 manufacturing interests, chiefly from the wool textile sector, occupied three in ten of the council places, while cloth merchants, excluding retailers, averaged 24% of the council membership. From 1875 onwards there was a substantiual representation of the retail trades and it was not until the 1890's that employee craftsmen began to be elected following the changes in the franchise in 1882. Table 46 shows that in 1847, 46 of the 56 councillors lived in the inner area of the town, but by the end of the century when there were 76 councillors, the majority lived in the outer suburbs or outside the Borough from which we may conclude that the councillor-decision-makers were less willing to live in the environments they were administering.

## Table 46 The Geographical Distribution of the Residences of Bradford Councillors 1847-1900

| Year | Number of councillors | | | | |
|------|-------------------------|------------------------|-------------------------|--------------------------|-------|
|      | Living in inner urban area | Living in inner Suburbs | lving in outer suburbs | Living outside Bradford | Total |
| 1847 | 18 | 28 | 8  | 2 | 56 |
| 1853 | 10 | 28 | 12 | 6 | 56 |
| 1860 | 7  | 30 | 22 | 3 | 56 |
| 1867 | 11 | 25 | 16 | 4 | 56 |
| 1875 | 7  | 22 | 22 | 7 | 60 |
| 1890 | 4  | 26 | 27 | 3 | 60 |
| 1900 | 2  | 25 | 44 | 5 | 76 |

In the closing years of the 19th and the early years of the 20th century a number of important laws affecting town and country government were passed. The Local Government Act of 1888 created a system of elected county councils and county boroughs. Bradford became a county borough with responsibilities under the Act including public health and highways; and its regulatory powers covered water supply, proper drainage, the prevention and removal of nuisances including air pollution, healthy housing in well-lit well ordered streets, the inspection of food, proper provision for burial and suppression of the causes of disease.[27] It will be noted that Bradford already had these powers under its private acts. The Local Government Act 1894 created the rural and urban authorities. By the time of the Royal Commission 1966-69 the Bradford region consisted of Keighley Municipal Borough, the Urban Districts of Baildon, Bingley, Ilkley, Queensbury and Shelf, Shipley and Silsden with the parts of the Rural Districts of Wharfedale and Skipton.[28] Until the passing of the Local Government Act 1973 the local government structure reflected the view that urban and rural communities were different from each other and should be administered separately. The fragmentation failed to recognise the changes in mobility of people, and that rural areas were dormitory extensions of the towns where people worked and shopped. It did not therefore take into account the interaction and interdependence of urban and rural areas with the increasingly urbanised population. Thus the administrative separation of urban and rural government had less meaning in the way urban regions functioned. The Local Government Act 1973 had the urban region as its basis, and the Bradford Metropolitan District, incorporating the seven urban districts and the parish of Addingham, came into existence. (Originally the parishes of Kildwick, Steeton with Eastburn, and other parts of Skipton Rural District were included, but these were later transferred to Craven District).

The Housing and Town Plannng Act 1909 introduced the idea that government, both local and central, should intervene to ensure the orderly development of towns. Amongst others, it gave planning powers to local authorities, and was an early recognition of the interaction between urban areas and their rural surroundings. Although there had already been legislation to deal with the housing and health matters, the form and structure of the towns had been decided almost entirely by the action of private individuals and businesses. In this the ownership of property was a major determinant of land utilisation and location. Land acquired value from its location as well as its intrinsic worth. The competition between land users however, resulted in differences in land values, and through these, affected the way land was used. In the evolution of the planning system it was recognised that the the land market did not always produce the 'best social environment'. The significance of the housing and planning legislation as it developed during the 20th century showed the necessity of public authority intervention in such aspects as land use and the location of human activities. There were planning acts during the period leading up to the definitive 1948 Town and Country Planning Act. The planning system in the Region, both before and after the passing of the Act, was shared between the West Yorkshire County Council, which was responsible for the outer area, and Bradford-dale was covered by the Bradford County Borough Council. But the 1948 Planning Act had more teeth than the earlier planning legislation giving extensive powers to county and county borough councils to control development in the public interest. *Inter alia* it gave councils the responsibility of preparing town plans to ensure their orderly development and to exercise control through their powers to control land use and location. Thus through the planning system public authorities became directly involved in creating and influencing the geography of the towns and the countryside within their administrative areas. Through the designation of green belts the councils were able to protect the countryside, limit urban sprawl, and prevent the linking of towns by ribbon development. As housing authorities councils were responsible for purchasing land and developing estates; and as education authorities, they decided on the location of school and other educational esablishments. It was a characteristic of 20th century municipal history that local councils acquired these extensive powers because they were convenient local agencies to implement the social policies of central governments. This was particularly the case with housing, highway development and the limitation of the uncontrolled extensions of towns. By a variety of parliamentary acts, and especially under the 1973 Local Government Act, Bradford Metropolitan District Council, as a major land owner and land user, became directly involved with other land users in the evolution of Region's urban morphology and manager of its surrounding countryside.

The 19th century began with acts setting up weak local government in Bradford and Keighley. Later urban sanitary unions were established to cover the remaining townships of the region. The 20th century witnessed the creation of stronger elected public bodies with extensive powers in which local councils were directly involved in creating the geography of the areas they administered, not least they were better financed and therefore more able to carry out their responsibilities as environmental managers. Through the application of the planning system Bradford Council became a partner with the public and private developer in ordering the way its environment should develop. The 20th was the 'century of the welfare state' of which the planning system can be seen as a part, and the extension of the franchise which led to universal suffrage after 1928, introduced greater democracy in local and central governments which were therefore more representative of the population they served, and these administrative changes have had a major impact on the geography of towns and their associated rural catchmments.

# REFERENCES

1.  An Act for the Watching, Lighting and Improving of Bradford etc, 1803 (The Bradford Improvement Act).
2.  The Bradford Improvment Act.
3.  Dr W. McTurk  Letter to the Bradford Observer 12/8/1848.
4.  Roberts, J.R. *The Bradford Worsted Warehouse* 1975.
5.  Cudworth, Wm. *Historical Notes on Bradford Corporation* 1881 p.9.8
6.  Report of the Woolcombers Sanitary Committee  (Woolcombers Report  1845).
7.  Elliott, A. *The Establishment of Municipal Government in Bradford* 1830-35 Ph.D. Thesis  Bradford 1976.
8.  Report of the Poor Law Commissioners into the Sanitary Condition  of the  Labouring Population and the Bradford M.O.H. Reports for the years shown.
9.  Bradford M.O..H. Report 1884 p.108.
10. West, R. *Worstedopolis and the Waterworks*  (Unpublished dissertation in Bradford Central; Library).
11. Health of Towns Report p.xxxv.
12. Yorkshire Water Authority - Historical Survey.
13. Bradford Corporation Sewage Disposal  1870-1947.
15. Bradford Council Byelaws 1860 XIII.
16. Bradford Borough Byelaws 1897.
17. The Town Council of Bradford Borough Report of the Surveyor on the arterial and main sewers June 1859.
18. The Town Council of the Borough of Bradford Report June 1859 p.5.
19. Bradford M.O.H. Reports for the years shown.
20. Bradford Council Byelaws  from 1848 onwards.
21. Bradford Smoke Nuisance Inspector's Report 1867.
22. M.O.H. Report 1900 p.11.
23. M.O.H. Report 1908 p.143.
24. M.O.H. Report 1921 p.27.
25. Dr. W.M. Turner - Bradford News  October 1972.
26. Fenner Brockway *Socialism over 60 Years*  1946 p.50-53.
27. Royal Commission on Local Government 1966-69 Report p.24.
28. Royal Commission op. cit.

## CHAPTER ELEVEN

# THE EVOLUTION OF THE BRADFORD CITY REGION – TRANSPORT AND COMMUNICATIONS

By 1991 Bradford city had become the main centre of a region with a population of 457,344. Between 1901 and 1991 the region had changed from being a group of more or less self-contained free-standing towns to a linked multi-centred urbanised system, extending across the three Pennine Dales. During the 20th century there had been a major re-distribution of population as new housing extended outwards from the 19th century crowded streets to the suburbs. The process which began in the twenties and thirties, gathered momentum during the second half of the 20th century and it affected all the towns and villages in the Bradford region. Some of this peripheral development was the result of the re-housing of the inhabitants by local councils and their re-location in council-owned estates. But probably the most significant factor was the outward spread of private house development because of its effect in producing homogeneous social areas, as the more affluent population moved to more salubrious areas onto greenfield sites away from the poorer inner city localities. A characteristic of 19th century urbanisation was that people lived near their workplace. The shopkeeper literally lived 'over the shop'. Distances between home and workplace increased as population spread to the low-density suburbs of the existing towns, and further afield, outside the built-up limits of Bradford and Keighley. Changes in the distribution of income obviously made it possible for people to choose where they lived, but it was the developments in transport modes and associated infra-structure, that provided the physical means, contributing to the formation of the City Region, and at the same time transforming the socio-economic geography of the Bradford region. In this chapter the developments in communications and transport are examined, beginning with the railways.

Figure 13 in chapter five (page 55) shows the railway system at its maximum development c. 1880. In the closing decades of the 19th century, as well as carrying goods, the railways were providing significant commuter links between town centres and the residential areas. One of the last major rail developments in the Bradford region was the line from Bradford to Keighley through western Bradford-dale, which was completed in 1878, and by that date was carrying goods and passengers. Significantly it had been promoted as early as 1864 by Messrs Foster and Son of Queensbury, Messrs Crossley and Ackroyd of Halifax, and the Halifax Chamber of Commerce. Apart from providing a goods line between the villages in the western area of the Bradford-dale and Halifax and Keighley, it served as a commuter link, contributing to the integration of the Dale and the wider region. It was an expensive line to build, involving the construction of viaducts across three valleys, tunnels beneath Great Horton, Queensbury and Lees Moor, and stations at Great Horton, Clayton, Thornton, Queensbury, Denholme, Cullingworth and Ingrow.[1] In Wharfedale the Ilkley line was extended to Skipton in 1883. It linked Addingham with the rest of the region. Valuable as they were, the railways had limitations because they were confined to the gentler gradients of the valley bottoms, and road transport became more important in handling commuter traffic because of its convenience and its greater accessibility to homes and workplaces. Also it could cope with hills, which gave it greater flexibility, enabling the further spread of population to the higher outlying land. Further mobility came with the introduction of the tramway systems.

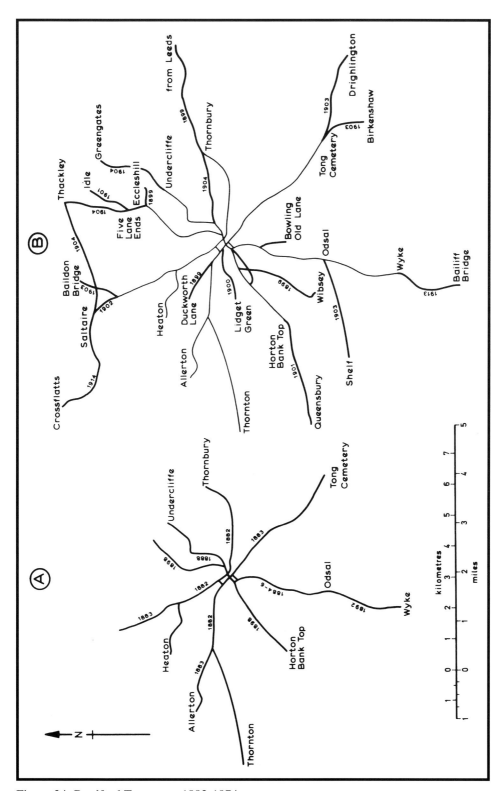

Figure 34. Bradford Tramways 1882-1974.

The first passenger tram service which ran from Bradford to Shipley was drawn by two horses. It operated from 1882 to 1888. Steam trams were introduced in 1883, running from North Parade in Bradford to Lister Park gates, a distance of 666 yards (609 m). By 1893 the line had been extended to include Frizinghall, Undercliffe, Thornbury and Saltaire. At the same time Shelf was joined to Bradford, and there was a service running from Bradford to Stanningley where it linked with the Leeds Corporation system. Figure 40A shows the development of the Bradford Corporation tramway network in 1974, and Figure 40B in 1882. The Bradford tramways were electrified in 1915, and Keighley introduced electricity in 1902. The first electricity works in Bradford was built in Houldsworth Street (off Bolton Road) in 1888 and the Valley Road works was commissioned in 1897. In the year 1912-1913 the Bradford Tramways had carried 62,005,976 passengers rising to 67,675,166 in the following year, and fares ranged from $1/2$d workman's fare to 5d within Bradford Borough.[4] The tram fare from the newly erected Faxfleet Council Estate to the City centre was one penny.

In 1911 there was an experiment with trackless vehicles (trolleybuses). Figure 40A shows the extent of the tramway coverage in 1915, by which time there were tram routes connecting the Aire valley towns with Crossflatts, Baildon Bridge, Tong and Bailiff Bridge. The system was enlarged in 1921 by the inclusion of routes to Thackley, Eccleshill, Idle, Lidget Green and Clayton. Motorbuses began to replace trams in 1928 and the last tram route to Odsal closed in 1950. On the eve of the Second World War, Crossflats could be reached by trolleybus; and by the mid-1950's Wibsey and Buttershaw also were on a trolleybus route. The trolleybus system developed well into the 1960s until it was discontinued as a result of the re-modelling of the City Centre. It closed in 1972 as the last system to operate in the U.K. The Keighley Corporation Omnibus Company's system linked with Bradford's at Bingley (see figure 34b)[2]. Its routes covered the Worth valley villages of Oakworth and Oxenhope, and the Aire valley route extended to Sutton, Kildwick and Crosshills. The flexibility of the system compared with rail routes can be seen in the Thwaites Brow and Laycock routes both of which involve steep hill climbs.[3]

The tram, trolleybus and omnibus services greatly facilitated urban expansion but they also contributed to ribbon development and urban sprawl. However, it provided a low cost means of transport for the residents in the large council estates such as Thorpe Edge and Allerton which were growing up away from the City centre and which would otherwise have been isolated. However it is the private car which has had the most profound effect on the extension of the sphere of influence of central Bradford. Indeed, in the closing decades of the 20th century it has indirectly threatened its retail economy because the more mobile car owners have greater choice to travel to Leeds, or to the supermarket where one-stop shopping and free car parking is more convenient than travel to the city centre. In the Bradford Region the car has become the chief mode of travel to work, far exceeding the numbers travelling by other means (see table 47). In 1971 nearly 40% of the total working population travelled to work by bus. This exceeded car use by 10%. By 1991 the proportion travelling by car had increased to 51.5%, and the numbers travelling to work by bus had fallen dramatically to 17.2%. Although there was a 21.4 percent increase in car usage during the twenty year period of the table it was still ten percent less than the West Yorkshire figure of 61% in 1991. As can be seen from table 48, the increase in car ownership matched the changes revealed in table 47. The generalised statistics of table 48 conceal the different distribution of car ownership between the inner and outer areas of the Keighley and Bradford travel to work areas. In 1991 the proportions of households with no car, in five of the wards of inner Bradford, occupied mainly by the Asian communities, were:

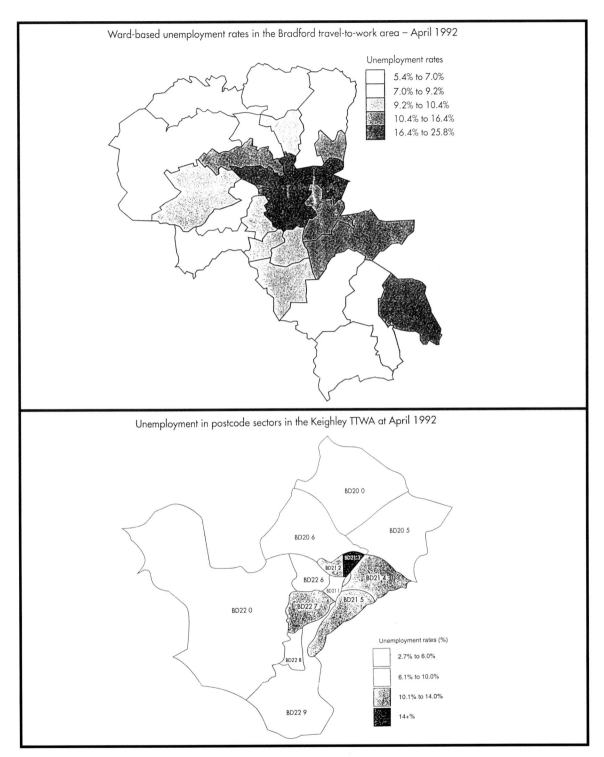

Figure 35. Travel to Work Areas in Bradford and Keighley 1992 (Reproduced from the 'Case for the Keighley Travel to Work Area' (TWA), and 'The Bradford TWA', published by and included with the permission of the City of Bradford Metropolitan Council's Corporate Services Strategic Management Section).

University 63.8%, Little Horton 68.3%, Bowling 58.2 %, Bradford Moor 57.6%, and in Keighley South Ward 56.8%. But the Tong ward with a large proportion of its residents in council housing had 57.9% lacking a car. These figures indicate a close relationship between income and car ownership, and contrast with the wards of Outer Bradford where those households with no car ownership is low e.g. Ilkley 23.7%, Rombalds 22.1%, Craven 24.4%, Bingley 33.4%, Bingley Rural 24.2%, Baildon 26.5%, Worth Valley 24.2%. It can be seen therefore that within the city region there are considerable differences influencing the mobility of its residents.

**Table 47 Travel to work 1971 - 1991  Bradford Region**[5]

| Year | Number of people travelling by: | | | | | | | | | | | |
| | Car | | Bus | | Rail | | Motor Cycle | | Pedal Cycle | | On foot | |
| | No | % | No. | % | No. | % | No. | % | No. | % | No. | % |
| 1971 | 61,970 | 30.1 | 81,250 | 39.5 | 1,730 | 0.8 | 1,590 | 7.7 | 950 | 0.46 | 43,200 | 21.0 |
| 1981 | 90,130 | 48.7 | 47,380 | 25.6 | 1,910 | 1.0 | 4,140 | 2.2 | 1,390 | 0.8 | 30,870 | 16.7 |
| 1991 | 96,300 | 51.5 | 32,170 | 17.2 | 3,570 | 1.9 | 1,520 | 0.8 | 1,500 | 0.8 | 23,640 | 12.6 |

**Table 48  Changes in car ownership in Bradford Metropolitan District 1971-1991**[5]

| Year | Households | | |
| | With no car | | With one car or more |
| | Number | Percent | Percent |
| 1971 | 84,300 | 52.7 | 48.3 |
| 1981 | 81,044 | 49.5 | 50.5 |
| 1991 | 84,537 | 48.6 | 51.4 |
| Change 1971-91 | | 4.1 | |

Figure 36 shows the commuting patterns within Bradford Metropolitan District. It is about interaction and movement between home and workplace within the region. The detail of the map measures this interaction in terms of work, but the same principle could apply to shopping and leisure journeys. These latter aspects were examined by the author and Brian Burkitt in 1972. They found that 31% of the people travelling to shop in the city centre of Bradford had come by car, and 61% by bus, they also noted that amongst the Bradford city centre shoppers between 1968 and 1971 there had been a 5% increase in the use of cars for the shopping journey. During the same period national car shopping travel had increased by 9%.[7]  In the work journey study of movement to the Bradford city centre in 1991 it was noted that an estimated 20,870 commuters lived in the  Bradford Metropolitan District, and about 7,000 lived outside the District.  It was also found that workers living further from the city centre tended to travel into the city by car and train, car travel being the most important.  There were 49.4% of car travellers compared with 3.7% travelling by train. The recorded percentage from Wharfedale travelling by car to work in the city centre were 62.1% and the corresponding figures for Bingley  were 58.6%, Keighley 56.9%, Shipley/Baildon 50.85 and workers living outside the M.D 69.4%. There have been other pressures on the city centre retail and business area, notably  the development of educational, cultural and leisure establishments, adding to the congestion in the commercial centre, and the demand for car parking space. It will be noted that the road system of Bradford radiates from the hub of the city retail/business centre, and the hilly topography of Bradford-dale limits areas of flat land for large space uses, such as car parks. In the 1960s an

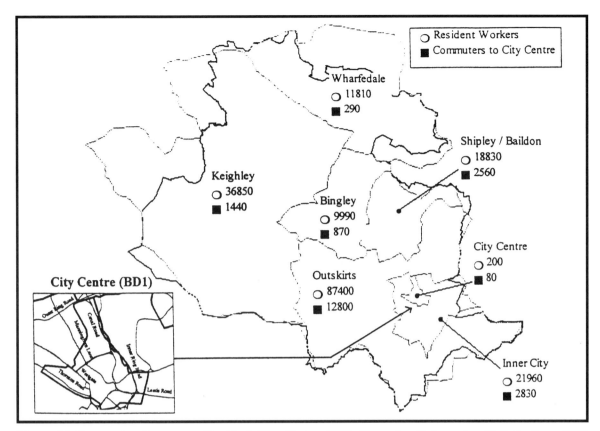

Figure 36 Commuting Patterns to Bradford City Centre 1995. From the 'Information Bulletin June 1997 published by the City of Bradford Metropolitan District Council's Corporate Services Strategic Management Section – reproduced with their permission.

attempt was made to cope with the concentration of vehicular traffic in the central area by building an inner ring road. The communication system was further modified by the construction of an outer ring road. During the closing decades of the 20th century the pressures of city centre traffic intensified and resulted in a shift of emphasis in retailing from the city centre to the outer ring for the weekly shopping trips in which the inadequacy of city centre car parking space had probably been a deciding factor. The geography of communications in the Aire valley also changed in response to the road traffic congestion in the centre of places like Bingley, where the daily work and holiday traffic passed through the town centre. It necessitated a by-pass, and the Aire Valley dual carriageway road built to motorway standards, was constructed to relieve the pressure by re-routing road traffic passing through the dale. The convenience of the motor car cannot be denied, but its use also produces conditions of noise, accident risk and pollution which have an adverse effect on the quality of life in town centres, where vehicular and pedestrian traffic come together. In Bradford itself, the need to separate pedestrians from motorised traffic resulted in the pedestrianisation of the main streets of the central business area. It was noted in the last chapter that air pollution from smoke was a major health hazard. Although atmospheric pollution from exhaust gases is less visible today than it was in the days before 1960, its existence is still evident when looking across the valley from the surrounding high land. A pall of brown pollution haze hangs over the town in the still air conditions associated with anticyclones. Keighley with a lower level of commuter/shopping traffic has been able to enhance its central shopping area.

The Royal Commission on Local Government in England noted that there were strong economic links between central Bradford and the urban areas of Airedale and Wharfedale thus recognising the existence of a Bradford city region. From the Commission's findings the Bradford Metropolitan District came into existence, reinforcing the central regional dominance of Bradford. This chapter has attempted to show how developments in transport and communication have contributed to the integration of the Bradford Region.

The idea of the region has always implied the common unifying characteristic of an area which gave it an identity and has contributed to its coherence. The Bradford Region over the past 140 years has benefitted from the development of communication links which have enhanced the central role of Bradford in drawing people from its outer area to the centre. At the same time the social and economic differences within the city region have developed. The separate identities of the outer urban centres were enhanced by the local government system inherited from the late 19th century and they remain to some extent today, but workers and shoppers 'voted with their feet', so that the reality of intra-regional spatial behaviour showed the underlying inter-connection of centre and outer zone. The mobility of the constituent population enabled the separation of home, workplace, shopping and leisure journeys, revealed in the commuter studies. There has been an 'ideological' change in thinking about the urban place. The Royal Commission on Local Government recognised this change, and its findings gave birth to the creation of the Bradford Metropolitan District with its elected democratic administration. The close correspondence of region formation and administrative district has been a common theme in the chapters of this book. The Bradford city region relates, as it should, to the spatial behaviour of its residents and the changes in transport and communications have provided the means to unify the region. Associated with this was the development of a hierarchy of market centres with the sub-regional apex centred on Bradford. The 19th century local government system did not pay due attention to the 'market' or the hierarchical relationship which was evolving between the Bradford centre and the constituent places to which it was linked by traffic and commuter flows. So the region can be treated as a unified multi-centred area linked by the communication networks and the traffic flows between places. The earlier concept of the town was of a built up area having its own 'set' of interests and human behavioural characteristics, with a clear break between it and the outer rural area. This had validity in an earlier transport age, but it is no longer a satisfactory definition of the city. In reality the outer area has come to be a commuter zone, involving movement and interaction between home, workplace, shopping and leisure area. As this chapter has attempted to show, the development of the transport and communication systems have played a dominant role in this process producing a more realistic definition of urban space, the Bradford city region.

# REFERENCES

1. Whitaker, A. *The Queensbury Triangle* 1979 p.7 and p.29 - 30.
2. Coates, D.M. *Bradford City Tramways 1882-1950* and Bradford Corporation - *Fleet History of Bradford Corporation Tramways*.
3. Keighley Corporation Omnibus Services Guide.
4. Bradford Corporation Tramways Report on Fares, 1914.
5. Sarah Hinds *Commuting and Transport to Work Trends* Appendix 3 -National Census 1971-1991 10% Sample Employed and Self-employed residents aged 16 and over- Special Workplace Statistics.

6.  National Census, op. cit. for the years shown.
7.  Richardson, C. and Burkitt, B. "Main Shopping Catchments of the West Yorkshire Conurbation" *European Journal of Marketing* Vol.6, No.L Spring 1972 p.56 1972'
8.  Bradford Council Strategic Management Unit Research Section - Information Bulletin, 1997.

# CHAPTER TWELVE

# THE CHANGING ECONOMY

By the close the twentieth century the economy of the Bradford Region had changed dramatically. This change matched the changes in Britain's global production and trading position. As shown later, Bradford's pre-eminence in the worsted textile sector enabled it to survive as an employer until the 1960s as it benefitted from the post war world shortages and 'lived on its industrial fat'. Table 49 shows that other sectors were similarly affected. But during the last three decades of the century the textile sector, once the region's main employer, was reduced to a relatively minor employer. The explanation of these changes lies largely with the changed position of Britain as a manufacturing and trading nation as much as by slowness of the industry to adjust. Britain had lost its privileged trading position with the Commonwealth whose members developed their own economies and established new trading partners, some with emerging third-world nations. Also, when Britain belatedly joined the European Union, its foreign trading orientation had become predominantly directed towards Europe. A combination of relatively high exchange and interest rates, and the increased competition by producers in other countries, and the slowness of the worsted industry to adjust to the new situation, also seriously weakened that sector's trading position.

To some extent however, the Region has responded to the new challenges, though as we see, they have had an impact on its industrial geography. Table 49 shows the Region's economic profile between 1971-73 and 1998 and compares it with the national picture. In 1961, 39.3% of the British workforce was employed in manufacturing. By 1978 the proportion had fallen to 32.0% and by 1998 it had only 20.7% engaged in this sector. The Bradford Metropolitan District experience was equally dramatic. In 1971 it had 47.3% in manufacturing and as table 49 shows the figure had fallen to 27.8%. Emphasis switched to the services sectors, which in Great Britain in 1971 employed 55.4%, compared with 78.1% in 1998 In the Bradford M.D the proportions were 48.1% in 1971-73 and 70.3% in 1998.

**Table 49 Structural Changes in Bradford Metropolitan District and in Great Britain between 1971-73 and 1998**[1]

| Industrial Group | Bradford M.D | | | Great Britain | |
| --- | --- | --- | --- | --- | --- |
| | 1971-73 | 1998 | | 1971-73 | 1998 |
| | Percent Employed | No. Employed | Percent | Percent | Percent |
| Primary | 0.3 | 2,712 | 1.4 | 3.7 | 1.4 |
| All manufacturing | 47.3 | 45,644 | 27.8 | 35.2 | 20.7 |
| Construction | 4.3 | 6,400 | 3.5 | 5.8 | 4.5 |
| All Services | 48.1 | 129,802 | 70.3 | 55.4 | 78.1 |

N.B. Figures do not add up exactly to 100% because of rounding

In spite of these changes the industrial geography of the Bradford Region showed a continuation of the valley-oriented pattern of Bradford-dale and Airedale, which typified the

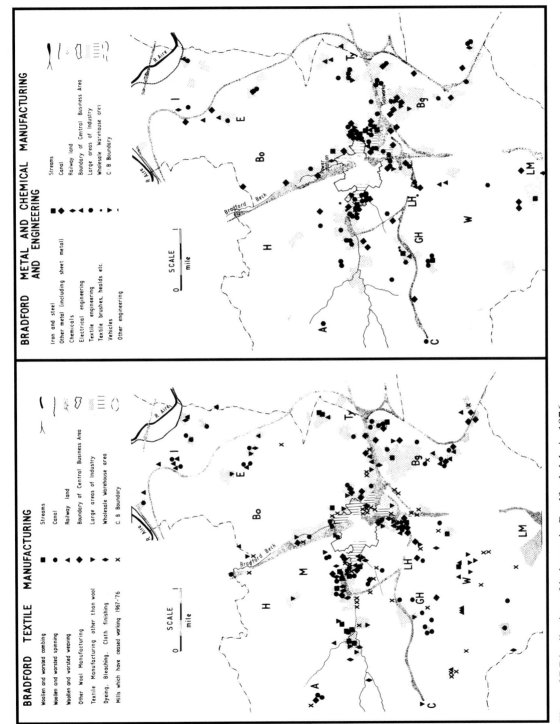

Figure 37.Distribution of industry in Bradford-dale in 1976.

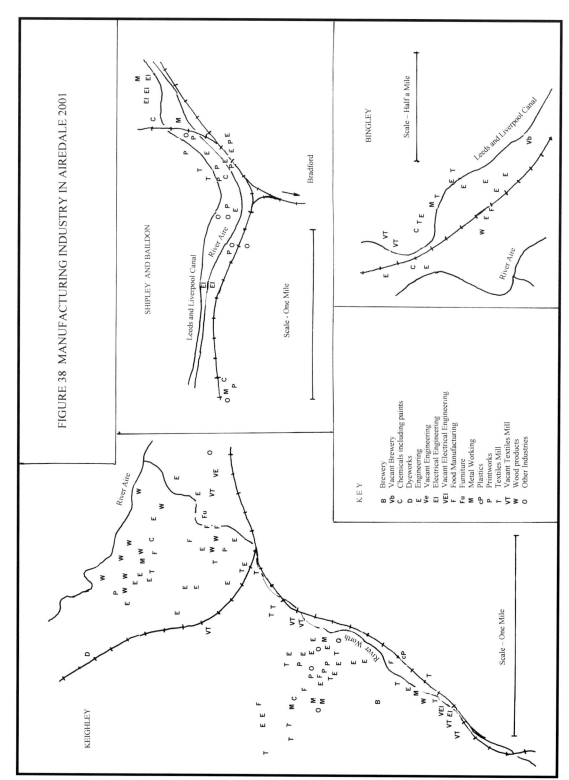

Figure 38. Manufacturing Industry in Airedale 2001

Region's industrial land use distribution during the 19th century. (See figures 37 and 38). In the past energy sites accessible to water power or coal influenced the location of industry, because they minimised production costs. Later electric power partially released industrial location from a dependence on coal, and helped to spread the distribution of factory sites. But for the most part the valley orientation continued. Entrepreneurs were the sole decision-makers throughout those early years. However in the 20th century governments, both central and local, entered the process when the statutory planning system came into being. This gave elected authorities power to control land development. Governmental agencies became locational facilitators in providing developed sites and factories, as well as financial assistance to businesses. As figures 37 and 38 show there have, however, been extensions of the established valley-oriented industrial concentrations. By the year 2001 the nature of production had changed in many ways as new industries had appeared and others had either ceased to be important, or had disappeared altogether. In particular the balance had begun to shift from the Region's traditional manufacturing sectors to the electronics, the chemical and the service industries.

The economic bases of coal and iron mining, which were so important in the 19th century industrial economy, had almost ceased to exist by the beginning of the 20th century, while the traditional industries of textiles and associated engineering sectors maintained their leading position in the Region's economy until the 1960s. Since then, however, they have experienced a major reduction in production and in the numbers employed. In spite of these changes the Region has maintained its importance as a manufacturing centre. In 1998 184,552 were employed in 15,846 firms, and 45,644 (24.7%) employees were in manufacturing, which is above the national percentage.[2] and [6] The detail for 1998 is shown in table 49.

In 1901, 211,729 (67%) of the total population of working age in the Bradford Region had been occupied, and manufacturing dominated the economy, but there are difficulties in making comparisons with later years because of changes in the working age and in the definition of the industrial categories. At the beginning of the century children aged 10 and over were included in the employment statistics, and some categories which at that time were organised as service industries, such as tailoring and dressmaking, have since become factory-based. By contrast with 1901, in 1991 71.4% were engaged in the services sector showing a major shift in the economy of the region.

At the beginning of the 20th century mining and iron manufacture occupied 6.8% of the Region's working population, and in the 'services' sector 19.5% were employed, leaving about 74% engaged in manufacturing. By 1961 manufacturing was occupying a smaller proportion of the working population. The Region was highly specialised in textiles. By 1960 22.8% were in the wool and worsted sector, but there were already signs that the industry was running down, as a few mills had already closed. As can be seen in table 50, the numbers in this industry fell rapidly from 1961 for the remainder of the century, until it occupied only 4.9% of the workforce by 1998.

There are many explanations for the continued dominance of textiles as an employer in the Region until the 1960 'watershed', and its striking fall in importance in the year 2001. During some of the years between 1945 and 1960 employment actually increased, although as has been noted, it was falling by 1960. The reasons for its survival and continued prosperity during that immediate post-war period were *inter alia*: post-war shortages of textile products, both nationally and internationally, and the availability of labour as immigrants came to Bradford and Keighley from what was called the New Commonwealth. The recruitment by the industry of people from the Indian sub-continent was important in covering the labour shortages to provide for what was a producer's market. A study of employment in the newly arrived migrants from the Indian sub-continent showed that in 1965 62% were employed in textiles (54% from Pakistan and 8% from the Indian Republic). They provided a pool of adaptable labour, willing to work shifts in uncomfortable conditions. But textile workers' wages were low, so production costs remained relatively low and for a time the industry was competitive.[3] Thus there was less of an incentive to instal modern plant and make the industry more competitive. In 1993 G. Bent in the Bradford Textile Journal, drew attention to obsolescence in the industry and the under-use of the most efficient, but expensive machinery, which contributed to Britain's less favourable market position. He also noted that new competitors were in low wage countries such as the Phillipines, Indonesia, Malaysia and Taiwan, which began to supply Britain's traditional markets, and that environmental and planning controls were less stringent in third world countries, e.g. in wool scouring, where environmental controls were weaker. Furthermore the high exchange value of the pound did not help exporters[6]

**Table 50. Employment in the Wool and Worsted Industry in the Bradford Region 1901-1998**[4]

| Year | 1901 | 1961 | 1965 | 1971 | 1978 | 1998 |
|---|---|---|---|---|---|---|
| Number | 73,710 | 72,901 | 41,356 | 38,216 | 27,461 | 9,068 |
| Percent of total employed | 34.8 | | | 8.3 | 6.05 | 4.9 |

In 2001 a review of the author's 1968 field survey of industry in Bradford C.B revealed that over 60 textile mills had either changed use or were no longer being recorded in the Bradford telephone directory, indicating an important change in the Region's industrial geography which matched the fall in textile employment. As changes in the workforce took place, the product also changed. The consumption of wool, the Region's traditional raw material, fell from 63.5 million kilos in 1960 to 33.7 million kilos in 1974, and at the same time, man-made fibre consumption rose from 33.1 to 46.1 million kilos[5]

The design of the worsted spinning mill consists of a tall multi-storeyed building which is not readily adaptable to other uses. While the typical worsted mills have large floor areas for spinning and weaving, there is little room around the mills for storage or car parking, so they remain as imposing, but sad monuments to the Region's past, as for example in the Ingrow mill cluster in Keighley. Nevertheless, notable uses of the former worsted mills include the Bradford Industrial Museum, Phoenix Mill used as part of the University, Salts's Mill in Saltaire, where the Hockney Gallery shares floors with the Pace and Filtronic electronics manufacturers. Another example is Damart's use of its Bowling Green Mill in Bingley, as its main office headquarters and shop; and part of the adjacent Albert Mill site is now used as flats. A further example is John Cawdra and Son's joinery works in Bradford Road, Keighley.

It has been noted that a large proportion of Asian workers were engaged in textiles and by 1991 many were unemployed. Thus a connection may be drawn between their unemployment rates and the run down of the industry. This is suggested by the pockets of higher than average unemployment rates in those areas where most of the Asian population was concentrated. For example in 1991, although the overall rate for the Bradford M.D was 10.9%, in the wards of Keighley where much of the Asian population lived, the rate ranged between 24% and 32% and in similar central wards of Bradford-dale they were between 30.4% and 35.1%.[7] Table 51 shows the position in 1998, when the total for the District was 6.3%.

## Table 51 Unemployment in Bradford District in 1998[8]

| Ethnic Group | White | Pakistani | Bangladeshi | Indian | Black | Other | Overall |
|---|---|---|---|---|---|---|---|
| Percent Unemployed | 5.2 | 21.0 | 21.2 | 9.0 | 12.4 | 12.9 | 6.3 |

Females which traditionally constituted 49% of the textile employment were also distributed more generally through other employment sectors, and were more readily absorbed in the distribution and other industries.

While employment statistics provide a readily available and significant measurement of the District's industrial structure in the nineteen nineties, there are other ways of evaluating the economy such as the capital value of firms, their turnover and profit levels. Both Bradford and Keighley have diverse industrial profiles as Table 52 and the following paragraphs show.

The Bradford Economic Development Unit (EDU) Bulletin of 1994 recorded that firms based in the Bradford Region had a market capitalisation of £14 billions[10] and in 1999 the total turnover of the fifty largest firms amounted to £7.356 bn.

## Table 52 - Examples of firms having the greatest capital value, greatest turnover and producing the highest pre-tax profits - 1992 -1993[11]

| Company | Capital Value  £m | Turnover £m | Pre-tax Profits £m |
|---|---|---|---|
| Wm Morrison Supermarkets plc | 855 | 1,370 | 384 |
| Allied Colloids | 700.1 | 210 | |
| Cyanomid of Gt Britain | | 220 | 17 |
| Grattan Mail Order | | 403 | |
| Empire Stores, Mail Order | | 222 | |
| Fine Art Development | 404.4 | 312 | 34 |
| Pace Micro-Technology | | 90 | 5 |
| Peter Black, Keighley | | 209 | |
| Kone Escalators, Keighley | | 35 | |
| Transtechnology at Glusburn | | 25 | |
| Landis Lund Ltd, MachineTools | | 39 | |
| John Haggas | | 43 | |

By the year 2000 Morrisons annual turnover was £3,300m, Grattan £523m, Pace £378m, Magnet £250m, Peter Black £209m, Kone Escalators £44m and John Haggas £36m.

Generally speaking, most firms in the Region were in the small to medium size categories. In 1994 the largest employers in the Bradford District were Grattan (2,912), Wm. Morrison (2,650), Yorkshire Co-op (2,500), Allied Colloids (1,900), Bradford and Bingley Building Society (1,700), Fine Art Development plc (1,200), Drummond Group (900), Magnet (815), P.Black (800), Illingworth Morris (800), Pace Micro-Technology (770), Empire Stores (750), Kosset Carpets(710), British Mohair (686), Field Packaging (670) Robert McBride (650), W. and S.Whitehead (650), Spring Ram (640), Watmoughs (550), John Haggas (500), Damart Thermwear (420), Marks (410), Syltone (367), Microvitek (342) Bulmer and Lumb (240).[11]

In addition to the traditional textiles industry this list covers the chemical, electronics, printing and packaging, mail order, food and distributive industries, indicating the District's diversity.[9] By 2000 Morrisons employment total had increased to 2800 and Pace to 1000.[11]

Keighley has a diverse industrial profile with a few large firms, including clothing and footwear, Peter Black (400), engineering, Kone Escalators (250), Transtechnology at Glusburn (535) and Landis & Lund Ltd, Machine Tools (390), textiles John Haggas (480), metal pipes, clips etc Wask-Rmf steel tubes (100), and manufacture of anaesthetics equipment Ohmeda. Other large employers include Magnet Joinery and Bolivar Stamping Company.[11]

Exports from Bradford in 1994 amounted to £619,3 millions, and the main exporters were the textile companies of Parkland Group, W & J Whitehead, John Foster & Son plc, Drummond Group plc and British Mohair Holdings plc; in chemicals - Allied Colloids plc, and Ellis & Everard plc; the engineering firm of Syltone plc; the printers - Fine Art Developments plc, Watmough plc and ISA International[12]

As can be seen at the same time as the textile industry declined, new and established, 'growth' industries were expanding. In particular, extra jobs were created in the firms with good prospects like those engaged in the electrical and electronics, chemicals and pharmaceuticals industries; and the financial services, the distribution, and the mail order sectors. In 1999 the Bradford 'Telegraph and Argus' reported that *Bradford is at the hub of the electronics sector, accounting for 38% of the region's jobs in this industry*.[9]

The new extensions of the traditional industrial concentrations noted above, reveal a preference for level ground, accommodating single storey structures. Also areas with substantial amounts of ground space are required to accommodate modern industrial development which contrasts with the tight clustering of mills in valley-bottom sites, typical of the earlier textile industrial development. Modern industry also requires good road access. Car parking space is often an essential reqirement. Most of the traditional industrial concentrations of the Bradford Region are entrenched in the valleys of the Pennine plateau, and there are few large areas of flat land. Thus Aire-side sites in Keighley and Shipley and the flatter parts of the plateau in south Bradford are more suited to the needs of modern industry. It is in these areas that Bradford Council's Regeneration Division has developed industrial and business parks. These are shown in figure 39. They are specially suited to small and growing firms which also often qualify as 'growth' businesses. Here the Council, as facilitator, has provided accommodation in well-serviced industrial sites occupied by one-storey buildings to add to the industrial map of the Region. In addition to the purpose-built industrial estates, use has been made of the redundant textile mills, amongst which the Knowle Mill, Keighley, now a business centre, and Salt's Mill in Saltaire may be noted. Appropriately sited, adjacent to the University of Bradford, is the Council-owned Lister Hill Science Park, where many firms connected with the electronics and computer industry are located, and the Carlisle Business Centre has computer firms among its tenants.

The creation of the University of Bradford merits special mention, not only in its employment effect, but also in changing the geography of the inner city with the development of the campus. The main buildings were constructed on what had been the sites of terraced housing, and its first halls of residence were constructed on open land in the Trinity Road area adjacent to the Margaret McMillan College of Education. It had 2,694 students and 415 staff at its foundation in 1966 and 564 places in halls, so over 2,000 students depended on rented accommodation from private landlords. Further growth took place so that by 1996 there were 6,784 students and 2,041 places in halls of residence. It can be seen that the University has had a major effect in generating income and with the extension of the campus, has changed the geography of the City. Together with the Bradford College, it has formed a large educational precinct west of the City centre. As can be seen above, it has also influenced the siting and development of the Listerhills Science Park.

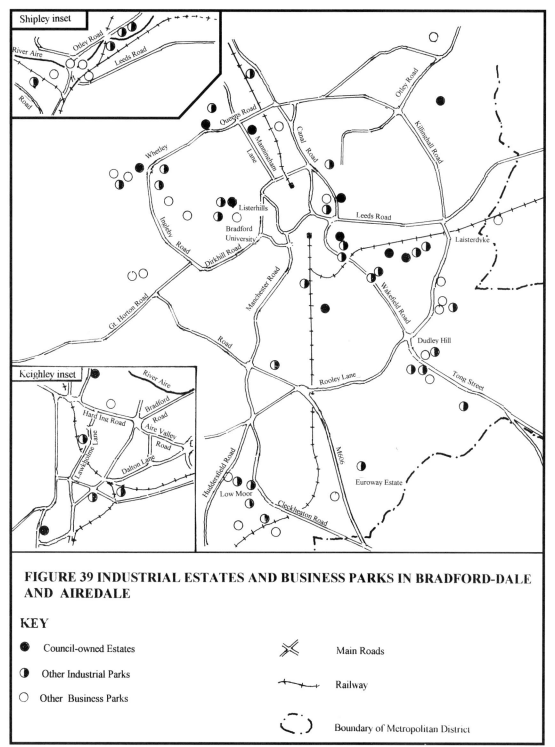

**FIGURE 39 INDUSTRIAL ESTATES AND BUSINESS PARKS IN BRADFORD-DALE AND AIREDALE**

**KEY**

| | | | |
|---|---|---|---|
| ● | Council-owned Estates | ✕ | Main Roads |
| ◑ | Other Industrial Parks | ┼─┼─┼ | Railway |
| ○ | Other Business Parks | ⌐ ⌐ | Boundary of Metropolitan District |

Figure 39 Industrial Estates and Business Parks in Bradford-dale and Airedale
Reproduced from the map issued by the Land and Property Section – Copyright – Bradford Metropolitan District Council.

Part of the time there were three educational colleges in the Region, at Bingley, Ilkley and Bradford, the latter becoming the Bradford College. An interesting example of the industrial conversion of former mills resulting from the rundown of the textile industry, was the use by Keighley Technical College for some of its technology teaching at the Dalton Mill in Dalton Lane.

Employment in the services sector increased rapidly during the 20th century until it has become one of the most important components in the economic profile of the Bradford Region. Its expansion has helped to soften the impact of the reduction in employment in the textile industry. It is divided between public and private agencies. A large part of this change in the local labour economy can be related to the extension of government involvement in industrial location and in the development of the welfare state. From the beginning of the century local councils were given extensive statutory powers and responsibilities to own and manage property, resulting in increases in employment in the public services. The pace quickened after the Second World War. For example additional staff was required *inter alia,* to manage council estates, to take responsibility for social care, to run and staff the educational service following the extension of the school leaving age; and to staff the housing, welfare and the planning systems. At one time Bradford Council was the largest employer in the Bradford District, with 25,000 employees.

The greater role of public authorities as land-owners and users also has had a geographical impact on the urban morphology, notably in the creation of large council-owned estates mostly using greenfield sites on the periphery of the towns to replace the slum clearance of the inner urban areas. At the same time new upper school campusses located on former farmland away from the congested central areas have been created. Perhaps the most important land use change was the construction of the educational precinct incorporating the University, its halls of residence, and the Bradford and Ilkley College, which occupy the large tract of land west of the city centre of Bradford. New residences involving conversion of redundant college land in Bingley and Ilkley represents a further example of public authority involvement in shaping the urban as well as the economic geography of the Region.

The second half of the 20th century also witnessed the formation of the National Health Service. Health and social work employment occupied 21,339 people in 1997. In addition, the utilities sector, including gas and water supply, employed 2,636 in the district in 1991. Yorkshire Water has its headquarters in South Bradford.

In the private sector there were also structural and locational changes, notably in the distribution industry, and especially in the mail order and the supermarket divisions. As with education, the services sector has its own geography. Land use changes paralleled the changes in employment as has been demonstrated.

The transport and communications sector engaged a significant number of workers throughout the twentieth century. It had 11,755 aged 10 and over or 3.7% of the total Regional employment in 1901, 3.8% in 1966 and 7,110 employees (3.9%) in 1991, but these generalised statistics hide the huge changes in transport technology, the closure of rail branch lines and the development of new highways.

Turning to the private sector, distribution, mail order shopping, warehousing, and supermarkets are particularly important, not only as employers, but also as major land users. Grattan mail order business with 2910 employees in 1994, Empire Stores (750), and Thermawear (Damart) (420) represent a significant division of the distribution industry which had its origins in the 19th century, again providing employment as other industries declined. The

Grattan and Empire Stores companies had their origins as far back as the 1830s, when Emilio Fattorini, an ex-soldier, came to Bradford to set up a jewellery business. He sold his wares in local inns on a credit basis and made small regular collections from his clients until the items were paid for. The mail order business began in 1898, and by 1912 was fully established. A family split occurred at the later date and Enrico Fattorini left the family business of Empire Stores to start Grattan, which became one of Bradford's largest employers. By the late 1990s it had become part of the German-based Otto Versant (GMBH) organisation. At one time Grattan's business was distributed at several locations but during the late 1980s it concentrated its main business in a modern distribution centre adjacent to Thornton Road in Bradford.[14]

According to the 1991 Census 21,340 were occupied in retailing in the Bradford Region. Its organisation includes large scale establishments such as the supermarkets and small family businesses. The Bradford-based Wm Morrison Supermarket plc with 2,560 employees in 1994 is the largest employer in retailing in the Bradford District, while the convenience shop is a significant element at the small business end of the market.

Supermarkets are a major post-war retailing development, suited to the motor age. In general their site requirements include large areas of flat land to accommodate the single storey shopping and storage area, and the car parks which ideally should be located near the ring roads so as to be accessible to the undertaking's suppliers and to customers, most of whom live in the large public and private housing areas away from the City centre. However, there is the exception of Morrisons at the Westgate site. There has been some deterioration of the shopping provision in Bradford's City Centre in the loss of some large departmental stores. This could be due to the ascendancy of Leeds in the metropolitan shopping economy, and to the greater mobility of former Bradford central area customers, who travel to other centres. In addition, the development of the supermarket and hypermarkets has had an impact on Bradford's Central Business Area. But one bright development is the conversion of the Wool Exchange, once the regional centre of the worsted trade, into shops and offices.

The family-managed shops, largely provided by the Asian population, are important economically. They not only serve their Asian customers, but also the remainder of the Region's population, where they provide the convenience of street corner shops in the suburbs. The 'ethnic' shop is often more than a specialist establishment dealing with such commodities as halal meat and Asian foods, it frequently acts as a post office and/or newsagency and off-licence, to serve a wider clientele. To the numerous Asian-managed shops may be added the Asian restaurants, which might also be treated as part of the leisure industry as the Bradford curry houses have a national reputation. In the 1991 10% sample census, the catering division, which includes more than the Asian establishments, showed that 3,140 were employed in that sub-sector.[15] For the distribution of Asian businesses in Bradford see figure 51 on page 164.

In Bradford the cultural and leisure facilities are important not just because of the number of people they engage, but as an economic resource in the tourist industry. Undoubtedly they contribute substantially to the quality of life in the Region as well as bringing in wealth. To the many museums and cultural attractions, may be added the scenic attractions of the three dales. Each of the dales has its own areas of rural beauty, including extensive moorlands and valleys rich in scenic, archaeological and historical interest, that draw people from areas far outside the Bradford Region who require hotel accommodation as well as other needs. Even the heavily urbanised Bradford-dale has its attractive rural areas, and Airedale and Wharfedale are scenic gateways to the Yorkshire Dales National Park. Ilkley has a history as a resort, a function it still retains. Haworth with its association with the Brontës, draws people to the region from all parts of the world. Nor should the Haworth's importance to railway enthusiasts be forgotten. During the 20th century places like Bradford developed and publicised tourism to serve a national and international public as well as providing cultural and entertainment facilities for its own regional inhabitants. A number of new hotels were built and the annual overnight stays in Bradford regional hotels increased to 2 millon in the year 2000 amounting to an increase of 14% between 1998 and September 2000.[16]

Amongst Bradford's treasures are the St George's Hall concert hall which is a significant part of the city's architectural heritage. The establishment in Bradford of the National Photographic, Film and Television Museum, as part of the National Science Museum, has brought enormous economic benefits to the District because it serves a wide regional and extra-regional population. To these has been added the re-furbished Bradford Alhambra theatre - a major asset, enabling the staging of performances by the largest national opera, ballet, and drama companies.

There are museums in other parts of the Region, amongst which Keighley's Cliffe Castle with its excellent geological and natural history department, and the Manor House Museum in Ilkley should be noted. As well as having considerable educational value, they are also part of the leisure industry.

The increased ownership of the motor car, and the arrival of the television has changed people's leisure habits affecting the entertainment industry, including the use of the city parks. In the first half of the 20th century the 'Victorian' routine of Sunday strolls in the park, listening to the band and enjoying the gardens has begun to give way to the car trip and televiewing. Economic stringency has affected the way the parks are maintained, so they are used less than formerly, but the provision of leisure swimming pools, such as that in Keighley and the Richard Dunn Centre, have been effective in reviving interest in the parks. Lister Park, which is also the site of the Cartwright Museum and Art Gallery, is well used, as is the Cliffe Castle museum and park at Keighley.

Reviewing the changing economy and its geographical effects, we have noted the reduced importance of manufacturing generally, the dramatic fall in the numbers employed in textiles, and the consequent increase in redundant mills. At the same time it has been possible to adapt some industrial premises to new uses involving other industries, educational and cultural institutions, and commercial businesses. The most profound change has been the growth of the service sectors, a change the Region shares with other national industrial centres. Even so, manufacturing is still important and its exports make a substantial contribution to the nation's balance of trade. There are also encouraging signs that the Region is adapting to the modern industrial trends which is evident in the shift towards the 'growth ' sectors of the electrical, electronic and chemical industries. The development of the University in the 1960s has had employment effects and has influenced the re-shaping of its urban geography as the educational precinct has taken shape. Employment in the National Health Service, together with post-primary educational developments have considerably transformed the employment structural profile of the region when compared with the position at the beginning of the 20th century. These, along with the leisure sector, have brought wealth into the Region's economy. The enlargement of local government corresponding to the increased powers and responsibilities central governments have imposed on it, has also added to the numbers in employment. It has been, noted in particular, that through the control of development under the planning system, mostly since the 1948 Planning Act, local and central government have shared with the entrepreneur developer, housing, industrial and other locational decisions. In spite of evidence of resilience provided chiefly by the additonal work opportunities in the retailing and other sectors, some pockets of unemployment persist. These seem to be located in the areas where the Asian population is concentrated in Bradford and Keighley and in the large council estates.

## REFERENCES

1 Office of National Statistics - *Economic profile* Vol.3 1998 and *Regional Trends* 2001 Edition U.K. No.36.

1a Richardson, C. *Geography* ibid Maps on pp.129, and 132.

2 Bradford Council - Annual Employment Survey, 1998 p.13.

3 Allen, S., Bentley, S. and Bornat, J. *Work, Race and Immigrants 1977* Table 2.9 p.51.

4 Decennial Censuses of Great Britain and Sample Censuses for the years shown.

5 Bradford M.D.C. *District Profile* 1975, Table 3 p.23.

6 Bent, George, Director of Schlumberger and Co., in the *Journal of the Bradford Textiles Society* 1993-94 pp.8-10.

7 Census of Great Britain 1991 in Bradford M.D.C. Ward Digest, Table 15.

8 Bradford M.D.C.Training and Enterprising Council *Economic Profile* Vol. 6, 2000.

9 Bradford *Telegraph and Argus*, 2 January 1999.

10 Bradford Council Economic Development Unit *Information Bulletin* (EDU) quoting the *Financial Times*. Exports from the region amounted to £619.3m.

11 Bradford M.D.C. Library Business Review 2000 Key Firms with over 50 employees.

12 Bradford Coucil EDU Ibid. Figures from a review of Yorkshire and Humberside's major eleven exporters by Barclays Bank and the *Yorkshire Post*.

12 *Yorkshire Post* 1995.

13 Bradford Council Regeneration Division *Bradford - City of Opportunity* Examples of firms connected with the micro-electronics and the computer industry include Belgravium, Elonex, Computer Softwear, Gane International Ltd and Maindec Ltd Computers Ltd; The Acorn, the Fieldhead, the Carlisle Road Business Centre and the Angel Way Parks are other estates where computer services are situated.

14 Richardson, C. *Geography* ibid. p.136.

15 The 1991 Census 10% sample recorded 314 employees in catering, 55 hairdressers and 784 sales assistants in the Region, giving an approximate total of 21,430.

16 Bradford, M.D. Council Report - *Best Value Performance 2001-2002* p.43.

# CHAPTER THIRTEEN

# DEMOGRAPHY – SOCIAL AND ETHNIC GEOGRAPHY

The human geographer is not simply concerned with the mapping of differential spatial phenomena, but also the processes which influence their distribution. In searching for an explanation of the spacing of different social or ethnic populations it is necessary to consider the underlying forces affecting residential locational choice, and this requires an economic and a social approach. The demand for living space may be seen as a function of income and the price of dwellings, but it also involves a number of important intangibles related to people's views of socially desirable and satisfying neighbourhoods. The affluent groups are better able to choose and to separate themselves from areas which they consider would adversely affect the quality of life and/or their social standing. In this, social class and ethnicity become important motivants. There are economic indicators from which income can be inferred, but these alone do not entirely explain why some areas are avoided by the affluent population or, for that matter, the ethnic minorities. The reason for the separation of social or ethnic groups may lie in negative social interaction between different classes and/or different ethnic groups.

In this study of the population geography of the Bradford Region two major aspects may be singled out. Firstly, the huge change in the composition of its population, and secondly, its re-location, especially since the second World War.  As figure 40 shows, growth was positive throughout the 20th century, partly due to natural increase, but also due to the immigration of people from Europe and other parts of the world. In explaining the re-distribution of population it is possible to identify both the effect of administrative action and the operation of 'voluntary' locational decisions by private individuals. The re-location of the residents of the inner streets of the main urban centres and their being re-housed in the council estates in the outer areas, was the result of the local councils' slum clearance and re-development schemes of the inter-war, and post-war periods. This created homogeneous social areas, generally peripheral to the main built-up areas of the constituent towns of the Bradford Region. On the other hand, the 'voluntary' process where the more affluent population moved out of the inner areas to the outer areas of Bradford and Keighley, had much to do with income status which enabled the wealthier intra-regional migrants to choose where to live. At the same time, new incomers, often long-distance migrants, moved into the remaining inner streets to form single status neighbourhoods. The effect of these changes has been to produce the contrasting division of social status and ethnicity between the inner and the outer areas of the Region so evident in the map figures of this chapter. In doing so it is helpful to remember the close correspondence of the Regional area covered by this book to the area of the Bradford Metropolitan District, because it enables us to measure the population characteristics of the study area by providing reliable statistical data to construct the maps and the other figures.

In 1901 the population of the study area was 420,000,  by 1931 it had grown to 440,000, and it  remained near this level until 1961.[1] As can be seen in figure 40  during the first 30 years of the 20th century the Region experienced population and industrial growth. In 1901 families were larger, the average household size was 4.43 persons, compared with the 3.18 person per house in 1951 and 2.76  in 2001. Its population structure was  youthful, birth rates were high, and in spite of  high death rates, and the losses of the two world wars, the Region's population continued to grow. As was noted in chapter 12, since 1961 manufacturing in Bradford has

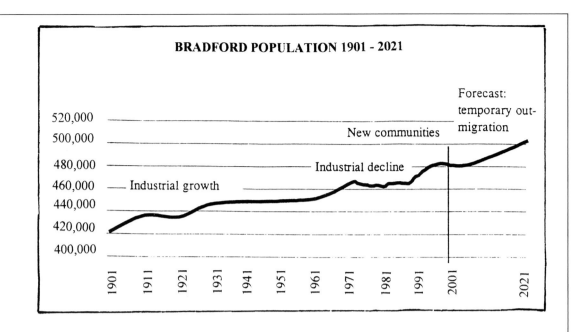

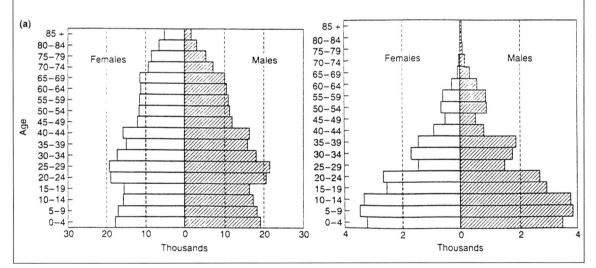

Figure 40. **A.** Total population (total 457,500, 26% under 18) **B.** Pakistani population (total 49,000, 50% under 18). Comparing the mainly European profile of distribution of **A**, which corresponds broadly to that of the National population, displaying a generally older population, with the Pakistani population of profile **B** (with half its number under 18) and showing a more youthful characteristic, confirms the expectation of continued growth to 2021 shown in figure 40.

Source: Census 1991 CROWN COPYRIGHT

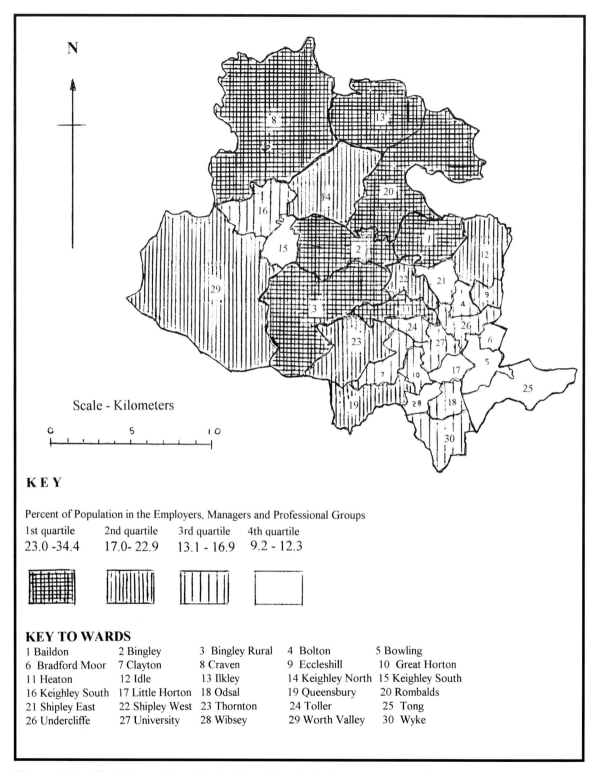

**KEY**

Percent of Population in the Employers, Managers and Professional Groups

| 1st quartile | 2nd quartile | 3rd quartile | 4th quartile |
|---|---|---|---|
| 23.0 -34.4 | 17.0- 22.9 | 13.1 - 16.9 | 9.2 - 12.3 |

**KEY TO WARDS**

| | | | | |
|---|---|---|---|---|
| 1 Baildon | 2 Bingley | 3 Bingley Rural | 4 Bolton | 5 Bowling |
| 6 Bradford Moor | 7 Clayton | 8 Craven | 9 Eccleshill | 10 Great Horton |
| 11 Heaton | 12 Idle | 13 Ilkley | 14 Keighley North | 15 Keighley South |
| 16 Keighley South | 17 Little Horton | 18 Odsal | 19 Queensbury | 20 Rombalds |
| 21 Shipley East | 22 Shipley West | 23 Thornton | 24 Toller | 25 Tong |
| 26 Undercliffe | 27 University | 28 Wibsey | 29 Worth Valley | 30 Wyke |

Figure 41. Bradford Metropolitan District. Population in the Managers and Professional Group.
Source: 1991 Census Local Base Statistics 10% sample. CROWN COPYRIGHT.

declined, but in spite of this, its population has continued to grow. There had been some small scale immigration into the area before the First World War but the greatest movement occurred towards the end of the Second World War, when refugees and ex-soldiers from eastern Europe and a few from South Asia began to settle in the inner wards of Bradford and Keighley, beginning a process which increased in the post-war period.

As new immigrants moved into the inner ward streets, and inner suburbs, their former occupants moved out to the commuter towns and villages. This has had the effect of producing an inner less-wealthy concentration of people and an outer area of more prosperous communities. Table 53 on page 152 shows the distribution of population in the thirty wards making up the Bradford Metropolitan District in 1991. The population of the District in the year 2001 was 480,000 indicating an increase of 60,000 during the century, and the forecast predicts continued growth in spite of economic decline in its main industries. Although the former County Borough area lost 6,201 of its population during the period 1931 to 1951, anticipating the trend in the post 1951 period, this was more than balanced by increases in the outer districts of Bradford and Keighley namely, Baildon, Bingley, Craven, Ilkley, Queensbury, Shipley and Silsden.

The Bradford Region's total population age-sex profile illustrated in figure 40 shows the more typical 'beehive' shape of the national population with fewer people in the 0-20 age cohorts and a large number in the post-65 age groups. Due to higher mortality rates of males compared with females there are fewer males in the post-retirement age categories. Also fertility in the 'host' population is lower than in the immigrant population. The contrasting south Asian profile is discussed below.

The socio-economic characteristics of the Region's population are shown in the maps of figures 41 to 46. Probably the best indicators of wealth are given by the occupational data of the 1991 census and the proportion of ward population in receipt of income support, (see figures 41 and 43). The wards with the highest percentage of their population in the high income occupational group were: Baildon, Bingley, Bingley Rural, Craven, Ilkley, Rombalds and Worth Valley, where the range was between 24.9% and 36.6% in 1991. This contrasts with the less affluent inner urban wards of Bowling, Bradford Moor, Keighley South, Little Horton and Shipley East, Tong and University, all of which had less than 11% of their residents in the high occupational category and may be compared with figure 42, which shows a high proportion in the combined un-skilled and semi-skilled worker groups. The data mapped in figure 43 show the ward population percentage in receipt of income support. The cluster of wards of inner Bradford, Bowling, Bradford Moor, Little Horton, Toller, Tong, Undercliffe, University, and in Keighley South, have a large number of claimants ranging from 10.9% to 14.1%, whereas the outer wards of Baildon, Bingley Rural, Craven, Ilkley, Rombalds and Worth Valley have very few in this poverty indicator. The latter group of wards also has high level of owner occupation with rates between 73.5% and 86.1%, also suggesting contrasting levels of wealth when compared with the detail of figure 44, where it can be seen that the proportion in the 'Bowling-University' group in rented accommodation ranged from 26.5% to 57.4% in 1991. Amongst these the Tong, Little Horton, Braithwaite/Guardhouse in Keighley and Shipley East wards include large council estates. These socio-economic class differences may be correlated with other social indicators. Thus the two-car ownership map of figure 45 suggests a higher income status for the ward population of the outer wards where the highest percentage categories range between 15.7% and 29.9% compared with values ranging from 3.2% to 8.7% in the poorest ward populations of the 'Bowling-University' group. It will be noted that this same group of wards had high levels of unemployment where there was between 16.3% and 31.3% of

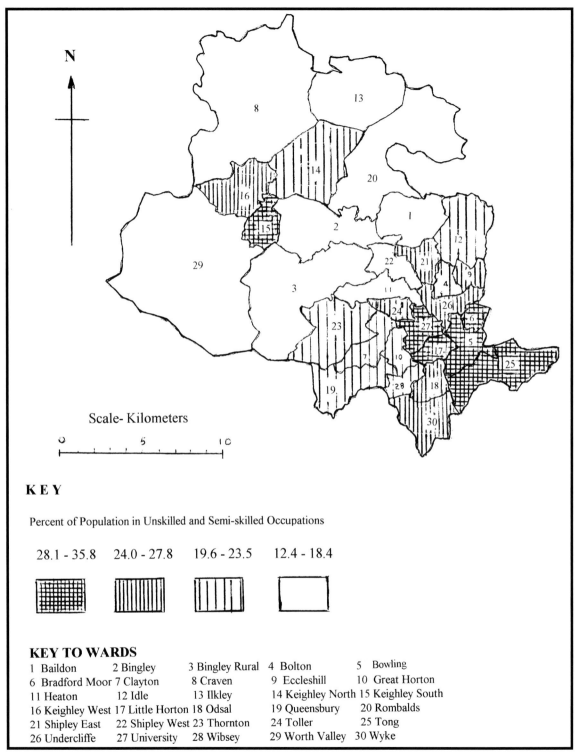

KEY

Percent of Population in Unskilled and Semi-skilled Occupations

28.1 - 35.8    24.0 - 27.8    19.6 - 23.5    12.4 - 18.4

**KEY TO WARDS**

| | | | | |
|---|---|---|---|---|
| 1 Baildon | 2 Bingley | 3 Bingley Rural | 4 Bolton | 5 Bowling |
| 6 Bradford Moor | 7 Clayton | 8 Craven | 9 Eccleshill | 10 Great Horton |
| 11 Heaton | 12 Idle | 13 Ilkley | 14 Keighley North | 15 Keighley South |
| 16 Keighley West | 17 Little Horton | 18 Odsal | 19 Queensbury | 20 Rombalds |
| 21 Shipley East | 22 Shipley West | 23 Thornton | 24 Toller | 25 Tong |
| 26 Undercliffe | 27 University | 28 Wibsey | 29 Worth Valley | 30 Wyke |

Figure 42. Bradford Metropolitan District. Population in Unskilled and Semi-skilled occupations.
Source: 1991 Census Local Base Statistics 10% sample. CROWN COPYRIGHT.

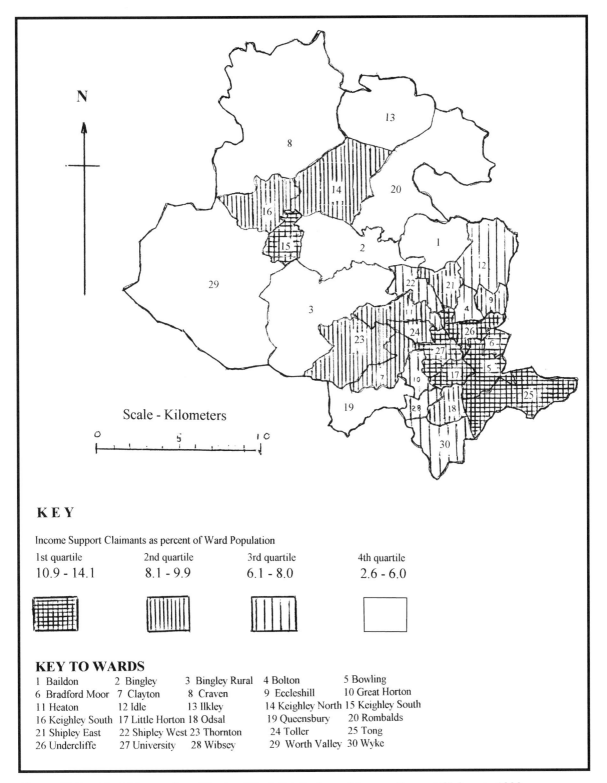

N

Scale - Kilometers

0        5        10

**K E Y**

Income Support Claimants as percent of Ward Population

| 1st quartile | 2nd quartile | 3rd quartile | 4th quartile |
|---|---|---|---|
| 10.9 - 14.1 | 8.1 - 9.9 | 6.1 - 8.0 | 2.6 - 6.0 |

**KEY TO WARDS**

| | | | | |
|---|---|---|---|---|
| 1 Baildon | 2 Bingley | 3 Bingley Rural | 4 Bolton | 5 Bowling |
| 6 Bradford Moor | 7 Clayton | 8 Craven | 9 Eccleshill | 10 Great Horton |
| 11 Heaton | 12 Idle | 13 Ilkley | 14 Keighley North | 15 Keighley South |
| 16 Keighley South | 17 Little Horton | 18 Odsal | 19 Queensbury | 20 Rombalds |
| 21 Shipley East | 22 Shipley West | 23 Thornton | 24 Toller | 25 Tong |
| 26 Undercliffe | 27 University | 28 Wibsey | 29 Worth Valley | 30 Wyke |

Figure 43. Bradford Metropolitan District. Ward distribution of Income Support Claimants 1998.
Source: Office of National Survey (2001) Neighbourhood Statistics. CROWN COPYRIGHT.

their populations who were unemployed at the time of the 1991 census. (Figure 46)

**Table 53 The population of the thirty wards of Bradford Metropolitan District in 1991**[3] **and total in 2000**

| Ward | Total 1991 | Male 1991 | Female 1991 | Total in 2000 | Increase 1991-2000 |
|------|-----------|-----------|-------------|---------------|--------------------|
| Baildon | 15,385 | 7,406 | 7,979 | 15,590 | 210 |
| Bingley | 12,898 | 6,229 | 6,669 | 13,260 | 360 |
| Bingley Rural | 15,298 | 7,418 | 7,880 | 15,580 | 380 |
| Bolton | 13,171 | 6,363 | 6,808 | 14,060 | 890 |
| Bowling | 17,770 | 8,591 | 9,179 | 18,620 | 850 |
| Bradford Moor | 16,393 | 8,075 | 8,318 | 19,480 | 3,070 |
| Clayton | 13,104 | 6,259 | 6,845 | 14,220 | 1,100 |
| Craven | 14,310 | 6,771 | 7,539 | 15,420 | 1,110 |
| Eccleshill | 14,864 | 7,097 | 7,767 | 13,840 | - 1,020 |
| Great Horton | 15,211 | 7,390 | 7,821 | 16,010 | 930 |
| Heaton | 16,856 | 8,162 | 8,694 | 17,190 | 930 |
| Idle | 14,052 | 6,736 | 7,316 | 15,690 | 1,540 |
| Ilkley | 13,530 | 6,189 | 7,341 | 13,660 | 130 |
| Keighley North | 15,460 | 7,649 | 7,811 | 15,970 | 510 |
| Keighley South | 13,289 | 6,211 | 7,078 | 13,130 | -160 |
| Keighley West | 16,371 | 7,817 | 8,584 | 16,620 | 240 |
| Little Horton | 16,792 | 8,069 | 8,723 | 18,640 | 1,850 |
| Odsal | 16,836 | 8,151 | 8,685 | 17,330 | 490 |
| Queensbury | 16,241 | 7,838 | 8,403 | 17,450 | 1,210 |
| Rombalds | 15,258 | 7,250 | 8,008 | 16,040 | 780 |
| Shipley East | 14,332 | 6,871 | 7,461 | 13,580 | - 750 |
| Shipley West | 15,421 | 7,358 | 8,063 | 15,640 | 220 |
| Thornton | 13,830 | 6,598 | 7,232 | 13,150 | - 680 |
| Toller | 17,599 | 8,606 | 8,993 | 19,760 | 2,160 |
| Tong | 14,106 | 6,794 | 7,312 | 13,700 | -410 |
| Undercliffe | 15,515 | 7,608 | 7,907 | 16,690 | 1,180 |
| University | 18,898 | 9,726 | 9,172 | 24,880 | 6,980 |
| Wibsey | 13,835 | 6,554 | 7,281 | 13,540 | - 300 |
| Worth Valley | 13,788 | 6,715 | 7,073 | 14,870 | 1,080 |
| Wyke | 16,931 | 8,201 | 8,730 | 16,510 | -420 |
| TOTAL BRADFORD M.D. | 457,344 | 220,702 | 236,642 | 481,020 | 23,676 |

There has been considerable movement since the second World War from the inner city areas of Bradford and Keighley. The wards showing the greatest growth include Bingley Rural, Craven, Keighley North, Queensbury, Rombalds, and Worth Valley in the outer areas and Bolton, Bradford Moor, Heaton, Idle, Great Horton, Keighley South, Little Horton, Odsal, and University in the inner area. The latter may be explained by the influx of migrants to Bradford and Keighley, whereas the movement from inner to the outer areas involved former inner ward residents.

Demographers have referred to the 'push'- 'pull' effect in explaining both inward and outward migration. For example, at one time, as was noted earlier, people were moving out of the unhealthy inner city neighbourhoods to seek the healthier areas away from the congested smoke-laden atmosphere, to live in the more attractive environment of the outer suburbs and the open country localities away from the built-up urban centres. The maps discussed above point

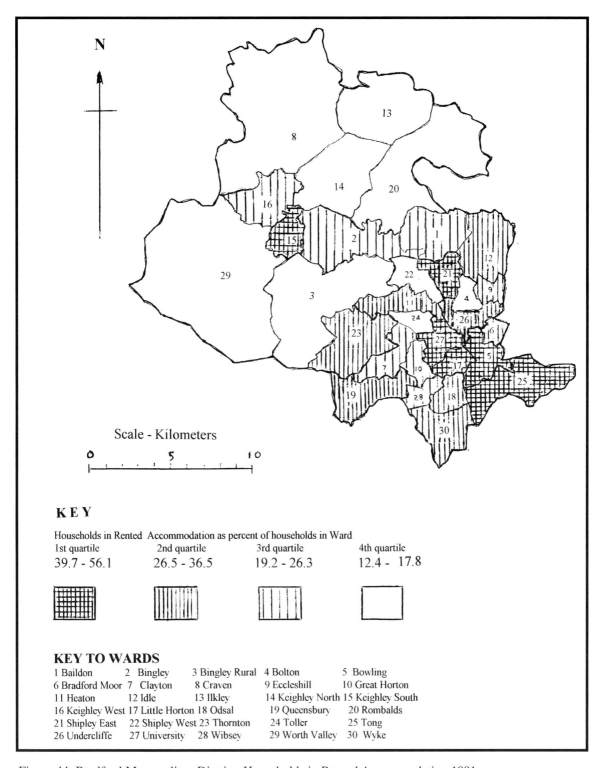

Scale - Kilometers

0    5    10

**KEY**

Households in Rented Accommodation as percent of households in Ward

| 1st quartile | 2nd quartile | 3rd quartile | 4th quartile |
|---|---|---|---|
| 39.7 - 56.1 | 26.5 - 36.5 | 19.2 - 26.3 | 12.4 - 17.8 |

**KEY TO WARDS**

| | | | | |
|---|---|---|---|---|
| 1 Baildon | 2 Bingley | 3 Bingley Rural | 4 Bolton | 5 Bowling |
| 6 Bradford Moor | 7 Clayton | 8 Craven | 9 Eccleshill | 10 Great Horton |
| 11 Heaton | 12 Idle | 13 Ilkley | 14 Keighley North | 15 Keighley South |
| 16 Keighley West | 17 Little Horton | 18 Odsal | 19 Queensbury | 20 Rombalds |
| 21 Shipley East | 22 Shipley West | 23 Thornton | 24 Toller | 25 Tong |
| 26 Undercliffe | 27 University | 28 Wibsey | 29 Worth Valley | 30 Wyke |

Figure 44. Bradford Metropolitan District. Households in Rented Accommodation 1991.
Source: 1991 Census Local Base Statistics. CROWN COPYRIGHT.

to the social and ethnic separation of the more residentially mobile high social class population. This may include people seeking to move into the catchment of what is perceived as a "good" state school in the outer areas. However, whatever the motivation, it is the relative wealth that makes such choice possible. The wealthy can afford to move, the poor have less choice where to live.

**Table 54 Main languages, other than English, spoken by Bradford pupils**[5]

| Ethic group | Number of children who speak this langauge at home | | |
| --- | --- | --- | --- |
| | 1981 | 1985 | 1995 |
| Punjabi | 6,899 | | |
| Urdu | 2,701 | 13,947 | 15,223 |
| Punjabi (Gurmukhi) | 585 | 1,684 | 3,317 |
| Gujarati | 1,251 | 1,360 | 1,038 |
| Bengali | 449 | 944 | 1,593 |
| Pushto | 415 | 577 | * |
| Italian | 367 | 196 | 39 |
| Polish | 190 | 148 | * |
| Cantonese | 148 | 144 | 204 |
| Hindi | 176 | 139 | 106 |
| Creole | 146 | 44 | * |
| Ukrainian | 104 | 75 | * |
| French | 75 | 31 | * |
| German | 77 | 25 | * |
| Spanish | 54 | 31 | 4 |
| Serbo-Croat | 68 | 27 | * |
| Other languages | 498 | 228 | 1,928 |
| All languages | 14,207 | 19,600 | 23,452 |
| % of all pupils | 18% | 23% | 31% |

Notes: Both Punjabi and Urdu are spoken by many Muslim pupils with family origins in Pakistan, where Punjabi has no written form, and were for this reason combined as one response since 1985. Punjabi (Gurmukhi) refers to Punjabi spoken mainly by Sikh families with origins in India, where a written form is expressed in the Gurmukhi script. Languages marked with * were not separately identified.

The evidence of the decennial censuses showed that Irish settlement discussed in chapter eight continued into the 20th century and that the Region's population contained small numbers of Germans and Italians. However, the second World War brought new groups to Bradford and Keighley, when ex-soldiers, refugees and émigré communities began to arrive from the territories in eastern Europe which had been incorporated in the Soviet Union. This population of Poles, Ukrainians, Latvians, Lithuanians and Estonians was augmented by groups from Hungary and Yugoslavia following the upheavals in those two countries in the late 40s and the 50s. The largest group came from Poland and the Ukraine. Together they made up the majority of the non-Commonwealth Europeans in 1971. The presence of eastern rites Catholic churches, Polish clubs and the continued existence of cultural organisations in the Region are an enduring feature of this part of Bradford's ethnic history. But the changes in the home language detail of table 54 also suggests that there was some linguistic assimilation of this group of people as the numbers using their ancestral language in the home had fallen by 1995. The earliest settler-locality in this group was in the inner wards of Bradford, but examination of the electoral

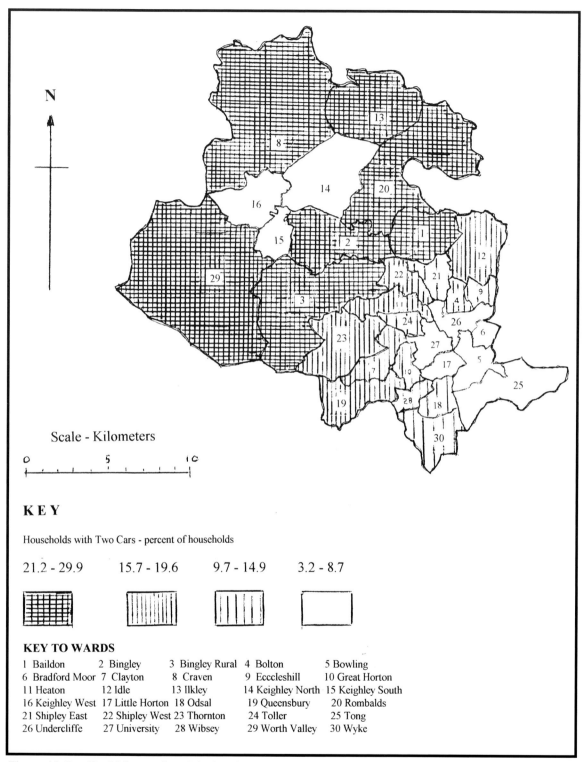

N

Scale - Kilometers

0          5          10

**K E Y**

Households with Two Cars - percent of households

21.2 - 29.9          15.7 - 19.6          9.7 - 14.9          3.2 - 8.7

**KEY TO WARDS**

| | | | | |
|---|---|---|---|---|
| 1 Baildon | 2 Bingley | 3 Bingley Rural | 4 Bolton | 5 Bowling |
| 6 Bradford Moor | 7 Clayton | 8 Craven | 9 Ecccleshill | 10 Great Horton |
| 11 Heaton | 12 Idle | 13 Ilkley | 14 Keighley North | 15 Keighley South |
| 16 Keighley West | 17 Little Horton | 18 Odsal | 19 Queensbury | 20 Rombalds |
| 21 Shipley East | 22 Shipley West | 23 Thornton | 24 Toller | 25 Tong |
| 26 Undercliffe | 27 University | 28 Wibsey | 29 Worth Valley | 30 Wyke |

Figure 45. Bradford Metropolitan District. Car availability - Households with two cars
Source: 1991 Census of Population Base Statistics 10% sample. CROWN COPYRIGHT.

registers shows a dispersal of this ethnic category to the outer suburbs and commuter areas.

At the same time as the east European migrants were settling in Bradford, Afro Caribbean communities were arriving, some of these were Creole speaking, and a few were French speaking, but as the pupil-language table suggests, the numbers using the West Indian language in the home had fallen by 1995. This ethnic group included population 'born in America' in the national census, numbered 984 in Bradford in 1961, and 1,980(67%) in the 1971 census of the City. While table 54 shows a reduction in the number of non-Asian pupils whose ancestral language-use in the home was diminishing, the number using Bengali and Punjabi in the home was increasing. Figure 47 shows areas in the Indian sub-continent from which emigration to Bradford has taken place. The partition of India following the British withdrawal, resulted in large scale communal conflict which generated migratory pressure in such areas as Kashmir and Bengal and Gujarat. Bengal was formerly East Pakistan. It became Bangladesh after its separation from West Pakistan. This conflict was not the only 'push' factor in the migration equation. The researcher Stephen Barton estimated that 95% of the Bangladeshi community in Bradford came from the area of Sylhet (see figure 47).[7] These were peasant cultivators in an area where pressure on the land was great and land prices were increasing. The tradition both in Bangladesh and Gujarat was for the sons of families to work as seaman in the British merchant navy and remit some of their earnings back to the family in India in order to relieve the poverty and the pressure on the family's land. Barton identified four phases of migration from the Sylhet region, but the sequence he described could apply to other parts of the sub-continent. He stated that phase one - the 'pioneer phase', covered the period from the 19th century to 1945; phase two 1945-1960, involved mass migration of unskilled workers; phase three 1968-1978, was a phase of family re-union which coincided with the change in the British government's immigration policy to limit male entry, but which gave preference to allow the wives and children to join their menfolk already resident in Britain (a point of some significance in perpetuating the kinship and village concentrations of the initial settler groups); and phase four from 1970 onwards, involved the emergence of a British educated second generation population which tended towards dispersal.[8] Confirming Barton's findings, Badra Dahya, in an earlier study of Bradford's Asian migrants, noted a 'pioneer' phase as early as 1944, when there were about 30 former Asian seamen lodging in the city.[9] This pioneer group consisted predominantly of Muslim men who lodged in houses owned by Poles in Howard Street in Bradford. The Asian population remained a tiny minority in the City for several years. There were about 350 in 1953, but by 1961 the numbers had grown to 3,457 Pakistanis and 1,512 Indians.

**Table 55 Known and predicted change rates among Bradford's ethnic population 1991-2011**[13]

| Ethnic Group | 1991 | 2001 | 2011 |
|---|---|---|---|
| Afro-Caribbean | 1.2% | 1.3% | 1.3% |
| Bangladeshi | 0.8% | 1.2% | 1.5% |
| Indian | 2.7% | 2.8% | 2.9% |
| Pakistani | 10.3% | 14.4% | 20.0% |
| Other | 1.1% | 1.3% | 1.6% |

The 'riots' Commission Report of 1996[13] expressed concern about the implications of the high growth rates among Bradford's Asian population because of its implication for job creation.

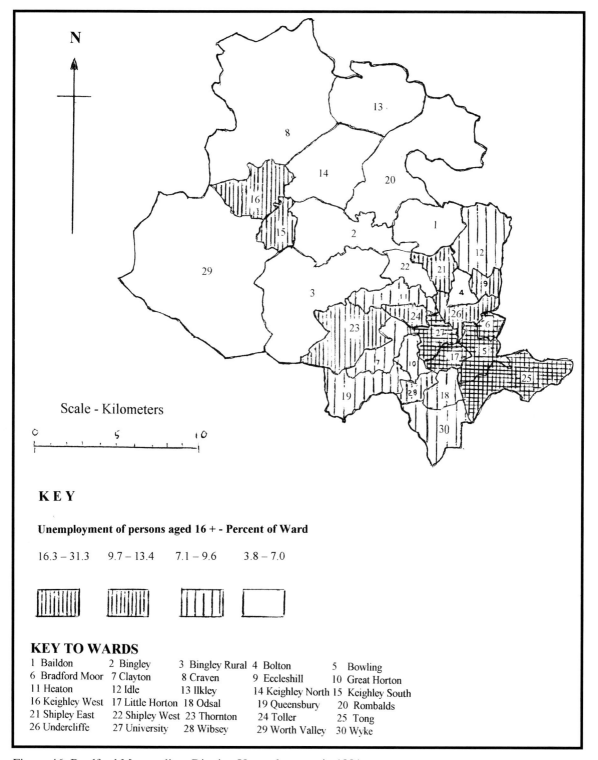

**N**

Scale - Kilometers

0                5                10

**KEY**

**Unemployment of persons aged 16 + - Percent of Ward**

16.3 – 31.3      9.7 – 13.4      7.1 – 9.6      3.8 – 7.0

**KEY TO WARDS**

| | | | | |
|---|---|---|---|---|
| 1 Baildon | 2 Bingley | 3 Bingley Rural | 4 Bolton | 5 Bowling |
| 6 Bradford Moor | 7 Clayton | 8 Craven | 9 Eccleshill | 10 Great Horton |
| 11 Heaton | 12 Idle | 13 Ilkley | 14 Keighley North | 15 Keighley South |
| 16 Keighley West | 17 Little Horton | 18 Odsal | 19 Queensbury | 20 Rombalds |
| 21 Shipley East | 22 Shipley West | 23 Thornton | 24 Toller | 25 Tong |
| 26 Undercliffe | 27 University | 28 Wibsey | 29 Worth Valley | 30 Wyke |

Figure 46. Bradford Metropolitan District. Unemployment in 1991.
Source: 1991 Census of Population Base Statistics 10% sample. CROWN COPYRIGHT.

Figure 47. Indian sub-continent showing areas from which emigration to Bradford has taken place. Source: 'Why should I care?' - City of Bradford Metropolitan Council.

The Commission estimated that between 700 and 1,000 new jobs per year would be needed to maintain current levels of employment.

The Region's Asian population is ethnically very diverse, not only in its having originated in the communities from different parts of the Indian sub-continent and of Africa from which they came, but also in their linguistic and religious differences. This is of great significance in influencing neighbourhood formation within the Asian population, revealed by the examination of the finer detail of the ethnic distributions in Keighley and Bradford. Ramindar Singh and his collaborator, Sadhi Ram, in their small sample study of Indians in Bradford, found that the communities consisted of four main religious groups: 50.6% Hindu, 46.9% Sikh, 2.3% Muslim and 0.2% Christian. They also found that immigration to Britain had either been direct from India or from Africa, mainly Kenya and Uganda in East Africa. Of the Bradford sample 91% of the Sikhs, had come directly from India, and of the Hindus 58.6% were from India, and 37.1% from East Africa. Of the Indian population 57.0% were Gujarati, concentrated in the University ward, and most of the remainder of this ethnic group were in the Great Horton and Little Horton wards, but the Punjabis were strongly represented (30%) in the Bradford Moor, Bowling, Toller and University ward, indicating a wider dispersal than the Pakistani and Bangladeshi communities.[10]

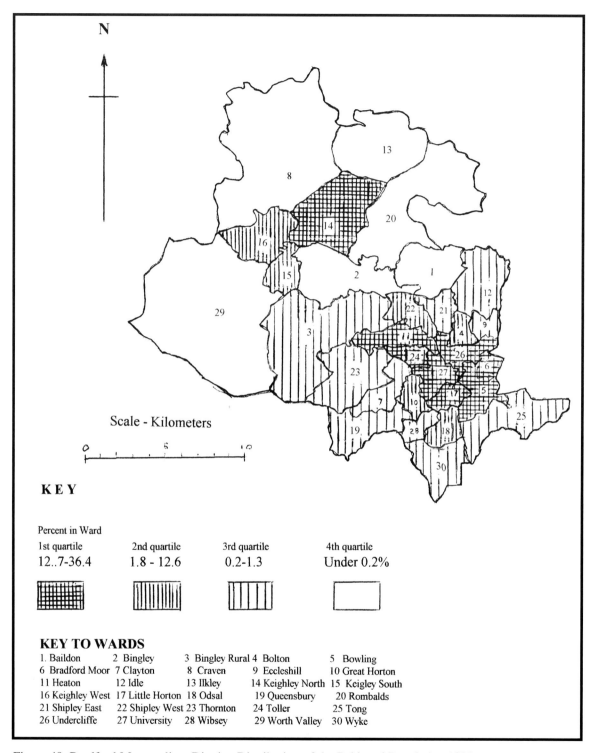

KEY

Percent in Ward

| 1st quartile | 2nd quartile | 3rd quartile | 4th quartile |
|---|---|---|---|
| 12..7-36.4 | 1.8 - 12.6 | 0.2-1.3 | Under 0.2% |

**KEY TO WARDS**

| | | | | |
|---|---|---|---|---|
| 1. Baildon | 2 Bingley | 3 Bingley Rural | 4 Bolton | 5 Bowling |
| 6 Bradford Moor | 7 Clayton | 8 Craven | 9 Eccleshill | 10 Great Horton |
| 11 Heaton | 12 Idle | 13 Ilkley | 14 Keighley North | 15 Keigley South |
| 16 Keighley West | 17 Little Horton | 18 Odsal | 19 Queensbury | 20 Rombalds |
| 21 Shipley East | 22 Shipley West | 23 Thornton | 24 Toller | 25 Tong |
| 26 Undercliffe | 27 University | 28 Wibsey | 29 Worth Valley | 30 Wyke |

Figure 48. Bradford Metropolitan District. Distribution of the Pakistani Population 1991
Source: 1991 Census of Population Base Statistics 10% sample. CROWN COPYRIGHT.

159

The Bradford Region's Pakistani population in 1991 was 45,280 and its distribution is shown in figure 48, from which its concentration in the inner wards of Bradford and Keighley can be seen. The youthful nature of this population is evident from the profile in figure 40B on page 147. 30% were under the age of 18 in 1991, compared with only 26% in the District as a whole. Also, only 1% were over the age of 65, and the smaller ratio of females to males compared with that of the District's profile, suggests that the imbalance of earlier years has not yet worked through.

The detailed distribution of the Pakistani population indicates that the largest concentration with 9,973, was in the University ward, and there were substantial numbers of this ethnic group in Bradford Moor 972, Heaton 3,651, Little Horton 3,593, Keighley North 2,541, Bowling 2,253, Undercliffe 1,979, Great Horton 1,686, Shipley West 1,422, Keighley West 1,389, Odsal, 1,354, Keighley South 744; and in each of the other seventeen wards of the District they made up less than 0.5% of the ward population.

An even tighter concentration of the 3,653 Bangladeshis is evident from figure 49. The largest community was in the Undercliffe ward with 792, other principal locations were: Keighley North 602, Bowling 578, University 434, Keighley South 361, Bradford Moor 337, Little Horton 325, and the remaining 264 were distributed in the other twelve wards of Bradford-dale. In twelve of the outer Bradford wards the 1991 census did not record any Bangladeshis in their population.

In general, the 11,713 Indians (figure 50) are more widely spread than the Pakistani and Bangladeshi populations, the main clusters being University 2,193, Bradford Moor 1,512, Great Horton 1,391, Bowling 1049, Bolton 786, Little Horton 699, Toller 695, Heaton 671, Undercliffe 406, Shipley West 239, Wibsey 153, Queensbury 152, Wyke 143 and Thornton 104. Each of the remaining wards in the District had fewer than 100 in their population.

There are economic, social and cultural reasons for the localisation of the Asian communities in the inner wards of Bradford and Keighley. It should be remembered however, that *Muslim groups maintain much tighter and more inward looking social control networks, even in diaspora than do Sikhs and Hindus'.*[14] Thus the latter are more widely spread than the predominantly Muslim Bangladeshhi and Pakistani commumnties. Even so, the main Asian groupings are in the inner wards which contain the main stock of low-priced housing. Many of the Asian population were in low-paid employment such as the textile industry, which was always poorly paid. As already noted, the Asian groups it occupied, have a high unemployment rate; and many are employed in transport and in foundrywork which are also less well-paid. Language difficulties together with a lack of industrial skills, limit the occupations open to first generation migrants, coming as they do from predominantly agricultural environments. Thus the Asian population is amongst the poorest section of the Bradford Region's population and is less able to afford expensive housing. But in addition to the economic factors leading to the clustering of the poorer ethnic groups in the inner wards, the cultural effects of family, the network of clan and kinship relationships draw people together, and these cultural differences are more likely to inhibit dispersal. Social forces also play a part in the formation of the inner ethnic areas where there may be friendly environments, where there are kinsfolk, and clubs and other institutions. Dahya noted the strength of the segregative and aggregative forces. He said: *'No Bangladeshi lives with those from Pakistan' .....Within the Pakistan bloc, there are cleavages based on areas of origin, e.g. between Mirpuris and Punjabis, between Chaachhis and Pathans and so on'.* [16]

It is noteworthy that Bradford's first mosque is located in the central 'pioneer' settlement of

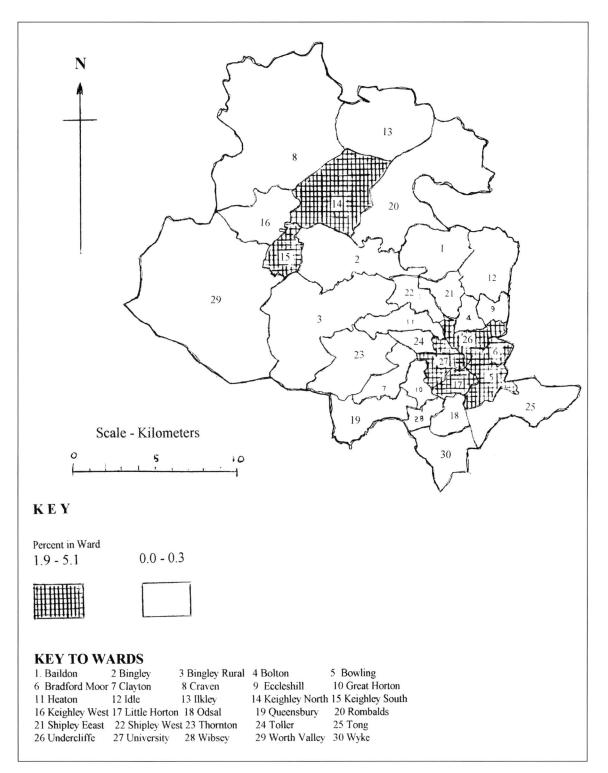

N

Scale - Kilometers

0          5          10

**KEY**

Percent in Ward
1.9 - 5.1                    0.0 - 0.3

**KEY TO WARDS**

| | | | | |
|---|---|---|---|---|
| 1. Baildon | 2 Bingley | 3 Bingley Rural | 4 Bolton | 5 Bowling |
| 6 Bradford Moor | 7 Clayton | 8 Craven | 9 Eccleshill | 10 Great Horton |
| 11 Heaton | 12 Idle | 13 Ilkley | 14 Keighley North | 15 Keighley South |
| 16 Keighley West | 17 Little Horton | 18 Odsal | 19 Queensbury | 20 Rombalds |
| 21 Shipley Eeast | 22 Shipley West | 23 Thornton | 24 Toller | 25 Tong |
| 26 Undercliffe | 27 University | 28 Wibsey | 29 Worth Valley | 30 Wyke |

Figure 49. Bradford Metropolitan District. Distrtibution of Bangladeshi Population 1991.
Source: 1991 Census of Population Base Statistics 10% sample. CROWN COPYRIGHT.

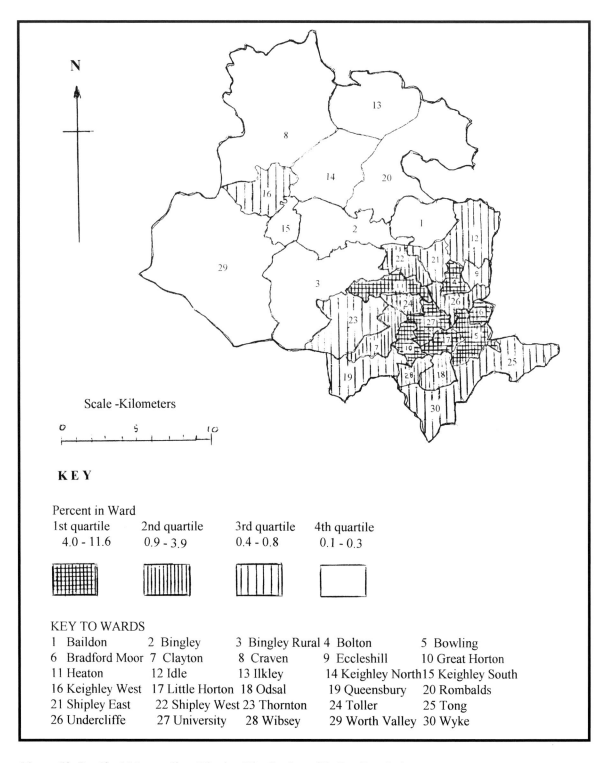

**N**

Scale -Kilometers

0          5          10

**K E Y**

Percent in Ward

| 1st quartile | 2nd quartile | 3rd quartile | 4th quartile |
|---|---|---|---|
| 4.0 - 11.6 | 0.9 - 3.9 | 0.4 - 0.8 | 0.1 - 0.3 |

KEY TO WARDS

| | | | | |
|---|---|---|---|---|
| 1  Baildon | 2  Bingley | 3  Bingley Rural | 4  Bolton | 5  Bowling |
| 6  Bradford Moor | 7  Clayton | 8  Craven | 9  Eccleshill | 10 Great Horton |
| 11 Heaton | 12 Idle | 13 Ilkley | 14 Keighley North | 15 Keighley South |
| 16 Keighley West | 17 Little Horton | 18 Odsal | 19 Queensbury | 20 Rombalds |
| 21 Shipley East | 22 Shipley West | 23 Thornton | 24 Toller | 25 Tong |
| 26 Undercliffe | 27 University | 28 Wibsey | 29 Worth Valley | 30 Wyke |

Figure 50. Bradford Metropolitan District. Distribution of Indian Population
Source: 1991 Census of Population Base Statistics 10% sample. CROWN COPYRIGHT.

Howard Street, where the first settlers lodged, and from which large scale immigration developed. There are obvious advantages of an inner urban residence to a non-car-owning population in facilitating easy access to a frequent bus service linking it with town-centre services. It may also be noted that the larger Victorian houses of the central wards favour adaptation to the needs of the extended family, and consequently the dormer attic extension is a common feature of the landscape of the urban Asian neighbourhoods.

The Asian neighbourhoods in Bradford and Keighley are sufficiently numerous to support a complete range of specialised shops and other economic and social institutions. These are mapped in figure 51 and 52 showing the position in Bradford in 1974, and in Keighley in 2001 in figure 53. The shops, especially food shops, are an essential part of the cultural landscape, not only in connection with the special dietary needs of particular groups, for example ritually slaughtered meat, but also for distributing information. This includes notices on religious events, cinema programmes and employment. The business proprietors may also be represented on the local mosque committees, which act as sectarian pressure groups. The range of Asian shopping and other facilities in Bradford may be seen in figure 51. The significance of this provision means that the adult Asian community, apart from work, need to have little contact with the host population, and is better able to maintain its cultural identity. The build-up of Asian shopping and other businesses has proceeded rapidly since 1959, when there were two butchery-grocery businesses and three cafes, roughly one establishment to every 143 Asians. There were 260 businesses in 1971, justifying the existence of eleven wholesale businesses and one canning factory. By 2001 there were 250 Asian restaurants, earning Bradford the title of the 'curry capital of England'. From figure 51 it can be seen that the greatest concentration of Asian businesses was in the Manningham and University wards. (Since then there has been a revision of ward boundaires and the map now includes University and Toller wards); and another group extends along Leeds Road, and more recently, Great Horton Road. Barton's phase two covered what was a mainly bachelor population, and who at that time expected to return to their home areas in the Indian sub-continent. The establishment of such a comprehensive provision of shops and other businesses is a strong indication of permanent settlement. Figure 52 shows the cultural establishments. Since the map's preparation, the efforts of religious pressure groups have resulted in the setting up of a single sex school for Muslim girls, and a recent study following the Manningham and Lidget Green disturbances, drew attention to the position of some of Bradford's inner schools which are almost entirely Asian. The localisation of the clubs and the places of worship in 1974 corresponded closely to the concentrations of Hindus and Sikhs in the eastern, and the Muslims in the western part of the city. [16] In 2001 Bradford Metropolitan Council had thirteen Asian councillors and one member of parliament, the Sikh, Marsha Singh.

Figure 53 shows how tightly drawn are the Keighley Asian neighbourhoods. Both concentrations illustrated on the map are near to the main shopping centre of this more compact town. In contrast to the large number of Asian businesses so evident in the midst of the Asian areas of Bradford, Keighley has only a few neighbourhood shops and other businesses, so that the neighbourhoods are almost entirely residential. This may be partly due to their close proximity to the main shopping centre of Keighley, as well as the town having a smaller Asian population. This indicates a less self-sufficent local concentration in Keighley compared with Bradford. The six Muslim religious establishments include community and religious educational centres

Largely using the data of census of population and other sources for the Bradford

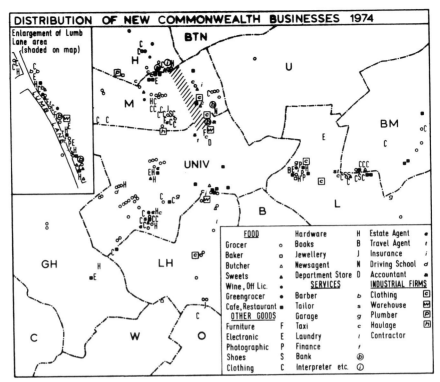

Figure 51. Distribution of Asian businesses in central Bradford 1974

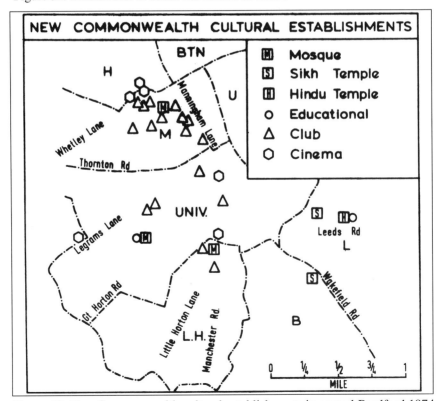

Figure 52. New Commonwealth cultural establishments in central Bradford 1974

164

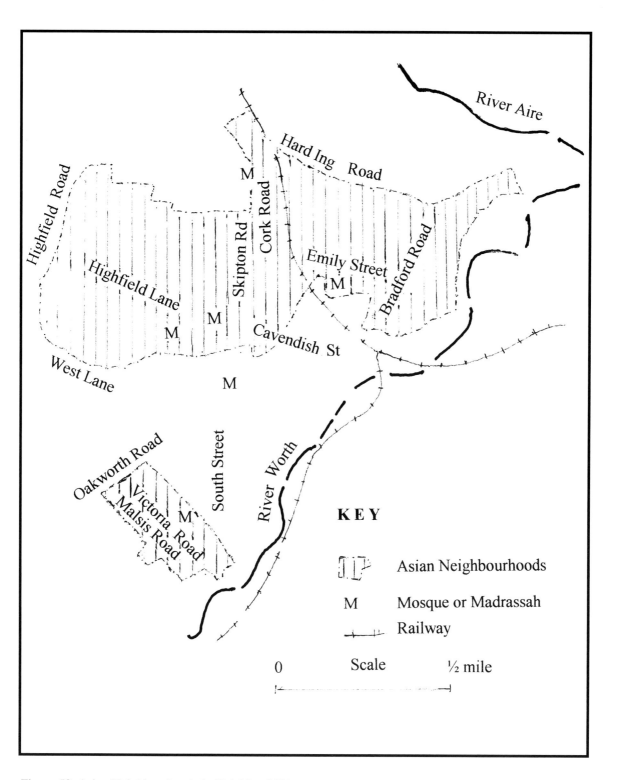

Figure 53. Asian Neighbourhoods in Keighley 2001.

Metropolitan District, this study of the demographic geography of the Bradford Region reveals a clear difference in wealth and socio-economic indicators between the inner and the outer areas of the Region. The significance of this for the future well-being of its population should concern all who have the Region's long-term interest at heart. It has noted that the cultural viability of the areas of Asian settlement in the inner wards of Bradford and Keighley is a function of the size of the ethnic concentrations. Some of the post-war immigrant groups, particularly those of European origin, and the Indian and African-Caribbeans, are residentially more mobile, showing an increased tendency to move away from the central inner ward localities of Barton's 'pioneer' phase of settlement, leading to a greater degree of mixing with 'white' neighbours. On the other hand, the largely Muslim Asian communities are more inward-looking, and because of their higher numbers there is a considerable degree of economic and cultural self-sufficiency. There are indications that this clustering will continue, as the contacts with the core areas in the Indian sub-continent remain strong. As Niaghat Talmuri stated in reviewing the Bradford disturbances in 1995 *'Asian sub groups organise themselves around their particular kinship ties, and follow separate paths in socio-cultural and religious life's.*[17] The presence of sectarian schools in which most of their pupils are from one social or ethnic neighbourhood increases the likelihood of the continuation of the divisions described in this study, whether social or ethnic.

## REFERENCES

1   The Population of the Bradford Metropolitan District.
2   Bradford Council Information Bulletin February 2000.
3   Simpson Stephen Demography and Ethnicity : case studies from Bradford, in *New Communities (January 1997 p.100.)*
4   Census of Population 1991 Local Base Studies.
5   From Simpson, Stephen, op.cit., quoting 1981 and 1985 City of Bradford Metropolitan Council Education Directorate Languages Survey 1985, (21 November 1985).
6   Richardson, C. *Geography of Bradford* p.167.
7   Barton, Stephen Wm. *The Bengali Muslims of Bradford* 1986, p.25.
8   Barton, Stephen Wm. Op. cit. p.55.
9   Dahya Badra, 'The Nature of Pakistani Ethnicity in Industrial Cities of Britain'. Published as a monograph in *Urban Ethnicity* (1974).
10  Ramindar Singh (in collaboration with Sadi Ram) *Indians in Bradford* 1986.
11  Richardson, C. *Geography* ibid. p.174.
12  Richardson, C. *Geography* ibid. p.174.
13  The Bradford Commission Report (on the 1995 riots) Stationery Office November 1996, p.20.
14  Lewis, Philip *Islamic Britain* 1994 p.20.
15  Dahya Badra Britain - Transients or Settlers? *Race* Vol XIV, No.3 July, 1972, p.244.
16  Richardson, C. *Geography* p.174 - 175.
17  Niaghar Talmuri *The June 1995 Manningham Riots - Root causes and future directions*, p.8-9.
18  Based on field survey and the distribution of Asian names recorded on the Electoral Register for 2001.

# CHAPTER FOURTEEN

# THE BRADFORD REGION
# FIVE THOUSAND YEARS OF CHANGE

These studies of the Bradford Region have focused on the interaction between its inhabitants and their environment. They have been about the changes in the physical setting and the evolution of the human landscape covering more than five thousand years of mankind's presence in the Region.

Geography centres on spatial differences, spatial processes and spatial interaction. Obviously it sets out to answer questions about WHERE spatial phenomena are distributed. But it is also concerned with the question of WHY there are differences in the spatial patterns. It is not therefore merely descriptive. It involves the analysis of the physical, economic and social processes which explain spatial differences. Coming to modern times, geographical explanation becomes a behavioural study as we try to understand how groups and individuals interact and, through their interaction, how they decide on the location of their activities and their residences. As was noted in a number of the chapters, technological developments produce their own geographical dynamic too, not only in providing the means of developing the region's resources, but in mobilising those resources to assist in its economic and demographic growth.

## BEFORE PRE-HISTORIC MAN

Long before the age of man, the rock material which underlies the surface of the Bradford Region was being removed from an older land, to be deposited over millions of years into the seas, the lagoons, the lakes and the valleys, to be consolidated into its rocks and minerals. Around the margins of these ancient seas, forests once flourished, lived, died and rotted, to form the coal beds on which the region's prosperity came to depend. At the same time iron in solution percolating through the sediments, aggregated to become the iron beds, to provide a further source of wealth to generations of Bradfordians during the age of man. Through the ages our restless planet experienced upheavals, which disturbed the rock strata beneath the ancient waters, causing them to be raised up later to form dry land, only to be re-buried and to be raised again, to form the uplands of the Pennines. The violence of these earth movements fractured and displaced the various strata, sometimes making them accessible to the miner and the quarryman, sometimes burying them deep in the earth beyond economic reach.

The processes of sub-aerial denudation removed large amounts of the overlying younger rocks and carved out ancient valleys. As time passed, it reduced the resultant undulating surface, and created the peneplain we know today. During the lifetime of our area, ice masses occupied the surface of the region, deepening the three valleys of Bradford-dale, Airedale and Wharfedale, moving material to be dumped along the valleys and providing the mineral content of its soils. These same dumps provided the better drained sites in the lower-lying areas of the region for its human settlers.

## WHAT IS HUMAN GEOGRAPHY?

The raw surface left behind at the end of the Ice Age has undergone many vegetational stages of colonisation in which climate and human intervention have played a part.

The studies of the Bradford Region have drawn on the discoveries and the analytical and interpretive skills of the archeaologists, from which it can be inferred how the earliest settlers evaluated, utilised and interacted with the environment. In this we are also reminded that immigration is no new phenomenon in the humanising of our share of the Pennine mass. To the earliest settlers it was its value as a hunting and gathering ground that the upland was most important, and the high Pennine surface apparently had religious significance to the Megalithic and Bronze age peoples on which we can speculate today. With the arrival of the Iron Age communities, changes in the vegetational cover became recognisable, as well as the existence of a rudimentary farmscape and the beginning of a settlement pattern associated with a higher level of social organisation. In the examination of the political geography of the Romano-British period we are reminded that our region was part of the military zone, extending to the area of the present day Scottish border. This tract was served by military roads and fortresses like Olicana (Ilkley), which were intended to protect the region and the more fertile land to the east and south.

From about the 6th century A.D teutonic invaders from the east established themselves in clearings of the forest and the waste, to create an embryonic road and track system, and a fieldscape consisting of a scatter of tiny settlements which laid the foundation of the Region's mediaeval, and more recent geography. Here land-management decisons were based on a customary collective process, which contrasts with the individual entrepreneurial decision-making of later years. In the study of the geography of the region in the Middle Ages various approaches were adopted to describe the man-land relationship of the period, to re-construct past geography, and to show how much past geography survives and influences the present day landscape. The open field system with its unfenced strip field pattern, farmed in common, inhibited innovation and experimentation. It lasted until a new kind of decision-maker came on the scene in the form of the individual capitalist land-owner who had benefitted from the sale of the monastic and chantry lands.

These 'new men' of the 16th and 17th centuries began to extend private land ownership and to fence their holdings, no longer fettered by the collectivist custom of the mediaeval manor. In so doing they contributed to the creation of the field systems of modern times and at the same time became sufficiently wealthy to invest in the local economy.

Meanwhile the demands of the builder, the charcoal burner, the grazier and the farmer resulted in more of the remaining waste being cleared and fenced. But the significance of the change to private ownership lay in its giving owners the freedom to develop their possession as they pleased. Property amongst the tribes of prehistory had been a territorial concept of group ownership of tribal land, and the principle of group decision-making informed mediaeval land-use managerial practice. The monasteries possessed land and enjoyed the freedom that it provided. Though they were corporations with connections with an international trading system which called for different ways of using land, in other respects they were still part of the mediaeval land system.The dissolved monasteries were replaced by the individual land-owning trader most strikingly exemplified by the independent merchant trader in raw wool and cloth.

Markets had existed on a limited scale during mediaeval times, and from these small-scale commercial territories it is possible to see the beginnings of the city region of modern times. The cloth-workers' smallholdings of the Pennines were linked by causeways traversed by trains of packhorses linking the domestic producer with the cloth halls of Leeds, Bradford and Halifax, thus contributing further to the evolution of their city regions.

The improvement in communications in the 18th century, especially the construction of the

Leeds and Liverpool Canal, changed the economic potential of Bradford-dale and Airedale, reducing the villages' isolation, giving them low-cost access to raw materials and providing them with an outlet to a wide national market which led to rapid urban growth. The capitalist innovators noted earlier, provided the financial means as well as the entrepreneurial drive and skill to revolutionise the transport and communication geography of the region. The transport revolution and the contemporaneous inventions related to the use of coal in manufacturing, resulted in the major development of the region's coal and iron resources. The foundries and the engineering works of Bradford and its urban neighbours gave new significance to the mineral wealth of the region. At the same time developments in textile machinery changed the worsted industry from a cottage to a factory industry and the concentration of production in more compact urban areas.

Immigrants from all parts of the British Isles swelled the population of the dales, mostly coming in response to the pressures of industrial and agrarian change. Amongst these were the poverty stricken incomers from Ireland, who clustered in the slums of Bradford and Keighley. Towns expanded beyond control to create the unhealthy urban environments as population increased.

During the 19th century new decision-making bodies had come into being. These began to intervene in the shaping and the management of the towns and so to make their impact on the human geography of the region. There had been critics of the unregulated growth of urban places, first in the form of the sanitary movements and later, by the town and country planning theorists. This ideological development coincided with the arrival of more democratic political forces coinciding with changes in the franchise. New ways of financing development made it possible for local councils to become land developers. These developments may be related to the development of the welfare state and the evolution of a planning system, the ideals of which, affected the geography of the region when applied to the location of buildings, the use of land, and the communications infrastructure.

It had been recognised that the land market, in which the land-owners were free to develop their property as they pleased, resulted in conflict between the developers and the wider public. The geographical outcome of these ideological and political changes was a change in the way land use and locational decisions were made. Instead of the developers having absolute freedom to decide how land was used, regardless of the impact their activities made on the community and the environment, their actions were subject to control by the planning authorities acting in the public interest. The planning of land and resources was accompanied by the new powers of local governments to own and develop land and provide housing and other community facilities. That responsibility also included the setting of limits to the disordered organic expansion of towns, by restricting ribbon development, the creation of the green belt, the protection of the countryside, and the designation of areas of great landscape value. Today, therefore, there exists the shared role of the private developer and the public authority in the shaping of the towns and the countryside.

The distribution and differentiation of population must be an essential element in any study of the human geography of the Region whether it involves consideration of its social or its ethnic characteristics. The evolving transport system of roads, railways, bus routes and private motor transport, and facilitated movement which allowed those who could afford to do so, to choose where to live. The richer sections of the Region's population were able to make residential locational decisons which contributed to the geographical division between the affluent outer area and inner areas of poverty in Bradford and Keighley.

It was noted that the localities of the main migrant concentrations also included the lowest income categories. To undersand this dichotomy of the Region into poor and rich areas it is necessary to examine the spatial behaviour of the social and the ethnic groups. It reveals both social and ethnic aggregation or separation. In the case of the ethnic concentrations the explanation demands more than the mere comparison of income and housing costs, though these criteria are obviously relevant. Language and culture play an important part. People choose to be in a more friendly and satisfying cultural environment, where there are appropriate facilities of shops and cultural establishments.

Migrants from Ireland, the Italians and the east Europeans have spread away from the centres of pioneer settlement and are more dispersed and integrated with the other communities of the Region. There are hopeful signs too, that the Indian and the Sikh populations are more dispersed and less confined to the inner urban areas. This dispersal has much to do with the greater fluency in English of the established populations. As noted however, the Muslim populations constitute a substantial minority which is largely clustered in the inner areas of Bradford and Keighley, amounting almost to culturally self-sufficient concentrations. To explain this spatial separation it is necessary to understand the social, economic, linguistic, and religious aspirations and fears of the populations, and the desire to preserve their cultural identity. It is the search also for cultural security that must contribute both to the creation of homogeneous ethnic areas, which apart from work, are separated socially from the other cultural groups of the Region. The hope for a harmonious future lies in the education of the host and the immigrant communities, so that the geographical and socio-ethnic divisions revealed in this study may be less sharply defined.

# INDEX

Saxon, 24
Saxton, Robert, 33, 37
Scandinavian, 24
Schofield R.A., 86, 87, 89, 94
Scholes, 61
Scoresby, Revd., 97
Scotland, 22, 75, 84, 107
Screw Mill, Keighley, 73
Sectarian schools, 165
Selby, 54
Selby Abbey, 30
Senlender, William, 36
Serbo-Croat, 154
Service industries, 5, 137
Sewage Purification 1871-1932, 119
Sheeran, George, 93
Shelf, 49, 53, 54, 58, 64, 66, 123, 128
Sheppard, Frere, 21, 22
Shertcliffe Coal, 12, 63
Shibden, 33
Shipley, 3, 16, 19, 20, 24, 26, 27, 30, 41, 42, 43, 44, 45, 49, 52, 54, 55, 56, 57, 58, 64, 80, 82, 83, 84, 85, 86, 88, 93, 99, 102, 105, 123, 128, 130, 140, 149, 160
Shipley East, 149, 152
Shipley West, 149, 152, 160
Shuttleworth, John, 94
Siemens-Martin, 66
Sites of special scientific interest, 16
Sigsworth E.M, 42, 45, 81, 103, 108
Sikhs, 158, 160, 163
Silks, 73, 76, 78, 79
Silsden, 9, 14, 20, 21, 22, 24, 25, 30, 45, 52, 83, 123, 149
Simon, Charles, 85
Simpson Stephen "Demography and Ethnicity", 166
Sissons, J.B., 16
Sindi, 27
Skaife, R.H., 36, 45
Skipton, 12, 16, 23, 44, 46, 52, 54, 56, 123, 126
Skipton Rural District, 123
Sligo, 88, 91, 93
Slum Clearance - Council Housing, 120
Smeaton, 51
Smith, A.H. - Place Names, 33, 36
Smith, Robert, 36
Smith, Sir Swire, 93
Smoke Prevention Committee of Bradford, 63, 120
Snail Green, 58
Soft Bed Coal, 9
Soap drawback, 74
Soils, 15
Somerset, 85
South Street, Keighley, 91

South Ward, Bradford, 93
South Ward, Keighley, 93, 149, 152, 160
Spanish, 154
Speight, H., 36
Spinning, 42, 43, 69, 74, 78, 79, 80, 81, 137
Spring Bank, Bradford, 93
Springhead Mill, Keighley, 73, 77, 99
Springhead Clubhouses, Keighley, 99
Springhead Pits, Queensbury, 73, 103
Spring Ram, 39
St Andrews, Keighley, 100
St Anne's Roman Catholic Church, Keighley, 88, 100
St George's Hall, 95, 144
St. Ives, 30
St John's, Baildon, 100
St Mary On The Hill, 87, 95
St Patricks, Bradford, 95
St Paul's Road, 93
Staffordshire, 85
Stainulf, 27
Stanbury, 9, 17, 36
Stanningley, 128
Steeton, 93, 123
Steeton Manor, 93
Stockbridge, 52
Stott Hill, 87
Stubbing Farm, 25
Stubden, 7, 14, 115
Sub-Atlantic climatic period, 19, 20
Sub-boreal climatic period, 19
Suffolk, 84
Sunshine, 14
Sun Street, Keighley, 99
Supermarkets, 139, 143
Sutton, 128
Sylhet, 156
Syltone plc, 139, 140

**T**
Tadcaster, 21
Taiwan, 138
Temperature, 13
Tempest, Sir Richard, 38
Tempest, Tristram, 43
Tenter ground, 42
Teutonic invaders, 22
Thackley, 128
Thackley Common, 41
Thermawear (Damart), 142
Thirtysix Yard Coal, 12
Thomas (Archbishop), 25
Thompson's Buildings, 79, 99, 117
Thompson's Mill, 77, 79, 99